MEASURING IMM

Social Inquiry and the Problem of Illegitimacy

Why do conservative politicians and scholars in Britain,
Australia and the United States continue to view rising rates
of out-of-wedlock births and teenage pregnancies as a threat
to civilised society? This book examines the process by which
social science transforms a biological event – a birth –
into a social and moral problem. Drawing on Foucault's
'archaeology of knowledge', Reekie stresses the role
of statistics and other social–scientific discourses in the
emergence of the illegitimacy 'problem' in the early
nineteenth century and its continuing cultural significance.
The book illustrates the continuity in concerns about
illegitimacy, including pressure on the welfare system,
associations with racial and intellectual inferiority, the
dangers of fatherless families, and the supposed selfishness
of excessively independent women.

Gail Reekie wrote *Measuring Immorality* while an Australian
Research Council Research Fellow attached to the History
Program in the Research School of Social Sciences at the
Australian National University. She is the author of
Temptations: Sex, Selling and the Department Store (1993),
editor of *On the Edge: Women's Experiences of Queensland*
and co-editor of *Uncertain Beginnings* (1993),
an Australian studies textbook.

MEASURING IMMORALITY

Social Inquiry and the Problem of Illegitimacy

GAIL REEKIE

CAMBRIDGE
UNIVERSITY PRESS

PUBLISHED BY THE PRESS SYNDICATE OF THE UNIVERSITY OF CAMBRIDGE
The Pitt Building, Trumpington Street, Cambridge, United Kingdom

CAMBRIDGE UNIVERSITY PRESS
The Edinburgh Building, Cambridge CB2 2RU, UK   http://www.cup.cam.ac.uk
40 West 20th Street, New York, NY 10011–4211, USA   http://www.cup.org
10 Stamford Road, Oakleigh, Melbourne 3166, Australia

First published 1998

Printed in China by L. Rex Printing Company Ltd.

Typeset in Baskerville 10/12 pt

A catalogue record for this book is available from the British Library

National Library of Australia Cataloguing in Publication data

Reekie, Gail.
Measuring immorality: social inquiry and the problem
of illegitimacy.
Bibliography.
Includes index.
ISBN 0 521 62974 8 (pbk.).
ISBN 0 521 62034 1.
1. Illegitimacy – Social aspects – History. 2. Single-
parent family – Social aspects. 3. Single-parent family –
Economic aspects. I. Title
362.8294

ISBN 0 521 62034 1 hardback
ISBN 0 521 62974 8 paperback

Contents

Acknowledgements

This book began its life as part of a pilot project funded by the Australian Research Council (ARC) and was made possible by a five-year ARC Australian Research Fellowship. I am very grateful to the Australian Government for its financial support.

The History Program, Division of Historical Studies, Research School of Social Sciences at the Australian National University provided invaluable institutional support. Not only is the Research School an ideal physical environment in which to research, write and think free of distractions, it attracts a constant flow of distinguished visiting scholars, many of whom generously made time to discuss my project with me, attend seminars and read draft papers. I thank all my colleagues and the administrative staff of the History Program, staff and postgraduates in the History Department (Faculty of Arts), Women's Studies, Political Science and elsewhere in the university for their sustained support over the five years of my fellowship.

For their practical assistance, encouragement and good ideas I am grateful to Carol Bacchi, Alison Mackinnon, Katharine Massam, Margot Harker, Jonathan Fulcher, Janice Aldridge, Helen Sutton, Beverly Gallina, Anthea Bundock, Eileen Yeo, Joanna Innes, Christine Owen, Pat Jalland, Rosanne Kennedy, Helen Walker, Joanna Bourke, Jennifer MacCulloch, Beverley Biglia, Linda Butler, Barbara Sullivan, Nicole McLennan, Helen Keane, Heather Brook, Jill Julius Matthews, Sarah Lloyd, Ann Curthoys, Michael Young, Marivic Wyndham, Carol Johnson, Gillian Swanson, Maureen Perkins, Bill Reekie, Anne Jenkins, Ian Buchanan, Dipesh Chakrabarty, Lorraine Sheather-Smith, Philip Barker, Tony Bennett, Joy Puls, Lynnette Finch, Susan Magarey, Shurlee Swain, Marion Stell, Gail Tulloch, Peter Cochrane, Renate Howe and Rosemary Berreen.

My thanks also to the staffs of the Institute for Research on Women at Rutgers University and the Center for Advanced Feminist Studies at the University of Minnesota for their interest in this project and their generous administrative support.

I obtained most of my sources through the Australian National University Library and the National Library of Australia. Valuable additional material came from the British Library, the Library of the Wellcome Institute for the History of Medicine and the libraries of Rutgers University and the University of Minnesota. My thanks to the skilled staff of all institutions. I am particularly indebted to the ANU Library for providing excellent on-line database search facilities and an efficient inter-library loans service.

Parts of chapter 2 were published in *Just Policy. A Journal of Australian Social Policy* (10, June 1997), parts of chapter 6 in *Arena Magazine* (31, Oct./Nov. 1997), and parts of chapters 5 and 6 in *Australian Feminist Studies* 12 (25, 1997).

INTRODUCTION

Assessing the Problem

America's social problems have their roots in the spread of unmarried parenthood, according to the President of the United States, Bill Clinton.

> For decades we have seen a stunning and simultaneous erosion of the institutions that give our lives structure and keep us strong: work, family and neighbourhood. There is no more troubling outgrowth of this social breakdown than the increase in teen pregnancy and out-of-wedlock births in recent decades. We know that children who are born into homes where there is no marriage are more likely to drop out of school, get involved in crime and drugs and end up in poverty. That's why I've worked so hard to demand responsibility from young people and reduce teen pregnancies. (White House 1996a, p. 1.)

Clinton is not alone in his concern about the social consequences of an increase in out-of-wedlock births. Consider the following fairly typical stories taken from newspapers and current affairs magazines. From the *Sunday Times*, England: 'My life has been hell for as long as I can remember', a single mother tells the *Birmingham Post*.

> Our estate is made up of 60% single parent families. Many of my neighbours are always angry. There are literally hundreds of kids who run wild with no parental control. Last week, my nine-year-old son was chased by two 13-year-olds wielding knives. They threatened him simply because he had a new pair of trainers. Bullying and extreme violence are an everyday occurrence here. (Jones 1993, p. 5.)

From an editorial in the *Australian* newspaper, commenting on a report 'Mother-headed families and why they have increased' by Ailsa Burns and Cath Scott:

the poverty in which many single mothers eke out a distressed existence is intolerable and destructive. It is destructive of the woman, and as the report shows, has a deleterious effect upon the child's development and education. There are areas where a culture of despair has developed or threatens to. The US experience of an underclass must be averted in Australia. (Reproduced in Healey 1995, p. 26.)

From the *US News and World Report* in Waterloo, Iowa, a 'white underclass neighborhood', a 28-year-old woman opens the newspaper to discover that a man just arrested for sixteen burglaries is the unwed father of her two youngest children. Her own mother was only 14 when she was born and she grew up in poverty. She dropped out of school at 13, had five children whom she supported with welfare and food stamps for nine years. All of her children are now fostered out to relatives, either at her own or the court's request (Whitman and Friedman et al. 1994, p. 45).

I was motivated to write this book by a paradox at the heart of contemporary western culture. On the one hand, the women's and sexual liberation movements have produced a more tolerant attitude towards non-marital heterosexual intercourse and the formation of families that do not conform to the married, two-parent, nuclear ideal. On the other hand, most political leaders, many opinion-shapers and a significant proportion of the general public react negatively to evidence of high rates of out-of-wedlock pregnancies and births. Many conservative social critics link the rise in what they call the 'illegitimacy rate' to a decline in moral values. This tendency to view births to women who are not married as socially deviant persists, even while statistics suggest that in some communities they outnumber legitimate births. Despite a relatively liberal social climate and the widespread acceptance of changing sexual and reproductive practices, many people continue to perceive unmarried parenthood as undesirable, disturbing, potentially troublesome, or just plain wrong. This ambivalence was evident in Clinton's 1996 'statement on teen pregnancy':

> We know there are an awful lot of good, single parents out there doing their best, but we also know it would be better if no teenager ever had a child out of wedlock; that it is not the right thing to do, and it is not a good thing for the children's future and for the future of our country. (White House 1996a, p. 2.)

As a culture, we are reluctant to morally condemn or penalise individual women and children, yet we easily judge as bad the abstract social phenomenon of single parenthood.

Today, the political issue of single parenthood is typically associated not with sexual immorality but with more tangible social ills, such as spiralling welfare costs, the spread of poverty, social disharmony and rising crime levels. In 1996 the United States federal government passed legislation restricting access to welfare payments in the hope that it would 'move people from welfare to work'. A major justification for Clinton's welfare reform measures was the widespread understanding that rising levels of teenage and out-of-wedlock births cause or contribute significantly to drug use, declining levels of educational achievement, violent crime, gang activity and dependency on state assistance 'as a way of life' (White House 1995a, p. 6).

In Britain during the period of Conservative Party rule and particularly around 1993, party members and government ministers expressed concern about spiralling welfare expenditure, the number of fatherless families living on council estates, and single teenage women apparently getting pregnant so that they could jump the queue for council housing (for example, Laws 1996). Although members of the Labour Party, elected in 1997, generally held more liberal views on family issues, Prime Minister Tony Blair signalled his intention of instituting changes to the welfare system that would encourage single mothers to re-enter the workforce. Conservative members of parliament still consider it acceptable to refer disparagingly to the 'bastard children' of their Labour opponents (*Daily Telegraph* 1997b).

Single parenthood is not a major political issue in Australia but the topic raises the odd political hackle. Few years have passed since the late 1980s without at least one rogue Independent, Liberal or National Party (that is, conservative) politician implying that women have babies solely in order to become eligible for the Sole Parent Pension (for example, Daley, P. 1997). The possibility was raised in 1997 of subjecting sole parents in receipt of state assistance to the same 'sudden death' assets test that applies to the parenting allowance (Australian Labor Party 1997). Talk-show hosts express outrage at the increase in the illegitimacy rate, from 5 per cent of the total birth-rate in 1973 to almost 25 per cent in 1997, and lament the fact that the word 'illegitimacy' has fallen victim to the 'political correctness' movement (Laws 1997).

There are differences in the political contexts and histories of each of these nations, the most obvious being greater prominence of racial issues in the United States. The single-parenthood issue rates highest in the United States, less prominently in Britain, and is barely detectable in Australia. As a general rule, the more conservative the party in government the more space out-of-wedlock births (or more widely, 'family breakdown') occupy as a political issue. In Australia, John

Howard's Government, for example, placed more stress than did its Labor predecessor on 'family values', welfare reform and the importance of catering to 'mainstream' Australia. On the other hand, Clinton's 1996 campaign to reduce teen pregnancy shows that the issue does not slip away with a shift towards a more liberal political agenda. In Britain, the so-called and as yet untried 'Blair Project' that helped New Labour win government in 1997 includes a vision of a moral society in the form of strong communities founded on respect for family life. Blair's 'strong families' are, it goes without saying, two-parent families (Carr Brown 1997).

Despite these national variations, the single-parenthood problem is basically the same wherever it is articulated. It has survived some major changes of political climate during the 1990s – from Republican Ronald Reagan's presidency to that of Democrat Bill Clinton in the United States, from the leadership of Labor's Paul Keating to the Liberal–National Party Coalition's John Howard in Australia, from Conservative John Major to New Labour Prime Minister Tony Blair in Britain. The single-parenthood problem can be seen as a bipartisan and transnational phenomenon.

The problem facing feminists, social liberals, single mothers and children brought up in sole-parent families is why the issue of illegitimacy still commands attention. Why is it possible in the 1990s for conservatives to reactivate the negative moral meanings of 'illegitimacy' when several generations of reformers have consistently struggled to dispel those moral prejudices and to improve the social, economic and legal status of the unmarried mother and her child? As early as the 1890s the English essayist and women's rights advocate Tennessee Celeste Cook (Lady Cook) argued that illegitimacy could coexist with 'much that is pure and moral', and was considered immoral only because 'morals are manners, and men make them' (Cook c. 1890, pp. 81–2). In a later essay on the same subject Cook observed that morality is a concept with 'no fixed value, no precise and invariable limits' (Cook 1900, p. 7).

Among the legions of female reformers and writers who, throughout the first half of the twentieth century, wrote about the various injustices and outdated prejudices experienced by unmarried mothers and their children were Ellen Key (Sweden), Jane Addams, Elsie Clews Parsons and Katharine Anthony (United States), Mrs W. F. Gallichan and Ivy Pinchbeck (Britain), and Rose Scott and Marion Piddington (Australia). The Bund fuer Mutterschutz in Germany (the Society for the Protection of Motherhood), established in 1905, included in its program of social reform a vigorous defence of the right of an unmarried woman to have children if she so wished (Wickert et al. 1982).

Women's organisations all over the western world took up the cause of unmarried motherhood, lobbying, often successfully, to protect the rights and improve the welfare of unmarried mothers and illegitimate children. In the 1970s and 1980s support organisations like (in Britain) the National Council for One Parent Families and (in Australia) the Council for the Single Mother and Her Child, among other reforms, introduced laws which abolished the legal status of 'illegitimacy' and removed discrimination against ex-nuptial children (West 1991). For at least a century, then, feminist scholars, writers and activists, not to mention large numbers of social and child welfare reformers, have publicly and often effectively disputed the idea that illegitimacy is equivalent to immorality.

Feminists' efforts to eradicate the concept of illegitimacy, or at least extract its moral connotations from it, and to integrate single mothers and ex-nuptial children into the wider population of mothers and children, now seem in danger of being reversed. Despite feminism's major achievements, especially over the past fifty years or so in the legal and economic spheres, it is clear that the notion of illegitimacy has retained its cultural power to function in public debate as a frightening sign of moral and social disorder. After two decades of dormancy, the concept of illegitimacy has re-emerged virtually unscathed, bringing with it moral meanings that reformers believed long dead.

This book questions the assumption that the birth of children to parents who are not married to one another is bad for society. It does so by looking at social inquiry's persistent obsession with illegitimacy. It centres on social inquiry because in post-Enlightenment cultures the task of assessing social vitality falls to the social sciences. Political debates, social policies and public opinions about single parenthood depend heavily for their empirical substance on the activities of sociologists, statisticians, demographers and social welfare experts. An enormous amount of scholarly effort is currently devoted to explaining, correcting, critiquing, revising, debating, supplementing, solving and elaborating the non-marital births question. The growing social–scientific interest in the topic has spread to every specialism from family therapy to anthropology, from population studies to paediatric nursing. Accounts of the out-of-wedlock births issue appear in textbooks, research monographs, television programs, informational videos, advice manuals, resource guides, articles in scholarly journals, current affairs periodicals, lifestyle magazines and daily newspapers. Social scientists approach the issue from a range of political perspectives, with anti-welfare and pro-family conservatives at one end of the spectrum and feminists and social progressives at the other. This unwieldy sprawl across various academic disciplines, professional practices, media and political movements helps explain the problem's resilient political profile. It also makes the illegitimacy problem a highly fragmented, mobile and indeterminate target.

Social inquiry's international interest in single parenthood ensures its vitality as a topic of political and social debate. The data, arguments and theoretical frameworks produced by the social–scientific disciplines indirectly shape debates concerning population growth, the welfare state, sexual behaviour, family structure, poverty, youth unemployment, sex education and contraceptive practices. Political claims about the situation, rights, prospects or effects of single parenthood are based, explicitly or implicitly, on the accredited, empirically supported, social 'truths' produced by social inquiry.

Although social scientists have a range of perspectives on the precise nature of the problem and how to solve it, they share one critical taken-for-granted notion. Social scientists (and lay persons) accept as self-evident that there is an actual, measurable distinction between marital and non-marital births. To most experts, the category of non-marital or ex-nuptial birth is simply what it says it is: a way of defining and counting those children born to mothers who are not married to the father of that child at the time of the birth, whether or not both parents are living together, whether or not the child is subsequently legitimised or adopted (Australian Bureau of Statistics 1997, p. 90). According to this rationale, the marital/non-marital distinction merely represents statistically the social reality that some babies are born to married parents, others are not. Out-of-wedlock births may not always be easy to calculate, compare or accurately represent, but potentially countable out-of-wedlock births (or, for historians, illegitimate births) do exist 'out there', somewhere.

Let me give one example of the ubiquity of this assumption from my discipline of history. Since the 1960s demographers and historical demographers have devoted considerable attention to the collection and analysis of statistical data showing regional and chronological variations in illegitimacy rates (for example, Basavarajappa 1968; Shorter et al. 1971; Smith and Hindus 1975; Laslett et al. 1980; Vinovskis 1988; Carmichael 1995; Adair 1996). Social historians working with less quantitative methodologies have examined possible causes *of* fluctuating illegitimacy rates, reasons *for*, treatment *of* and attitudes *towards* illegitimacy, single mothers and ex-nuptial children, and the social, political, policy and ideological contexts *of* illegitimacy and single motherhood (for example, Gill 1977; Gillis 1979; Brumberg 1984; Mitchison and Leneman 1989; Higginbotham 1989; Brignell 1990; Fuchs 1992; Solinger 1992; Blaikie 1993; Morton 1993; Kunzel 1993; Gordon 1994; Swain and Howe 1995). In the more recent of these studies it is not unusual for historians to point out that 'illegitimacy' is a historically-specific, socially-constructed concept or, more radically, to treat the 'single mother' as a discursive object (for example, Kunzel 1995). But few accounts, whether they originate from historical demography, social history or cultural history, suggest that 'an illegitimate birth' might be anything other than a real thing or an actual event existing outside of history and culture which can therefore be measured or at least estimated. Even histories of discourse that explicitly challenge essentialist views of sexuality (Weeks 1989, pp. 61–4; Weeks 1995, p. 36) or motherhood (Smart 1996, p. 51) treat 'illegitimacy rates' as a material given.

Instead of assuming that an illegitimate birth is a biological event common to all human cultures, it might be more helpful to think of the category 'illegitimate births' as something that was invented at a certain historical moment by, and specific to, European culture. The 'illegitimate child' and the 'unmarried mother' can be approached critically as particular social identities or subjectivities extruded as part of the cultural process of making and maintaining the illegitimate birth category. From this perspective we can view the legitimate/illegitimate distinction, not as a naturally-occurring demarcation but as a human artefact created for a particular purpose or purposes, to serve certain political or administrative ends.

My purpose here is to raise some important questions about social inquiry's habitual acceptance of the existence 'in nature' of a thing called a non-marital birth and, by extension, the social problem of unwed motherhood. Illegitimacy is a key concept in the conservative push to reinstate the traditional family. Social scientists are, I believe paradoxically, still trying to measure immorality, an abstraction as unmeasurable and as relative as good and evil. For feminists and other groups who support single motherhood – indeed, for anyone opposed to social conservativism – it may be time to develop alternatives to working with 'the single mother', 'the fatherless family' or 'the ex-nuptial child' as real, coherent human subjects with long and continuous histories. I would argue that not only are humanist assumptions difficult to sustain in the postmodern climate of the 1990s, but there are distinct political advantages for feminism in looking on reproductive identities as the products of a particular set of historically-specific academic and professional ideas about the nature of society.

My specific political target is the claim, first articulated by conservative social scientists in the late 1980s and early 1990s, that an 'epidemic' of illegitimacy is underway which will, if not halted, end in social disaster. The anti-illegitimacy argument is closely associated with the various right-wing 'think-tanks' of the United States (for example, the American Enterprise Institute, the Institute for American Values and the Heritage Foundation), Britain (the Institute for Economic Affairs), and Australia (the Institute for Public Affairs and the Centre for Independent Studies). The term 'conservative social science' is a little inexact, including as it does social scientists who may be members of the religious right, pro-family advocates, anti-welfare campaigners, opponents of state intervention, anti-feminists, moral crusaders, self-described moderates on family issues, communitarians and ethical socialists. For simplicity, by 'conservative' I generally mean in this book those who have some moral objection to illegitimacy.

It is this 'moral objection' that I want to examine more closely. The problem of illegitimacy lies at the heart of what is perceived to be a moral crisis facing western societies. Particularly in the United States, where fundamentalist Christian groups exert a well-organised influence on right-wing politics, public figures constantly assert that modern society must return to traditional moral values and standards. Clinton has described teenage pregnancy as 'a moral problem' (White House 1996a). Re-moralisation arguments are less mainstream but still evident in the more secular and moderate political environments of Australia and Britain. In 1983 Margaret Thatcher famously spoke with approval of 'Victorian values' and, more recently, Tony Blair has pledged to restore a moral dimension to government (Scruton 1997). In Australia, a public debate has emerged on the implications of a perceived 'moral shift' in Australian politics centred on socially-conservative politicians like Independent MP Brian Harradine, and the behind-the-scenes influence on government policy of pro-family Christian pressure groups such as the Lyons Forum (Davidson 1997).

Social scientists and other scholars provide essential empirical and intellectual support for the 're-moralisation of society' crusade. British academics, including several from Oxford University, published *The Loss of Virtue: Moral Confusion and Social Disorder in Britain and America* (Anderson 1992) amidst 'growing talk in Britain of a need for moral, not economic, solutions' (Bethell 1996). The Centre for Independent Studies in Australia recently produced a monograph on *Shaping the Social Virtues* (Popenoe, Norton and Maley 1994). In the United States, where social–scientific moralism is most robust, the call to reinstitute 'admirable human qualities that until lately have barely dared speak their names' has informed the anti-welfare campaign since at least the late 1980s (Murray 1989, 1994c). Conservative scholars believe that Americans have an innate moral sense (Wilson 1993) and that virtue and 'frankly moral language' is at last returning to public discourse (Krauthammer 1995, pp. 20–1).

The study of history and historical statistics of illegitimate births support the pro-moral campaign. Christie Davies, Professor of

Sociology at the University of Reading, finds, for example, a clear inverse relationship between the rise and fall of the Sunday school, and the fall and rise of deviant behaviour such as crime, social disorder and illegitimacy (Davies 1992, p. 10). Prominent social scientist and anti-welfare campaigner Charles Murray draws on parish records and civil registers to claim that in Britain until the mid-twentieth century about 95 per cent of children had been born to married parents 'for about 500 years' (1994c). In *The De-Moralization of American Society* (1995), American historian of British society, Gertrude Himmelfarb, argues that it was the exercise of the Victorian virtues and the Victorians' powerful social ethos of self-help, self-discipline and self-control that reduced crime and illegitimacy rates in the nineteenth century, and could do so again today. Himmelfarb's historical argument has slipped into the speeches of conservative politicians like Newt Gingrich (Seelye 1995, p. 19).

I also want to use history for explicitly political purposes, not to support a return to nineteenth-century moral certainties but to challenge them. By de-naturalising the illegitimacy problem and presenting it instead as a series of illegitimacy problems, each the mutable product of the historical conjunction of certain truth-telling discourses, my main objective is to question the authority with which the anti-illegitimacy movement speaks about a de-moralised society. This study investigates how it came to be possible to talk about illegitimacy as a social problem; how the problem has transmuted into different and often widely divergent shapes within different intellectual and professional contexts; and the effects of this discursive and historical legacy on today's debates about out-of-wedlock birth-rates, single parenthood and teenage pregnancy.

As my title, *Measuring Immorality*, indicates, I query social inquiry's claims to scientific credibility on this and other sexual-reproductive subjects by teasing out its ineradicable lineage as a moral science. The intimate intellectual relationship that existed between morality and social science in the nineteenth century has not, in the course of the twentieth century, been triumphantly overcome and expelled, as many of today's practitioners would argue. An implicit moral framework continues to structure the fundamental terms in which western cultures define and evaluate single parenthood as a social issue.

The second section of this Introduction sets out the methodological guidelines which have shaped the writing of this book. I define the problem – both political and epistemological – as I see it. I explain why I consider it important, in deconstructing this and other social problems, to move away from a materialist conception of history towards one based on Foucault's archaeological method of discourse analysis.

Chapter 1 suggests the discursive precedents for the emergence of illegitimacy as a social problem around the late eighteenth and early nineteenth centuries. Chapter 2 examines the close relationship between morality, statistics and the definition of the illegitimacy problem. Chapters 3 to 9 identify the different discursive histories of each subproblem: expense, racial inferiority, social disorder, death, mental incompetence, fatherlessness and selfishness. In chapter 10, I speculate on the wider cultural significance of the notion of illegitimacy.

Defining the Problem

My primary interest in this book is in pregnancy or parenthood arising from ex-nuptial conception. The social problem of rising proportions of children born to women who are not married overlaps with the problem usually known as 'single motherhood' or 'single parenthood', where these terms designate the birth of a child or children to a single (technically, 'never married') woman. The two issues are not precisely the same, however, as single or sole parenthood in current usage also refers to the result of desertion, separation or divorce. The category 'welfare mothers', in which the accent is on state expenditure, similarly includes but is not restricted to never married 'single mothers'.

Another area of overlap is with the problem of 'teenage pregnancy', 'adolescent pregnancy' or 'teenage motherhood'. Teenage pregnancy is almost always taken to mean teenagers who are not married. In addition to the question of marital status, the 'teenage pregnancy' problem foregrounds physical, emotional and social immaturity and the negative impact of early maternity on job skills and education, and is therefore not quite the same as the problem of an increase in ex-nuptial births.

I refer to single motherhood, single parenthood and teenage pregnancy where social scientists and politicians themselves use those terms to designate out-of-wedlock births. I agree with most feminists, liberals, social welfare practitioners and single-parent advocacy groups that the use of the term 'illegitimate' is retrograde, demeaning, offensive and hurtful to single mothers and their children. The majority of participants in the illegitimacy debate follow the legislative, professional and academic convention established in the 1970s of using 'morally neutral' terms to describe births occurring to parents who are not married. In Australia the most common demographic expression is 'ex-nuptial' births; in the United States it is usually 'out-of-wedlock births'; and in Britain 'non-marital births' or 'births outside of marriage'. Australians refer to 'single mothers', 'single parents', 'one-parent families' and (especially in the context of social policy) 'sole parents' or 'sole-parent families'. North Americans use the term 'single mothers', 'single-parent families', and sometimes 'welfare mothers'. The British talk about 'single mothers', 'one-parent families' or (particularly academics) 'lone' mothers, parents or families. At the risk of appearing inconsistent, I have tried to retain these national and professional variations in my discussions of the contemporary literature.

Generally throughout the book, however, I talk about 'the illegitimacy problem' because, for my purposes, it is a more specific linguistic formulation than its modern variants. Until the 1970s this is what social scientists routinely called 'the problem'. And 'illegitimacy', 'illegitimate births', 'unwed mothers' 'unmarried mothers' and 'illegitimate children' are the terms favoured today by British, Australian and, most often, American conservatives. A return to this older language will, they argue, revive the value judgements attached to the concept, express societal disapproval of behaviour that produces multiple social pathologies, and help restigmatise the institution of illegitimacy (Will 1993; Gingrich cited in Seelye 1995; Lamm 1997). The delinquent return of the illegitimate initiated by conservative writers appears at first to be no more than an innocent linguistic slip of the tongue, a simple and politically harmless reversion to obsolescent social mores that opponents can dismiss as inconsequential. But this benign view of language seriously underestimates the political effectiveness of remobilising a discursive object to which is attached some heavy cultural baggage. Illegitimacy's true moral colours are exposed only when the concept is systematically unpacked. When I use the language of illegitimacy, therefore, my intention is not to condone its usage but to expose and dismantle its inner workings as a taken-for-granted moral concept. I generally omit quotation marks when using *illegitimacy* or *problem* on the grounds that all social problems, identities and categories are inherently contestable social constructions (Edelman 1988).

I differ from many commentators in arguing that, despite the overwhelming social–scientific emphasis on the social and economic dimensions of single parenthood, illegitimacy still presents as a moral problem today. Illegitimacy's moral character is certainly less robust than it was in the nineteenth century and, except when it appears explicitly in the work of pro-moral conservatives, is typically submerged and elusive. The ubiquitous social disapproval of the loose sexual morals that were assumed to precede an illegitimate birth is much less evident now than it was a hundred years ago. Nevertheless, there is a widespread sense that it is wrong for a single woman to have a child, especially if she is poor, young, socially disadvantaged or black.

Illegitimacy is judged wrong according to a complicated mixture of unstated ethical standards governing individual sexual and social conduct, the expected role of government in fostering national wellbeing, and actions considered to be in 'the best interests of the child'. The morality and immorality with which this study is concerned are not the easily recognisable, fully elaborated and coherent 'grand morals' of philosophical discourse but a more informal, popular grid of shared values according to which citizens of western cultures decide what is right or wrong for society (meaning, usually, themselves). To this extent, all political questions can be framed as moral questions and all political positions, including my own feminist perspective on women's right to reproductive autonomy, can be said to contain an implicit moral imperative. The morality which social conservatives believe is crucial to social progress is distinctive in that it claims to be beyond politics – a universal, timeless foundation for all human conduct.

In order to speculate on the wider cultural significance of the illegitimacy problem, I have broadened the scope of this study to embrace the social–scientific literatures of Australia, the United States and Britain. The British literature tends to cover Britain as a whole, or Scotland, or England. I found very few Irish, Welsh or New Zealand studies of illegitimacy before the 1960s, and the North American literature is scant before World War I. Consequently, if readers notice an occasional geographical or chronological gap in the narrative, this is because I was unable to discover any significant body of social–scientific material on illegitimacy for that particular period or country.

The political and social structures of Australia, the United States and Britain do, of course, differ. Scientific accounts of the nature of society and social change in each country are nevertheless grounded in a common European intellectual heritage, one founded on the same Enlightenment principles of rational inquiry and a faith in the universality of scientific ideas and facts that transcend national boundaries and political ideologies. The social–scientific pursuit of knowledge about single parents – or, to be more precise, the way in which social–scientific language and conventions represent single parenthood as a social problem – is consequently very similar throughout the English-speaking world.

I am taking these three nations as representative of modern western culture, by which I mean the web of interdependent values characteristic of English-speaking industrialised societies of Anglo origin in which, historically, the principle of the natural superiority of the white race over the black, the middle classes over the working classes, men over women and the rational over the irrational has been axiomatic. The three-nation sweep is designed to suggest how endemic the legitimate/illegitimate distinction is to western culture, without losing sight of national idiosyncrasies where they occur. As an Australian scholar who necessarily reads the British and North American literatures as a semi-outsider (I lived in Britain until I migrated to Australia at the age of 22, and have spent several years in the United States as a graduate student and visiting scholar), I have the advantage of an Australian view of an issue often discussed as if it were uniquely American or British. The book's regional point of view is one of the (mostly American, partly British) centre from the (mostly Australian, partly British) periphery. As an Australian-trained historian immersed in the Australian literature on single parents, I was struck by the similarities in the process of problematisation at the centre and on the margins. I hope this book will show that colonial discourses are not simply derivative of, and dependent on, imperialist representations of the social world, but can be active elements in their own right.

The concept of illegitimacy emerges out of a number of sites of cultural production, including the law and the judicial system (legislation relating to child custody and property inheritance, for example), popular culture (film, television, women's magazines and popular music), literature (autobiography and fiction), state administration (employment and training schemes, provisions for social assistance), the parliamentary process (debates about welfare fraud) and religion (doctrinal emphases on chastity and purity). The question of ex-nuptial birth status lies scattered across these fields of cultural production. For example, in an issue of the Australian feminist magazine *Refractory Girl* (no. 52, 1997) the topic of illegitimacy appears in three separate contexts: in a commentary on Mike Leigh's film *Secrets and Lies*, in a review of Margaret Forster's family history *Hidden Lives: A Family Memoir*, and in an article on single heterosexual women and lesbians choosing artificial insemination as a way of having children.

Few studies of this question – and notably philosopher Jenny Teichman's (1982) groundbreaking account of how various social institutions produce the legitimacy/illegitimacy distinction – consider the crucial role of academic and professional knowledge in perpetuating the view that illegitimacy is a social problem. Social inquiry's contribution demands scrutiny because it determines 'how things really are'. It is its special brief to ascertain as closely as possible the truth or the reality of social problems. The products of social inquiry give lawmakers, politicians, film-makers, writers, church workers and government administrators a reliable image of social reality, the essential facts, figures and hard evidence they need to work with.

By 'social inquiry' I mean a broadly based intellectual enterprise, usually but not always academic, aimed at determining and publicly presenting a truthful account of the nature of society, social relationships, social problems and social behaviour. Social inquiry is generally motivated by a humanist impulse to improve social wellbeing and contribute to human happiness on the modernist principle that good research methods and sound analysis will ultimately contribute to social progress. It is conducted by members of the various 'helping' professions, academics, social commentators, and social-issues journalists.

Most of those engaged in social inquiry practise one or another of the social sciences. A social science – a category which in this book includes social medicine, population studies, psychology, psychoanalysis, sociology, demography, statistics, economics, eugenics, anthropology and sexology – represents itself as a specialised, empirical, usually quantitatively based, scientific procedure that adheres to specific techniques, methodologies, research procedures, protocols, key terms and concepts. In Michel Foucault's terms, each of the social sciences can be seen as both a discourse – a specific and regular system of thought accessible as a unique pattern of particular linguistic objects, statements, rules and conventions – and a discipline; that is, a specific technical knowledge that produces certain practices which discipline the body and manage populations (Foucault 1972; Foucault [1976] 1981; Goldstein 1984). Demographers, for example, typically produce knowledge about 'fertility' or 'mortality' through a system of graphs, tables, mathematical equations, methodological rationales, lists of relevant factors and statistical discussion. Demographic discourse directly or indirectly informs government policy aimed at reducing, increasing, moving or changing the economic profile of certain sections of the population.

Despite its claims to scientific objectivity, and often unintentionally, social inquiry is a deeply political process. Power relationships existing between different social groups produce, accredit, perpetuate and disseminate social–scientific knowledge. Once made public, social–scientific accounts of any given social problem become, whether social scientists want them to or not, the property of the political process, to be used as required by participants to score points or achieve desired legislative or electoral outcomes. 'Power', and 'power relations', which I consider to be discursive products (Jones 1996), are not the subject of this study. An acknowledgement of the inherently political nature of scientific knowledge and of 'power's' potentially devastating material effects on men, women and children is, nevertheless, implicit in my argument.

And while we are on the subject of power, a word about agency. Since the 1980s feminists have attempted to present women as agents of their own lives rather than as victims of patriarchy, colonialism, capitalism and other oppressive social institutions. The humanist concept of agency does not fit comfortably, however, with poststructuralist forms of analysis that assume that the various categories of womanhood – the 'black teenage mom', for example – are not coherent human subjects but particular discursively constituted and unstable subjectivities. My solution has been to try to make some space for the words attributed to those women that social scientists labelled 'unmarried mothers'. These voices are, of course, relatively rare and when detectable are neither pure nor undistorted. The contemporary reader hears them imperfectly through the discursive static of various experts who, for better or for worse, represent them in the public sphere. But neither is the delinquent unmarried mother utterly imprisoned within the official discourses of doctors, psychologists or social workers. Instead, as Michel de Certeau suggests of the speech of the 'possessed woman' at the centre of the sorcery epidemics of seventeenth-century Europe, I prefer to think of the unmarried mother and her variants as a source of feminine disturbance and uncertainty in texts in which there is perpetual oscillation between integration and transgression (1988, p. 251).

Analysing the Problem

A century ago, illegitimacy reform campaigner Lady Cook wrote: 'In discussing any social topic, we have to deal with engrained habits of thought bequeathed, as it were, from one generation to another' (1900, p. 7). In *Measuring Immorality* I examine those 'engrained habits of thought' about illegitimacy that have been bequeathed to us specifically by the social sciences. Because I am primarily interested in the relationship between how we (western culture) habitually think about single parenthood and related problems now, and how we have thought about illegitimacy in the past, the book is more historical in focus than most of the current feminist literature on the subject (for example, Cass 1993; Phoenix 1993; Burns and Scott 1994; Young 1994; Silva 1996; Sidel 1996; Dowd 1997). The book owes a large methodological debt to this non-historical feminist scholarship, however. My approach follows in the footsteps of various poststructuralist-feminist analyses of social problems, key concepts and public debates involving women (for example, Fraser 1989; Condit 1990; Dean 1991; Marcus 1992; Finch 1993; Johnson 1993; Fraser and Gordon 1994; Bell 1994; Luker 1996; Sullivan 1997).

The critical effectiveness of present-centred feminist discourse analysis can be considerably enhanced by adding an historical dimension to it. Andrew Blaikie (1996) has juxtaposed evidence from nineteenth-century Scotland with the current British debate about rising non-marital birth-rates, showing how the language of immorality has become the language of the underclass. Blaikie's work suggests that the historical analysis of illegitimacy can make an important and highly relevant contribution to feminist and progressive defences of single parents. Assuming that what is spoken or written in the present is always shaped, and capable of being endlessly reshaped, by its own discursive legacy, in this study I have tried to set up a dialogue between historical and contemporary discourses. As Judith Butler, feminist theorist and Professor of Rhetoric and Comparative Literature, argues in *Bodies That Matter* (1993), an analysis of the reiterative mechanism which produces cultural identities must acknowledge the historicity of discourse:

> The historicity of discourse implies the way in which history is constitutive of discourse itself. It is not simply that discourses are located *in* histories, but that they have their own constitutive historical character. Historicity is a term which directly implies the constitutive character of history in discursive practice, that is, a condition in which a 'practice' could not exist apart from the sedimentation of conventions by which it is produced and becomes legible. (Butler 1993, p. 282.)

Butler's own project, and those of most cultural critics, does not explore this historicity. It seems to me though, that cultural critique is likely to be most effective where it exposes the diachronic density and complexity of contemporary contests for meaning.

While this book depends heavily on historical analysis, unlike most other histories of illegitimacy and related subjects it does not confine itself exclusively to what happened or what was said or written in the past. Instead of assuming that something *has* happened, whether discursively or materially, I work from the premise that things *are* happening discursively in the cultural milieu in which I and my readers and the various participants in the illegitimacy debate are currently immersed, a milieu which is inescapably historical in character. I was initially influenced by the work of feminist scholars like Joan Scott (1988a; 1988b; 1991; 1993), Mary Poovey (1988a; 1988b; 1990; 1993), and Denise Riley (1988). While persuaded by their arguments for applying the poststructuralist technique of deconstruction to the study of history, what I wanted to analyse was a particular configuration of discourses, not the internal dynamics and tensions of individual texts. Consequently this study relies almost exclusively on discourse analysis.

This is a 'history of the present', in the sense that it aims to show that an apparently natural and taken-for-granted concept has a particular discursive history and that its existence is contingent upon certain discourses that, historically, provided the conditions for the emergence of the notion of illegitimacy as a social problem. Borrowing a useful technique from Foucault, *Measuring Immorality* re-problematises illegitimacy. Certain discursive practices problematise, or 'introduce something into the play of true and false and constitute it as an object for moral reflection, scientific knowledge or political analysis' (Foucault 1988, p. 257). Illegitimacy, as it happens, is currently constituted as all three objects simultaneously. To re-problematise is to examine the process of problematisation, to 'question over and over again what is postulated as self-evident, to disturb people's mental habits, the way they do and think things, to dissipate what is familiar and accepted, to re-examine rules and institutions ...'(Foucault 1988, p. 265).

To effect this re-examination I have adapted the method Foucault set out in *The Archaeology of Knowledge* (1972). *The Archaeology* is not as popular among historians and feminist scholars as Foucault's later work, perhaps because it is more a technical manual than a source of historical information, and even Foucault sympathisers appear unconvinced of the practical utility of its radical agenda. An iconoclastic, intelligent and comprehensive guide to discourse analysis and the critical analysis of systems of knowledge at their purest and in all their complexity, *The Archaeology* remains a critical yet largely untested textbook of poststructuralist technique. *Measuring Immorality*, an experimental foray into archaeological inquiry, attempts to reposition the somewhat neglected *Archaeology* more centrally in poststructuralist history.

We are about to embark on a guided expedition into the archive of illegitimacy. For Foucault, 'the archive' meant not the physical repository of historical documents or the sum of all texts that a culture has kept upon its person. The archive is:

> the law of what can be said, the system that governs the appearance of statements as unique events. But the archive is also that which determines that all these things said do not accumulate endlessly in an amorphous mass, nor are they inscribed in an unbroken linearity, nor do they disappear at the mercy of chance external accidents; but they are grouped together in distinct figures, composed together in accordance with multiple relations, maintained or blurred in accordance with specific regularities; that which determines that they do not withdraw at the same pace in time, but shine, as it were, like stars, some that seem close to us shining brightly from afar off, while others that are in fact close to us are already growing pale. The archive ... is that which differentiates discourses in their multiple existence and specifies them in their own duration. (Foucault 1972, p. 129.)

The subject of this book is the social–scientific archive of the problem of illegitimacy. Archaeology, as distinct from 'the history of ideas' or 'cultural history', is the technique with which I attempt to delineate that archive. Archaeology 'describes discourses as practices specified in the element of the archive' (Foucault 1972, p. 131). An archaeology is a variety of what Foucault would call effective history, a historical method that assumes discontinuity rather than continuity, that refuses to adopt the 'voiceless obstinacy toward a millennial ending' (Foucault 1977, p. 154). It proceeds on the principle that statements from 'discourses that have just ceased to be ours' survive and undergo regular modification in the present (Foucault 1972, p. 130).

Most Foucauldian historical studies tend to share Foucault's own ambivalence about the status of the non-discursive sphere. Historians conventionally explain discursive changes by referring to some underlying social force or material cause. From a poststructuralist perspective in which 'underlying social forces' are themselves conceptualised as the products of discourse, this automatic deference to overarching explanations grounded in 'material reality' becomes problematic, if not impossible. This is not to say that there are not, or were not, real women, children, pregnancies and births; or that certain political events, demographic changes or policy innovations bore no relationship to discursive constructions of illegitimacy; just that we can only ever know these material objects and events through discourse analysis.

In an effort to apply poststructuralist principles more consistently and rigorously to historical inquiry, I have chosen to conduct my own analytical work almost exclusively on discursive terrain, without reference to whatever economic, social and political structures and contexts and material preconditions may pertain to the illegitimacy problem, or that might account for the production of relevant social–scientific discourses. I do not follow the historical convention of relating illegitimacy to other social practices such as abortion, adoption, contraception, marriage or the maternal and infant welfare movement, because I view each of these as discursive objects with their own distinctive histories, yet to be written. Similarly, instead of 'using' statistics of illegitimate birth or single parenthood to signify the presence of an underlying and deterministic demographic reality, my concern is to analyse the contribution of statistical and demographic discourses to the constitution of illegitimacy as a social problem.

Readers used to historical and social–scientific writing may be troubled by the virtual absence of context, so let me add a few words of explanation. As Dominick LaCapra has argued, in much cultural history (and inevitably, in traditional history) context tends to function reductively. When historians produce an account of a text's context they reduce a complicated and heterogeneous network of texts to a single interpretive point in what LaCapra calls an 'insistent process of domestication, leveling, and reduction of the different to the same' (1989, p. 79). That artificial reduction then provides a (usually single) explanatory framework for whatever is going on in the text foregrounded by the discussion. Social analysis follows the same practice, using social–scientific texts as context. In my view, adopting an uncritical stance in relation to context diverts critical attention away from the discourse that is the subject of the analysis, thereby diluting the force of the analytical process. It also seems methodologically inconsistent for cultural analysts to adopt a critical stance in relation to one set of texts, those nominated as central to the analysis, or 'the discourse', while treating other texts, the 'secondary sources', historical 'background' or relevant statistics, say, as if they speak an unmediated and unquestionable truth.

In this book I try to present illegitimacy's discursive variety as a kaleidoscope of textual fragments. Each text is implicitly contextualised, not by some deeper external historical reality but by the texts that surround it synchronically and diachronically, and by its own linguistic references to other texts which signify elements of the 'outside' world. Although I tried not to rely heavily on context as explanation, occasional references to background or secondary sources (where it was impossible to directly consult primary documents, for example) proved unavoidable. Non-fictional writing sets up certain expectations, and readers (I include myself) trained in structuralist and humanist ways of interpretation cannot help but be curious about the world and people beyond the text. In the interests of telling a more satisfying story, and by way of a compromise between theoretical purity and readability, I have included some biographical, political or intellectual background, especially in the first few chapters.

I have organised my historical material in the form of eight separate narratives, each centred in the present controversy and each constituting one facet of illegitimacy's 'polyhedron of intelligibility' (Foucault [1976] 1981, p. 6). Chapters 2 to 9 should be read as case studies applying the methodological and theoretical principles set out in this Introduction. The aim is to define what Foucault calls the 'positivity' of a discourse; that is, 'to describe a group of statements, in order to rediscover not the moment or the trace of their origin, but the specific forms of an accumulation' (Foucault 1972, p. 125). This form of positivism does not assume a hidden totality of meaning or intention, a transcendental foundation; it stands for an analysis based on a specific group of identifiable verbal performances and the external relationships between them. These groupings do not comprise a closed totality but appear as 'an incomplete, fragmented figure' (Foucault 1972, p. 125).

The thematically organised discussions move back and forth between current representations of the illegitimacy problem and what Shannon Bell (1994) calls historical 'discursive domains' (as opposed to non-discursive historical 'periods'). The chronological distinction between 'past' and 'present' is inevitably an arbitrary one. I have assumed the turning point to be somewhere around the 1970s, on the grounds that the way that social scientists spoke about illegitimacy from the 1980s on sounds familiar to me in the 1990s, while how they spoke about it until the 1960s sounds different. This interweaving of present and past discourses is an attempt to reflect what I see as an active symbiotic relationship in everyday life. In social practice, in our endless attempts to make sense of the world, we constantly juxtapose truth statements of different historical origins. The continual and almost random movement between one discursive statement and another, some older than others, is how we actually navigate the sea of ideas and concepts in which we daily find ourselves as citizens of western culture. Historians can only draw meaning from their 'primary source material' by placing it, usually implicitly and informally, in dialogue with material from their own discursive environment. By interspersing contemporary and historical texts, then, I am trying to expose some of the machinery of history's production, to make my writing follow more closely the actual practice of history (de Certeau 1988, p. 86).

Michel de Certeau (1986, ch. 1) offers an intriguing psychoanalytic perspective on this active engagement between historical and contemporary discourses. He proposes that the present is haunted by the 'return of the repressed', an 'other' that has been eradicated in the process of writing, an other that comes back to disturb and unsettle the fixity of current meanings. The objective of this archaeological project is to make the repressed's return visible, explicit and disturbing. It recreates illegitimacy's own shady past in order to damage its credibility in current political discourse.

CHAPTER 1

Bastards and Children of the Parish

Illegitimacy has not always been a social problem. It has been a personal problem, a family problem, a community problem, a religious problem and a legal problem. The notion that illegitimacy is bad for society is distinct from and more recent than these other problems. There was a time, before the nineteenth century, when it did not occur to middle-class, educated men and women interested in questions of social and individual wellbeing that illegitimacy had to be measured, understood or solved. People who considered themselves respectable were, of course, concerned about the birth and legal status of illegitimate children, and disapproved of the illicit heterosexual behaviour which an illegitimate pregnancy inevitably signalled. But it took a particular constellation of intellectual and political developments in the late eighteenth and early nineteenth centuries to make people start to think of illegitimacy as more than an individual failing or an issue of concern for the local community, to think of it instead as a problem of national and international significance.

The notion that a birth is either legitimate or illegitimate is present in most known human cultures. However, illegitimacy can mean something different, or not mean as much, to non-Europeans. Among the adult members of some contemporary Aboriginal communities, for example, it makes people 'shame' if an adolescent girl has a 'single baby', but it is even more shameful for her to enter into a 'not straight' marriage; that is, a marriage that disregards traditional cultural laws governing who may marry whom. Some mothers forbid their pregnant daughters to marry if the father is not a correct marriage partner (Burbank 1989, pp. 232–3). Working-class African–American women do not necessarily view marriage and the stable presence of a male head-of-household as essential to the maintenance of strong families.

One study found in a group of such mothers 'an ideal of community-based independence involving shared care-giving and nonmarital partnerships with men' (Blum and Deussen 1996, p. 200). In Japan (where the category 'illegitimate birth' was invented only when European systems of registration were introduced in 1868) it is possible to indicate that someone is the child of a concubine, but there is no equivalent of the English word 'bastard' (Hayami 1980, p. 397).

Under Jewish law, the offspring of any marriage contracted between prohibited relatives, such as between relatives by marriage, is deemed a *mamzer*, or illegitimate child (Lewittes 1994, p. 21). Jewish law regarded extra-marital (illegitimate) relationships as almost equivalent to legitimate relationships, with the acknowledgement of the father being sufficient proof of descent. A *mamzer* can be a bastard, but the Talmud tends to limit the term to the offspring of incest, adultery, or forbidden marriages (*Universal Jewish Encyclopedia* 1948, pp. 309, 376). Any child of a Jewish marriage which is subsequently dissolved in a civil divorce, but not a religious divorce, is considered illegitimate even when the woman remarries (Jopson 1995).

Before the Middle Ages illegitimacy was not strongly associated with immorality. In Ancient Roman society the terms used to distinguish between different classes of illegitimates produced legal – not moral or social – categories of person, and little shame or secrecy was attached to illegitimate births. Illegitimacy primarily designated the lack of a father in the eyes of the law. Being born illegitimate was to exist outside the web of family rights and responsibilities and therefore to possess less than full rights to the support of a father. As the responsibility for the support of the illegitimate child in pre-Christian Rome rested with the mother or her family and not the state, illegitimacy was not viewed as a social problem (Rawson 1989; Teichman 1982, pp. 53–5).

Ancient Greco-Roman constructions of illegitimacy revolved around problems of inheritance and the importance of passing on the family name through legitimate male heirs. In the Middle Ages illegitimacy was associated with both property transmission and a Christian concern for purity (Chidester 1992, pp. 147–51). According to Foucault's *History of Sexuality* ([1976] 1981), until the end of the eighteenth century sexual practices were governed by canonical law, the Christian pastoral and civil law. These codes determined the division between licit and illicit sexual activity (Foucault [1976] 1981, pp. 37–8). A 'deployment of alliance' based on this system of rules defined what was permitted and what was forbidden. Marriage, the fixation and development of kinship ties, and the transmission of names and possessions were central to this alliance (Foucault [1976] 1981, p. 106). Any children conceived or born as a consequence of illicit sex were not only legally problematic but inevitably tainted with their parents' sin of debauchery.

In England the distinction between legitimate and illegitimate offspring was enshrined in the canon and common laws, and in provisions for the poor. A bastard child was legally *filius nullius*, or 'nobody's child', meaning that no person was obliged to care for him or her. Until the sixteenth century the 'fatherless poor' depended for their survival on the ministrations of monasteries and the distribution of town alms, while those who were illegitimately born to wealthy parents depended on the goodwill of their relations (Teichman 1982, pp. 53–60). The idea that the community had some responsibility to care for destitute children, whether legitimate or illegitimate, emerged with the enactment in the sixteenth century of the first English Poor Laws. These laws turned the children of nobody into the children of the parish. Poor, illegitimate children were considered to be a particularly heavy burden on parish expenditure. A statute of 1547 allowed justices of the peace to issue bastardy orders by which the parish could obtain money from the fathers of illegitimate children to help pay for their keep. Economic pressures and the popular and religious view that illegitimacy was an offence against morality contributed to a punitive attitude towards the illegitimate mother and her child during the sixteenth and seventeenth centuries (Teichman 1982, pp. 62–4).

The adjective 'illegitimate', meaning 'not born in lawful wedlock' (the earliest sense of the word in English), joined its predecessor 'bastard' in written English at about this time. The *Oxford English Dictionary* traces the use of 'illegitimate' to Shakespeare's *Henry VIII* (1536), in which Elizabeth is described as 'the kynges doughter illegyttimate borne under the same mariage [sic]'. By the early seventeenth century 'illegitimate' was a synonym for 'bastard', used descriptively to signify that a person's parents were not married at the time of the birth. The adjective applied to an individual, not to a group of persons with a shared characteristic, or to a specific category of birth. When the noun 'illegitimacy' did begin to be used in the late seventeenth century, it meant simply the state of being illegitimate.

Before the nineteenth century scholars appear not to have been very interested in illegitimacy. The classic studies of the seventeenth-century demography pioneers, John Graunt, William Petty and Gregory King, contain no reference to illegitimate births. If illegitimate children were sometimes mentioned in social surveys conducted by amateur English gentlemen sociologists in the second half of the seventeenth century, they were invariably viewed through the lens of pauperism. Poor, unmarried mothers were often unable to support their children financially and appeared regularly as an item of expenditure in parish accounts. The problem addressed by eighteenth-century social observers was therefore not so much illegitimacy or illegitimacy rates but the existence and costs of bastard children. Illegitimate children were a sub-set of the wider problem of the economic situation of the poor.

Observers of the English pauper question considered illegitimate children to be the 'fruit of an illicit connexion' (Eden [1797] 1966, p. 450). Critics of the Poor Laws argued that by supporting illegitimate children and unwed mothers the Poor Laws encouraged immorality and debauchery. Joseph Townsend's *Dissertation on the Poor Laws* ([1786] 1817) argued that the Poor Laws encouraged 'idleness and vice' and, instead of remedying the problem of pauperism, tended to multiply the poor ([1786] 1817, pp. 2–3). The only poor women mentioned in Townsend's pamphlet were widows, and the only poor children were orphans. Illegitimacy ranked lower on the scale of social problems in the eighteenth century than did the lack of industry and economy among the labouring poor.

Poor Law commentators made few references to actual numbers of illegitimate children. Eighteenth-century social observers did occasionally estimate the proportion of illegitimate children born in particular, discrete communities, in certain parishes for example, where local records were available and calculations manageable. These informal surveys were usually conducted for political purposes and their results presented, not as official statistics or as the results of scientific data collection and analysis, but as direct observations. For example, Jonas Hanway, Governor of the London Foundling Hospital, used the mortality records of some parishes in his published appeals for greater assistance for the children of the poor in the 1750s and 1760s (Hutchins 1940, pp. 188–90).

Illegitimate births were also countable in the early Australian penal colonies. Teichman argues that the social distinction between licit and illicit birth, normally rigidly observed, comes closest to breaking down in societies in which substantial numbers of men and women are without property and living in slavery or servitude (Teichman 1982, p. 58). The British Government displayed an intense interest in the moral and reproductive behaviour of the poor, white population of the Australian colonies, possibly 'one of the most observed, mapped and organised populations in the enlightened world' (Finch 1993, p. 29). Unlike its British counterpart, the white population of the Australian colonies was relatively contained and subject to strict government surveillance, so that government officials could at least attempt to enumerate the extent of illegitimacy in one whole society. Unusually large proportions of unmarried mothers were unlikely to be ignored by a government keen to encourage the growth of a 'respectable' and settled white colonial population. Samuel Marsden, Chaplain of New South Wales, reported in 1806 that there were 807 legitimate and 1025 illegitimate children in the colony (Finch 1993, p. 26). The British Select Committee on Transportation informed the British Government in 1812 that two-thirds of all children born in the first years of the colony of New South Wales were illegitimate (Douglas 1959, p. 790).

The main problem facing colonial governments was not that of understanding and solving the problem of illegitimacy, but of managing its subjects, instilling order and encouraging marriage and legitimate population growth. Early colonial correspondence suggests that some of the elements constituting what was to become the social problem of illegitimacy had begun to surface by the end of the eighteenth century but illegitimacy was more a governmental matter than a subject of scientific inquiry in its own right.

Another indicator of the low scientific currency of the term 'illegitimacy' in public discourse is its virtual invisibility in eighteenth- and early nineteenth-century encyclopaedias and dictionaries. There is no reference to illegitimacy in either the first edition of the *Encyclopaedia Britannica*, published in 1771, or in *The Politician's Dictionary* of 1775. This silence persisted despite an obvious interest in various questions concerning the population. Under the heading 'People', for example, *The Politician's Dictionary* referred to such problematic categories of the poor as the idle, the vagrant and the pickpocket. Bastards were not mentioned. On the question of population growth, the author of the *Dictionary* argued that 'in a debauched nation, addicted to sensuality and irregular amours', the population would be smaller than in those nations where people were frugal and virtuous. Populations only increased when people were encouraged to marry. This implies that only the 'fruitfulness of marriages', that is, legitimate births, were seen to constitute 'the population'. Illegitimate births literally did not count.

Signalling the advent of a more scientific approach to the question, the terms 'bastard' and 'bastardy' appeared in the second edition of the *Encyclopaedia Britannica* of 1791. The *Encyclopaedia Britannica* constructed illegitimacy as an individual not a social problem, drawing predominantly on legal discourse and, to a lesser extent, on those of government and philanthropy. A bastard was 'a natural child, or one begotten and born out of wedlock', and bastardy 'a defect of birth objected to one born out of wedlock'. After summarising Blackstone's legal commentary on the status and rights of bastard children under English civil and canon laws, the author argued that English law was morally superior to that of the Romans because it did not allow for the legitimation of a child born to parents who were unmarried at the time of its birth but who subsequently married. The English law thereby reaffirmed the social value of children conceived within marriage, and attempted to ensure that 'all future children will be begotten, as well as born, within the rules of honour and civil society'. Expressing sentiments with which the governors of the Australian colonies would no doubt have agreed, the *Encyclopaedia* suggested that legitimacy was indispensable to the making of a civilised nation.

The *Encyclopaedia Britannica* also constructed the bastard as an economic subject whose support created a problem for society. Parents had a duty to support their bastard children and Poor Law provisions secured maintenance from the father. The 'lewd' mother, however, represented a moral and social, as well as an economic, problem (the bastard's father was simply described as 'putative'). The author claimed that older laws – for example, a provision that women suffer death in the case of concealment of birth of a bastard – were too severe and that such penalties were unjustly inflicted only on the woman. The child itself, 'the innocent offspring of his parents' crimes', was free of moral blame and undeserving of any social penalty. This ambivalent vision of the unmarried mother as both culprit and victim and the assertion of the child's moral purity and blamelessness were necessary preconditions for the rational approach to illegitimacy that developed over the next century.

What makes the 1791 *Encyclopaedia Britannica* entry remarkable when compared with those that followed over the next two centuries is the absence of statistics. Parish registers provided notoriously inaccurate and incomplete records and reliable official figures of illegitimate births did not exist for Britain at this stage. National illegitimacy statistics were, however, available in France by 1800. The next chapter shows how the Revolutionary Government of France brought illegitimacy into the all-embracing gaze of the state, counted it, and entered it into the accounting of national wellbeing.

CHAPTER 2

Statistics and the Birth of a Social Problem

The discourse of statistics has been indispensable to the transformation of a biological event, an illegitimate birth, into a social problem. It is no coincidence that the illegitimacy problem was invented just when official illegitimacy statistics became available. The systematic nationwide collection of European birth statistics that began in the eighteenth century made it possible for English-speaking social scientists to start to think about illegitimate births as a national problem. Those first statistics were steeped in certain cultural assumptions about sexual propriety, marriage and the working class. The statistics of ex-nuptial births and single-parent family formation used so freely today by feminists, conservatives and liberals alike, are impregnated with the moral meanings that were automatically attached to illegitimacy statistics in the nineteenth century.

Eighteenth- and early nineteenth-century social observers engaged in the debate in England surrounding pauperism and the Poor Laws had to rely for figures on the records of foundling institutions (which took in legitimate as well as illegitimate infants) and parish registers. Parents did not always register the birth of a child with the parish, so the registers were typically incomplete. Clergy could be lax in their record-keeping duties, and some eighteenth-century parishes discouraged the poor from registering by imposing a fee. Sir John Sinclair, author of *The Statistical Account of Scotland*, observed that in one Scottish parish there was no register of burials or marriages and 'the register of baptisms is not very accurate: a shilling is paid for registering, and poor people have an interest in the omission' (Sinclair 1791, p. 141). Poor women with new-born illegitimate infants would have been especially reluctant to register the birth with the local clergy.

Illegitimate births were covered technically by the government censuses of several European countries, including Britain from 1831, and in musters conducted by the British Government in the Australian colonies in the early nineteenth century. However, British statistical experts regarded the preliminary figures collected as part of the 1831 census as too unreliable to be useful. According to the Registrar-General, many of the ministers of religion responsible for the returns stated the numbers baptised instead of those born, the result of which was to significantly underestimate the extent of illegitimacy (Registrar-General 1844). In the United States, illegitimate births were not systematically recorded until the mid-nineteenth century, and then only by the states of Massachusetts, Connecticut and Michigan. Thus until mid-century, European, North American and Australian illegitimacy statistics were limited and relevant only to particular, relatively contained or (in the case of New South Wales) socially abnormal populations.

National, official and reliable illegitimacy statistics emerged as a direct consequence of the political and social upheavals in Europe, especially France, in the late eighteenth century. French revolutionary rhetoric included an interest in illegitimacy. In harmony with a general social reform movement that sought to make all citizens equal, no matter how humble or tainted their origins, members of the first French Revolutionary Government attempted to improve the legal, social and economic status of the illegitimate child. These Revolutionary reforms grew logically out of Enlightenment thinking. Revolutionists wanted to dispense with the designation 'illegitimate' because they saw it as an unnatural social category. Their arguments drew on the rhetoric of equality and 'natural rights' articulated in the writings of the *philosophes*, especially Jean-Jacques Rousseau.

Jacques Peuchet, a member of the Council of Commerce and the main instigator of the reforms, believed that under Nature's undiscriminating gaze all children, whether born inside or outside marriage, were equal. Peuchet argued to the National Assembly in 1790 that: 'The errors of formal ethics, deliberate celibacy, accidents, personal mistakes, have created in society a persecuted class, hardly known to civil law, and which intolerance designates as "illegitimate", as if there were some men more "legitimate" than others!' (Peuchet cited in Brinton 1936, p. 22). Peuchet urged the Assembly to abolish the category of illegitimacy on the grounds that it was 'contrary to the rights of man, to natural law, to familial happiness, to filial love, and to domestic authority ... Regardless of the conditions under which they are born, all children should be equal in rights and duties' (Peuchet cited in Rodis 1968, pp. 181–2). Peuchet wanted the natural equality of the illegitimate and the legitimate child to be enshrined in laws relating to property. Legislation that guaranteed equal rights of property inheritance and which continued to allow women to undertake legal action for filiation against fathers who refused to admit paternity was approved in 1793 (Brinton 1936, pp. 22–30).

A more pressing concern for the Revolutionary Government was the practical question of how to reduce the high mortality rate and improve the welfare of infants left in the dubious care of foundling institution nurses and wet-nurses, many of who were themselves struggling to survive. By the late eighteenth century the increasing visibility and suffering of the poor made state intervention necessary (Fuchs 1992, p. 99). A 'menacingly large' number of illegitimate infants were being abandoned in the streets or in the basket of the local *hôpital*, threatening to swamp the resources of charitable religious institutions funded partly by government (Hufton 1974, p. 349).

For a number of reasons, members of the Revolutionary Government wanted to reform the system of Catholic philanthropy that had traditionally cared for foundlings. The rise of humanitarianism challenged ancient ecclesiastical concepts of self-help and personal salvation through good works (benevolence). Consistent with their anticlerical principles, the Revolutionists argued that the notion of benevolence perpetuated the superstitious belief that giving money to the poor secured the donor a place in heaven. They claimed that religious institutions such as the foundling hospitals run by the Sisters of Charity were mismanaged and inefficient and had created a large group of social parasites (Forrest 1981, pp. 16–19; Hufton 1992, pp. 61–3). According to the humanitarian principles favoured by the Revolutionary Government, the state had an obligation to provide for the general welfare of all its members. It was consequently the duty of society, not of the church or of individual benefactors, to resolve the problem of the large population of poor, unmarried mothers and abandoned infants (Rodis 1968, pp. 173–5). The government's efforts to bring the illegitimate into the compass of the social meshed neatly with the revolutionary goal of increasing the French population and with the move to secularise matters previously under ecclesiastical control, including marriage and divorce (Rodis 1968, pp. 187–90, 218; Proctor 1990, pp. 96–102).

The Constituent Assembly of 1790 directed the provinces to hand over to the state the responsibility for the maintenance of foundlings. The charitable religious orders were disbanded and replaced by a government committee dedicated to ascertaining and properly managing what its members deemed to be the nation's 'real' poor (Hufton 1992, ch. 2). The Constitution of 1791 affirmed the right of the indigent to assistance and the duty of the state to provide it. In 1793 another law mandated state assistance to illegitimate children and their mothers (Fuchs 1990, p. 100). An unmarried mother could go to a hospital for the delivery of her child at state expense, or the state would provide monetary support if she chose to keep and nurse her child. If it was impossible for her to keep the infant the state would arrange for it to be placed in a hospital or with a wet-nurse (McCloy 1946, p. 255). Wet-nurses were to be remunerated for work that Republican rhetoric transformed into a valuable and ennobling task performed in the service of the nation (Hufton 1992, pp. 64–5).

Social historians of Revolutionary France note that, because of insufficient funds, these welfare programs barely got off the ground, and the poverty and distress which characterised the lives of many unmarried mothers and their infants not only failed to improve but worsened in the Revolutionary period. In 1811 a Napoleonic decree abolished assistance to mothers and instead created a system of foundling homes and wet-nurses for abandoned infants which, according to some estimates, led to the death of over half of those children (Fuchs 1990, p. 100). The legal reforms of the early 1790s were overturned. The Napoleonic Code enacted in 1804 revoked the provision for the legal equality of legitimates and illegitimates and expressly forbade mothers from seeking child support from the fathers of their illegitimate children, thereby reversing a centuries-old legal requirement that a father financially support his child, whether he married the mother or not (Fuchs 1990, p. 37; Brinton 1936, pp. 81–4). The Revolutionists' reverence for bourgeois marriage and the family triumphed ultimately over egalitarian sentiment.

As many historians have pointed out there was a wide gulf between Revolutionary ideals and practice. The social policies and legal reforms of the 1790s did, however, set an important discursive precedent. Revolutionary language placed into discourse the relatively novel idea that illegitimate children and their mothers were valued and rights-bearing members of the Republic. The illegitimate population was transformed, even if briefly and rhetorically, into 'a precious human resource of potential soldiers and mothers' (Hufton 1992, p. 64) to be known by official decree as '*enfants de la patrie*' (McCloy 1946, pp. 255–6). It became possible to think about the illegitimate as citizens, contributors to the strength of the state and worthy recipients of state support.

As illegitimate births became redefined as events of national significance Revolutionary Government officials realised that they needed to count them and compare them to legitimate births. The same Enlightenment ideals that had driven the new turn in social policy produced the first statistics of illegitimate births. Countable illegitimacy was a by-product of the emergence in the eighteenth century of 'population' as an economic and political problem with, in Foucault's words, sex at its heart ([1976] 1981, pp. 24–6). The new population question ran parallel with a faith in the possibility of total knowledge, an enthusiasm for social facts and the pursuit of what were called the moral sciences. This new European science of society was founded on the assumption that man needed to be studied with the same methods and precision as the natural and physical sciences.

The connection between statistics and the state was stronger and established earlier in France than in any other country. In 1785 Jacques Necker, a financier who subsequently became an official of the French Royal Treasury, published a *Treatise on the Administration of the Finances of France* that included figures relating to birth-rates and infant mortality (James 1979, p. 311). After the collapse of the old regime and following the success of Necker's book, the Constituent Assembly gave priority to the collection of statistical data for administration purposes by establishing a board of statistics. Necker himself collected from each commune information on its population, produce and commerce (Peuchet 1815, p. 13). The Republican enthusiasm for statistical science extended to the committee with responsibility for the welfare of the poor, which used statistics provided by the eighty-five departments to categorise the poor according to income levels (Hufton 1992, pp. 68–70; Forrest 1981, p. 24). In a similar but larger project, Jean-Antoine Chaptal, Minister of the Interior from 1800 to 1804, instituted a grand 'statistical topography' based on data provided by the prefects of each department, whose purpose was to produce and classify a 'complete body of information' on the inhabitants of each geographical area 'in a reasoned manner' (Perrot and Woolf 1984, p. 87).

The purpose of this extensive and systematic information-gathering exercise was, as the officials put it, to document 'the splendid representation of the fortune and power of the French empire' (Peuchet 1815, p. 16). Effective government demanded knowledge about disadvantaged and potentially troublesome sections of the population. In addition to gathering essential information about finances and natural resources some surveys sought to assess the impact of the Revolution on 'the people' of France. Chaptal's topographies inquired into the social customs, private habits and practices of the different classes of French society, primarily the poor (Perrot and Woolf 1984; Woolf 1989).

Peuchet, the illegitimacy reformer, was one of the Revolutionary Government's most prolific statisticians and a leading exponent of new demographic techniques. According to Peuchet, statistical science was more exact than the older moral sociology and political economy models. Statistics provided 'the facts, the bases for calculation, the real picture of the wealth and strength of the state' (Perrot and Woolf 1984, p. 86). Peuchet included population statistics in his *Dictionnaire*

Universel de la Géographie Commercante on the grounds that 'men' not only constituted part of the wealth and strength of the state but were a means of increasing it (Peuchet 1799). Among those social factors influencing the size of the population, according to Peuchet, were laws relating to illegitimate children.

In 1800 at Chaptal's request, Peuchet produced *An Essay on the General Statistics of France*, a methodological treatise designed to provide a model for the new French statistical method by reinventing statistical systems of classification. Peuchet included Necker's original estimate, possibly contained in his 1785 *Treatise*, of the extent to which illegitimate births had been affected by the Revolution. According to Necker, the proportion of illegitimate births had risen from $1/47$th in 1780 to $1/11$th of the total number of births in the country (Peuchet 1815, p. 39).

Computing the extent of illegitimacy in different populations and determining how much it had risen or fallen over time was, as Foucault ([1976] 1981) suggests, only one of a number of new ways of speaking scientifically about sex. From the eighteenth century onwards the 'deployment of sexuality' was superimposed on the older 'deployment of alliance'. The deployment of sexuality 'has its reason for being, not in reproducing itself, but in proliferating, innovating, annexing, creating, and penetrating bodies in an increasingly detailed way, and in controlling populations in an increasingly comprehensive way' (Foucault [1976] 1981, p. 107).

The burgeoning statistical interest in illegitimacy in the second half of the nineteenth century exemplifies the interpenetration of the deployment of alliance and that of sexuality. The old problem of the transmission of wealth became intricately enmeshed within the new one of regulating bodily pleasures.

As the various European states created institutions to collect and disseminate statistics in the first few decades of the nineteenth century, figures relating to illegitimate births joined what Ian Hacking has called an 'avalanche of printed numbers' (1990, ch. 5). This proliferation of figures is evident in the Belgian statistician Adolphe Quetelet's statistical study of society, *A Treatise on Man and the Development of His Faculties* (published in French in 1835 and translated into English in 1842). The first part of the treatise examined 'all which relates to the life of man, his reproduction, and mortality' (Quetelet [1842] 1969, p. 10). The statistical study of illegitimate births had already assumed an international and comparative character. Quetelet's study included illegitimacy figures for France (69.7 illegitimate for every 1000 legitimate children), the Kingdom of Naples (48.4), Prussia (76.4), Westphalia (88.1), the cities of Westphalia (217.4), and Montpellier (91.6). Quetelet noted that although rates varied considerably in cities such as Stockholm, Leipzig and Berlin, overall the proportions of illegitimate births had increased over the past fifty years. He cited figures from as early as 1780 suggesting that France was not the only European state to begin to show an interest in illegitimacy at the end of the eighteenth century (Quetelet [1842] 1969, p. 22).

Illegitimate births were starting to be counted as part of the population. Quetelet pointed out that because some births were illegitimate, population growth did not correspond exactly to an increase in the number of marriages. When estimating marital fertility, therefore, scholars needed to compare *legitimate* births with the number of marriages (Quetelet [1842] 1969, p. 10). In his subsequent discussions of demographic phenomena such as the sex ratio, infant mortality and still-births, Quetelet carefully disaggregated legitimate from illegitimate births.

Quetelet placed his discussion of illegitimacy under the heading 'The influence of morality'. In the first half of the nineteenth century scholars habitually interpreted illegitimate births as a demographic outcome of immoral conduct. Simultaneously, statistical-social discourse transformed illegitimacy into a proper object of scientific analysis. Reassuringly concrete numbers turned a vexatious abstract moral problem into a measurable, discussable and potentially solvable 'thing'.

Statisticians refined their methods over the course of the nineteenth century, and the language in which they talked about illegitimate populations became statistically coded and formulaic. Statisticians routinely referred to the 'illegitimacy rate' or ratio; that is, the number of illegitimate births in relation to the total number of births, usually expressed in numbers per 100 or 1000 births, as a percentage, or as a ratio expressed in the formula 'one in every x number of births'. By the 1870s statisticians favoured what they viewed as a more accurate but more difficult calculation: the number of illegitimate births in relation to the number of unmarried women between the ages of 15 (or 20) and 45 in any given population (Farr 1877).

Aided by the introduction of civil registration procedures in the 1830s, British and colonial government officials began to systematically collect, compare and explain data relating to the illegitimacy rates of different regions and nations. The implementation of the British Registration Act of 1836 was overseen by the Registrar-General, William Farr. Farr was not only an eminent statistician, he was known as a rationalist and a reformist. He believed that poverty and disease were the result of poor living conditions that could partly be improved through sanitary measures, but would only be ameliorated by raising the poorer classes' standard of living. The General Register Office became a 'government-sponsored pulpit for reforming ideas' during Farr's incumbency (Cullen 1975, p. 38).

As both statistician and social observer Farr showed a particular interest in the measurement of illegitimacy. In his first detailed discussion of illegitimacy figures, in the 1844 report to the House of Commons, Farr noted the possible impact of recent amendments to the Poor Law which placed the responsibility for maintaining illegitimate offspring on their mothers. He drew the attention of the House to a number of other variables: seasonal variations in the illegitimacy ratio, the ratio of illegitimate boys to girls, the relative prevalence of illegitimacy (which he also calls by its older name of 'bastardy', a term still used up to the end of the nineteenth century) in the various English counties, comparisons with several states of Europe, numbers born in London compared with other large European cities, and high illegitimate death rates. Although Farr's report was a study in demography it indirectly raised political questions concerning the possible relationship between illegitimacy and religion, welfare assistance, provincial morals and the pernicious effects on national wellbeing of urban life and institutions such as foundling hospitals. Farr was anxious to distance the statistical study of illegitimacy from questions of sexual morality, claiming that the returns of illegitimacy could not be taken as an indicator of the state of morals or of the 'peculiarity in the manners of the people' of any particular district. If illegitimacy was implicated in immoral behaviour it was because the mortality rate among infants placed in 'Foreign Foundling Hospitals' was so high. It was in this sense that illegitimacy was a great social evil. Farr quoted his colleague, Christophe Bernouilli, a descendant of the famous Swiss family of scientists and mathematicians and the author of a study outlining the new science of 'populationistik' published in Germany in 1841:

> Who can doubt that their bringing up is much harder and more difficult? that [sic] the existence of a class of men, bound to society by few or no family ties, is not a matter of indifference to the State? The great majority of foundlings are illegitimate, which of itself shows how little, as a general rule, the mothers can or will care for these children. It is beyond doubt that fewer illegitimate children grow up to maturity; that they get through the world with more trouble; that more of them are poor; and that therefore more of them become criminals. Illegitimacy is in itself an evil to a man; and the State should seek to diminish the number of these births, and carefully inquire to what circumstances any increase is to be ascribed. (Registrar-General 1844, p. xxiv.)

Illegitimacy, in Farr's view, was an evil that governments must continue to count and explain because it produced death, poverty and social distress, not – or not just – because it was a product of immoral sexual behaviour.

Worried by manifest sexual impropriety in their own neighbourhoods, Farr's Australian colleagues were less forgiving. During the convict period high rates of illegitimacy were taken as an indicator of a dangerously unruly and unsettled population. Parish records of births were often incomplete, especially for the Roman Catholic population (Roman Catholic clergy were not appointed to New South Wales until 1820). The introduction of self-government provided both the facilities and a strong motive for collecting vital statistics in New South Wales, Victoria, Tasmania and South Australia in the 1850s. Victoria's first Registrar-General, W. H. Archer, completed his training in England at the height of the enthusiasm for the collection and analysis of statistical data (Forster and Hazlehurst n.d., pp. 4–21). Following the British example, Victorian legislation provided for the civil registration of births, deaths and marriages in 1853, and illegitimate births were included in the first reports from Victoria (1854), New South Wales (1857), and for the other colonies as soon as they were established.

Colonial officials linked illegitimacy explicitly to poor moral standards. The New South Wales Registrar-General remarked in 1869 that his colony's illegitimacy figures represented 'a proportional increase much to be lamented, and calling for the earnest interference of the conservators of public morals to check the growth of this affliction' (New South Wales 1869). His colleagues to the north were equally outspoken. The Queensland Registrar-General's report on vital statistics for 1893 described the colony's high illegitimacy rate as 'a blot on Social life in this Colony', and blamed the large number of women, particularly those afflicted with 'town life and habits', who had refused the responsibilities and duties of marriage and who were living in unlawful cohabitation (Queensland 1893). Although Australian government statisticians were more prone to make moral judgements than their British counterparts, they shared a preoccupation with urban/rural and regional variations and what these statistics might reveal about the morality of different sub-populations. Reports routinely pointed out that the figures for urban districts were artificially inflated by country women who came to the towns to 'hide their shame' and seek the help of lying-in hospitals, orphanages, benevolent asylums and other institutions for 'fallen women'.

Timothy Coghlan, appointed New South Wales Government Statist in 1886, included illegitimacy rates in his series on *The Wealth and Progress of New South Wales*. Historian Desley Deacon describes Coghlan, a public servant with an unusually high public profile, as 'one of the most respected authorities in New South Wales on social and political issues' (Deacon 1989, p. 113). Like many of his professional colleagues, Coghlan's main political interest was the welfare of the working classes. High infant mortality and illegitimate birth-rates indicated to Coghlan that the colony was failing to prosper. Coghlan argued that the statistical fact that in 1890 one child in every eight was born in the colony with 'the brand of illegitimacy' was both 'a serious reflection upon the morals of the community' and a matter of state concern, 'as a very large percentage of these unfortunate children become a burden to the country from their birth, and it is from such that the pauper population of the Colony is largely recruited' (Coghlan 1889–90, p. 447). Even though New South Wales had no Poor Laws, the Australian and English illegitimacy 'problem' was framed in very similar terms.

Statistics produced by government officials provided the empirical precondition for social–scientific theories of illegitimacy. The problem of illegitimacy was swept up in the 'era of enthusiasm in statistics' and the statistical movement of early Victorian Britain (Cullen 1975; Porter 1986; Gigerenzer et al. 1989). Government statisticians and professional social scientists, inspired by a new sense of the dynamism of 'society' as a source of both progress and instability and persuaded of the need for a 'social science' to understand it, produced a swelling stream of vital statistics. Official statistical offices proliferated and a number of statistical societies were established from the 1830s in France, Germany, the United States and especially in Britain (notably those of London and Manchester). Much of this statistical activity was prompted by a liberal temperament and a strong desire for social reform. Advocates of the science of statistics believed that 'the confusion of politics could be replaced by an orderly reign of facts' (Porter 1986, p. 27).

Recently, historians of gender have revealed the unstable and deeply political nature of statistical discourse and its authoritative contribution to particular constructions of male and female identities (Deacon 1985; Scott 1988a; Anderson 1992). Mary Poovey (1993) suggests that even in its nascent stages in the 1830s and 1840s the British statistical establishment's claims to scientific objectivity generated dispute and scepticism. A number of different groups, each of which looked at the various social questions of the day from a particular class, gender or political vantage point, made up the social–scientific establishment. According to Eileen Janes Yeo (1996), social–scientific knowledge was a site of contest between socialists, women, professional statisticians, doctors and social investigators. The inherent uncertainty of statistical discourse, together with constant disagreement over priorities and methods that would effect social and moral improvement, made mid-nineteenth-century social–scientific constructions of illegitimacy highly mobile.

Illegitimacy analysts Adolphe Quetelet and Thomas Robert Malthus were among the handful of prominent statisticians involved in setting up the Statistical Society of London in 1833. Illegitimacy was a minor preoccupation of the early statistical movement but members of the Statistical Society of London did occasionally present papers on the subject, either in its own right or, more typically, as it related to infant mortality. The social profile of the statistical society was 'distinctly middle-class' and included a majority of professional men, including civil servants and academics (Yeo 1996, p. 65). M.J. Cullen (1975, pp. 135–9) suggests that adherents of the statistical movement were primarily concerned with the ill-effects of urbanisation and the means of improving it through better public health and education. They expected that a concerted individual, corporate and government attack on the urban environment would lead to a more moral society.

Two important papers on illegitimacy were presented to the Statistical Society in this period. The first was William Acton's 1859 'Observations on Illegitimacy', as far as I can tell the first English-language sociological study devoted to the subject. It was based on an analysis of the unpublished returns of the Registrar-General relating to the deaths of children under 5 years of age born to unmarried women. Acton detailed the sex and age at death of each illegitimate infant, the cause of death, the occupation and age of the mother and the occupations of some of the fathers. He concluded that there was an excessively high mortality rate among illegitimate infants in certain London parishes and that the London Foundling Hospital was mismanaged and ineffective. Acton proposed establishing a government board that would take responsibility for the health and welfare of pregnant women and seek to 'recover damages' from the child's father.

Acton was a Member of the Royal College of Surgeons, a Fellow of the Statistical Society of London and a prominent advocate of social progress. In this article he represented himself as the brave bearer of the torch of reason in dangerously dark and unexplored moral territory. However 'disagreeable or repulsive the task' Acton proclaimed, illegitimacy like other 'social evils' – Acton most likely was thinking of another of his preoccupations, prostitution – demanded the attention of 'a body whose self-imposed task and duty is the careful collection of what I may fairly call the raw material of truths' (Acton 1859, p. 491). His defensive preface suggests that illegitimacy, traditionally only whispered about in polite society or seen as a matter for the church, was still barely a subject about which English gentlemen might speak in public. Perhaps anticipating criticism, Acton used statistical discourse to shield him against the possible charge that his investigation might be more scurrilous than scientific.

Acton's paper prompted a longer and more conventionally demographic study of the 'Statistics of Illegitimacy' by W. G. Lumley. Lumley was also a member of the Statistical Society, a barrister and an Assistant Secretary of the Poor Law Board. Designed to test statistically the common perception that illegitimacy was widespread in England, Lumley's objective was to 'ascertain what is the real extent of this social disorder in this country; how it differs in the various parts of the kingdom; and how, in this respect, England can bear a comparison with other countries' (Lumley 1862, p. 219). Lumley investigated the possible influence on illegitimacy rates of seasonal variations, the density of the population, the number of persons per household, education, religion, the extent of prostitution and 'prudential habits'. Lumley found that the amount of the 'evil' was less than generally estimated, and that England fared well by comparison with other countries. He found no clear relationship between any of the posited social variables and illegitimacy rates, and cautioned statisticians against making hasty theoretical judgements. Indeed, he concluded, illegitimacy rates were influenced by any number of political, moral, religious, social, legal and natural conditions, while the accuracy of the statistics themselves were affected by 'variations in the modes of obtaining and recording the facts' (1862, p. 274). Lumley's point was that it was difficult, if not impossible, to empirically determine illegitimacy rates and their causes.

These methodological caveats would be familiar to demographers today. Unlike contemporary statistical experts, however, Lumley was openly interested in moral questions. Lumley stated that the statistician's proper business was figures, not social or moral judgements. But he argued against legal provision for legitimisation on the grounds that it may induce a woman to 'submit to that conduct which in its first consequences produces distress and shame' (Lumley 1862, p. 263). He suggested that the shining examples of Queen Victoria and her consort, 'distinguished by their domestic virtues and the purity and decorum of their lives', had prevented England from following the downward moral course of her European neighbours. The extension of religious instruction and sanitary improvements among the lowest classes would, Lumley hoped, ensure that England would occupy first place in the international scale of morality (1862, p. 274).

Lumley's statistics played a leading role in Edmund Robertson's article on bastards for the 1875 edition of the *Encyclopaedia Britannica*. Encyclopaedia definitions are a useful barometer of the impact of statistical discourse on conceptualisations of illegitimacy. The 1854 *Encyclopaedia Britannica* entry for 'bastard' was the first to contain statistics. It supplemented the legal information given in 1791 with a statistical discussion based on the registration data for England and Wales and vital statistics for Scotland that had just become available. The 'bastard' entry in the 1853 *Standard Library Cyclopaedia of Political, Constitutional, Statistical and Forensic Knowledge* also used the new statistical material.

In the 1875 edition of the *Encyclopaedia Britannica*, 'bastard' is a legal category and is distinguished from the sub-topic of 'illegitimacy', which is primarily statistical and social in meaning. Robertson, a Professor of Roman Law, drew the reader's attention to observable statistical patterns in illegitimacy and their possible causes, referring to the conundrum represented by 'striking differences' in local and national rates alongside the 'steadiness with which the general average of illegitimacy is maintained' over time. In common with most of his colleagues, Robertson found that differences of religious belief or education did not explain national variations, but offered no alternative explanation. Robertson's definition stood unchanged for thirty-five years.

By the mid-nineteenth century the study of illegitimacy had started to attract scholars who described themselves as social scientists. Today we would probably call them amateur quantitative sociologists. The National Association for the Promotion of Social Science, established in England in 1857, included many members of the legal professions, with smaller numbers who were members of parliament, London businessmen, doctors, civil servants and aristocrats. Some members were female. According to Eileen Janes Yeo the annual Congresses, held in a different city each year, were major social events involving the local elite in soirées and social–scientific sightseeing, as well as engaging them in serious scholarly debate (Yeo 1996, pp. 153–5). In addition to extended discussions of infanticide and infant mortality, members of the Association presented papers specifically on illegitimacy, mostly in the 1860s. Subjects covered by male members included the laws of Belgium relating to illegitimate children and foundlings, the causes of illegitimacy in Scotland, bastardy in rural districts and the affiliation of illegitimate children. Women contributed their thoughts on a House of Shelter for Females and a proposed system of licensed nursing for illegitimate children.

Social scientists placed particular emphasis on the relationship between illegitimacy and the moral and social condition of the working classes. The result was often an eclectic mix of religion and science. In George Seton's 1860 pamphlet on *The Causes of Illegitimacy, Particularly in Scotland*, originally a paper read before the Social Science Association, theories influenced by Christian prohibitions on sexual impurity held equivalent intellectual status with those arising out of secular notions of the social. The publication in 1858 of the Scottish Registrar-General's first illegitimacy statistics sparked considerable speculation on the reasons for the country's particularly high rate of illegitimate births. An advocate (barrister) holding a Master of Arts degree from Oxford, Seton modestly described himself as a novice in the new science of 'social economy'. Nevertheless, Seton calculated that the extent of illegitimacy was considerably greater in Scotland than in England and most other European nations with the exception of Austria.

Seton used quotations from the Bible to support his sociological claims. Despite its scientific language of rates, percentages, proportions and comparisons, *The Causes of Illegitimacy* presented the problem of illegitimacy primarily as one of immorality among the working classes, and specifically as a problem of the lack of fit between religious principles and secular practices. Although many of the causes he identified were economic, Seton believed that the only way to eradicate illegitimacy was 'to elevate the moral and religious standard of the people'. Seton described illegitimacy as an 'evil', yet represented the consequences of illegitimacy – the production of unfortunate children who were likely to 'occupy a very prominent position in the records of poverty and crime' – as a social problem (Seton 1860, p. 23).

Early social scientists like Seton often referred to the uncertainty and relative novelty of statistical discourse. Seton's preface stated that he had made some concessions to 'readers who happen to entertain a horror of *ratios* and *percentages*' (Seton 1860, p. iv). He admitted that others may discover causes of illegitimacy that he had omitted, and that some of his own may actually 'jostle against' one another in what he called 'the paradoxes of Social Economy' (1860, p. iv). He cautioned against placing too much significance on figures:

> Speaking generally, … it must be acknowledged that the number of illegitimate births is not, as has been alleged by certain moralists, the exact mathematical expression of the corruption of society, nor the most convincing proof of the demoralization of the country in which they take place. There are unquestionably worse forms of vice than illegitimacy … If illegitimacy were to be taken as the gauge of morals, it is to be feared that very false inferences would in many instances be drawn; and guided by statistics alone, the most casual observer would surely hesitate to conclude that, in purity of manners, Palermo, Hamburg, and Amersterdam, are fully three, and London fully eight times better than Paris, Berlin, and Vienna. (Seton 1860, pp. 23–4.)

Despite a lack of formal training in statistics Seton and many of his contemporaries were alert to the slippery nature of the relationship between moral conduct and its arithmetical expression.

At about the time Seton was writing, statistics and sociology were starting to part company (Cullen 1975, pp. 148–9). Statistics were less often seen as the solution to social problems, more frequently located within the domain of mathematics. The National Association for the Promotion of Social Science collapsed in the mid-1880s. The waning of the mid-Victorian passion for moral arithmetic coincided with a lull in the sociological study of illegitimacy, which did not get off the ground again until the 1890s. In the course of the early statistical movement, however, social scientists had attached an arithmetical mantle to illegitimacy that proved to be permanent. If, by the end of the nineteenth century, statistics were no longer seen as the answer to the problem of illegitimacy, they had become indispensable to its public definition.

In 1892 Albert Leffingwell, a Doctor of Medicine, member of the International Congress of Hygiene and Demography and amateur sociologist, published (in both London and New York) what he claimed was the first treatise in the English language on the subject of illegitimacy. *Illegitimacy and the Influence of the Seasons Upon Conduct, Two Studies in Demography* extended and popularised the approach developed in the 1850s and 1860s by Acton, Seton and Lumley. Unambiguously sub-titled 'A Study in Morals', the book attributed the root of the illegitimacy problem to 'a lessened sensitivity to moral injunctions', 'moral delinquency', 'laxity of morals', 'ante-marital faults', 'moral susceptibility' or the absence of 'moral stamina'.

Alongside the moral terminology, however, Leffingwell frequently asserted his belief in scientific objectivity. Pointing out, as some of his predecessors had done, that low rates of illegitimacy did not necessarily imply a higher tone of morality, Leffingwell argued that illegitimacy statistics could only test the comparative sensitiveness of different people to moral laws 'when the totality of general environment is similar, as between cities or communities under the same general government' (Leffingwell 1892, pp. 86–7). The book was driven by an evangelistic belief in the social value of scientific methodologies and statistical facts. Leffingwell used statistics to refute commonly held 'unscientific' theories about the causes of illegitimacy, studding his text with diagrams, charts, tables and maps. Statistics, according to Leffingwell, were 'the record of events; not the building of hypotheses. In contemplation of them we stand, as it were, in audience with Truth itself, as distinct from that vague shadow of truth which the best opinion and most careful estimate – apart from the facts themselves – can only be to us' (1892, pp. 3–4). Leffingwell admitted that 'absolute accuracy cannot be hoped for, especially in respect to an event involving so much of shame and disgrace', but concluded optimistically that overall the effect of any errors was infinitesimal.

As proof of this accuracy Leffingwell pointed to the remarkable regularity with which illegitimate births occurred in any given locality, 'again and again, year after year, in almost precisely the same numbers, in almost exactly the same average frequency'. This 'event in human conduct' was akin to a law of Nature: invariable, regular and predictable. The same story of trouble and disgrace, anguish and remorse was repeated over and over again: 'For Nature does not more securely guarantee to the farmer the average product of his field than she gives to England, to Scotland, to Ireland, this annual harvest of sorrow and shame' (1892, p. 7). Statistics showed illegitimacy to be a natural phenomenon, one of the timeless patterns of human nature, rather than, as more conventional moralists would argue, an individual event located within the realm of the Divine. Leffingwell suggested that all natural laws, even those that were unhappy expressions of immoral and undesirable behaviour, served some social purpose.

Statistical analysis proved that illegitimacy and other moral issues were not the exclusive province of the churches but were amenable to rational explanation. Leffingwell's work was popular with the Legitimation League of London, a marriage reform organisation of free-thinkers founded in 1893 with the object of creating a means of acknowledging offspring born out of wedlock and securing their equal rights with legitimate children. The League's Secretary, Oswald Dawson, urged his followers to read Leffingwell's book. Another member, 'Agnosco', presented a paper in which he or she referred to statistical evidence of the influence of the seasons upon conduct (a subject investigated by Leffingwell in conjunction with his study of illegitimacy), and in particular upon the number of illegitimate births. Despite this evidence, Agnosco claimed:

> there will remain people who deny the rational physical theory of morality, and who are now, as ever, willing to absolutely ignore all the facts of the case, and to pretend that morality has had a divine and heaven-inspired origin, and that it is directed towards the well-being of humanity not in this world, which is most concerned in [sic] it, but in a land beyond the skies. (Legitimation League 1895, pp. 216–7.)

Agnosco's paper, which had appeared the previous year in the *Agnostic Journal*, suggests the critical role played by statistics in supporting the move towards a secular social science.

Although Leffingwell's 'rational physical theory of morality' was secular in tone, he was not anti-religious; on the contrary, he nominated the effect of religious belief as a major contributory factor to different rates of illegitimacy. But he was puzzled by evidence that, for example, strongly Calvinist Scotland exhibited such a high rate of illegitimate births. He accepted that religion, in general, was 'one of the most potent of agencies in checking the passions and proclivities of the human animal'. Yet comparing the statistics of different countries suggested that the influence of religion on illegitimacy had little to do with particular creeds or varieties of dogmatic teachings. Religion could be overruled by 'other and even stronger forces that move humanity toward action' (Leffingwell 1892, p. 42).

Leffingwell's *Illegitimacy* became a model for the objective, quantitative and theoretical study of illegitimacy, particularly within demography, one that has since been refined but not substantially altered. Social scientists referred to Leffingwell's study as an authoritative source well into the twentieth century and, to this day one or more copies of *Illegitimacy* can be found on library shelves throughout Australia, England and the United States.

Leffingwell was the main source on illegitimacy for the 1910 edition of the *Encyclopaedia Britannica*, the first to carry a separate entry for 'illegitimacy' (and another for 'legitimacy and legitimation') in addition to the 'bastard' essay that had been included since 1791. The topic was now irreversibly split into its legal and social–statistical aspects. The illegitimacy essay was written by Thomas Allan Ingram, Doctor of Laws, of Trinity College, Dublin. Ingram's sociological analysis incorporated twelve statistical tables, two of them occupying a whole page. It followed Leffingwell in stressing that the prevalence of illegitimacy in any community could not be taken as a guide to the morality of that community, and admitted that the reasons for its prevalence and extraordinary regional variations were not readily found. For an encyclopaedia reference, the tone of the account is surprisingly uncertain. The more sharply defined the statistical contours of the problem became, the more elusive was its truth.

The 1910 *Encyclopaedia Britannica* essay marks the moment at which illegitimacy, as a fully quantifiable if still puzzling social phenomenon, achieved the status of a coherent and self-contained object of western social-intellectual scrutiny. By the early twentieth century illegitimacy was a standard component of 'vital statistics'. The *New Dictionary of Statistics* (1911), for example, placed it between Bees and Building Societies as 'Births – Illegitimate'.

Twentieth-century discussions of illegitimacy statistics were increasingly dominated by methodological considerations. Thus the *New Dictionary of Statistics* pointed out that 'no very safe deductions' could be drawn from the table showing the average annual number of illegitimate births per 1000 live births because the figures needed to be compared with changes in the numbers of legitimate births. As Farr had pointed out in 1877, what needed to be compared was the ratio of illegitimate births to the numbers of unmarried women of childbearing ages. In the more codified statistical language of the twentieth century, this was the difference between 'corrected' and 'crude' rates of illegitimacy (*Encyclopaedia Britannica* 1910). Then, as now, statisticians were quick to criticise the temptation to jump to statistically unwarranted conclusions. By the second decade of the twentieth century the older moral framework had slipped into the background, giving way to a mathematical focus on statistical technique. Illegitimacy, according to W. F. Nixon in a paper delivered to the Royal Statistical Society, was 'affected by so many correlated circumstances that only by the use of technical methods can we hope to determine the part played by each one' (Nixon 1913–14, p. 862).

The advance of statistical representations of illegitimacy was geographically uneven. By the end of the nineteenth century the problem of illegitimacy occupied a secure niche within British and Australian statistical discourse and within statistically grounded British sociology. Australia in the nineteenth century had no indigenous sociology to speak of. Illegitimacy's position within the corresponding nineteenth-century American literature was also tenuous. Middle-class, educated white Americans undoubtedly disapproved of illegitimacy. But if the contents of its early sociology journals are any guide, American social scientists did not at this stage take much of a professional interest in the subject. Thus an article on 'The moral statistics of the United States' in the American *Journal of Social Science* (Woolsey 1881) referred to abortion, infanticide, divorce, seduction and concubinage – but not illegitimacy. This scholarly inattention may have had something to do with the absence in the United States of a tradition of Poor Law debates. The United States did not witness a flurry of activity on the same scale as that set in motion by members of the early statistical movement of Victorian Britain. Possibly American social observers had other more pressing social issues to worry about: the rising tide of immigrant births, for example, may have been a greater cause of concern than illegitimate increases in the white population.

The discursive silence was most likely due to the absence of widely available national official statistics of the kind which, by the 1850s, were being routinely collected by British and Australian government statisticians. It was not until 1915 that the Bureau of the Census of the Federal Government of the United States established a national system of birth registration, and 1933 before all forty-eight States were included and a complete national series of vital statistics produced. Illegitimacy statistics for some States were first made available by the Federal Government in 1917 (National Office of Vital Statistics 1947, pp. v–vii, xxiii–xxv). Only a few States had actually published their figures on illegitimacy by the early 1920s (Mangold 1921, p. 20). They made their first appearance in the *Statistical Abstract of the United States* in 1923 in the form of a table showing the number of births and still-births by legitimacy for each registration State (United States Bureau of the Census 1923, p. 70). Not until the 1920s could American social scientists quantify, and hence talk seriously about, the nation's illegitimacy problem.

It was not long before the United States caught up with the British and Australian registration systems. The recording and publication of illegitimate births has since become a routine practice of western governments. Official terminology now refers not to illegitimate births but to ex-nuptial births (Australia), 'births outside marriage' (Britain), or 'births to unmarried women' (United States). But the signified is essentially the same. To give one example, the Australian Bureau of Statistics *Year Book Australia* for 1996 reports that according to the last census single-parent families comprised 13 per cent of all families, and that the 'long-established upward trend in the proportion of births that are ex-nuptial is continuing', comprising 15 per cent of all registered births in 1984 and 26 per cent in 1994 (Australian Bureau of Statistics 1996, pp. 86–9). In 1995 almost one in three Australian children were born out of wedlock (Australian Bureau of Statistics 1997). These statistics are provided, according to Australian statistician Ian Castles, because 'the social and economic well-being of lone parents and their children is an issue of great current concern in Australian society' and statistics relating to one-parent families can contribute to 'informed public debate' (Australian Bureau of Statistics 1991, p. v). Social policy personnel, social analysts, welfare professionals, educationists, charity workers, housing and urban planners, market researchers, social reformers, politicians and even the 'person in the street' still consider it necessary to know exactly how many children are born outside of marriage. Today there is barely a book or article on the subject that does not at least begin with a paragraph citing relevant statistical information. Without statistics, scholarly conversations about social problems become virtually impossible: effectively there would be no problem, or at least not one that can be talked about in public.

Alongside the practical, generally sympathetic and welfare-related reasons why governments continue to differentiate nuptial from ex-nuptial births, illegitimacy statistics carry with them some of their older moral and social meanings. Illegitimacy rates continue to have something to say about social wellbeing. They are eminently newsworthy. The latest official figures are leapt upon by newspapers producing headlines like 'Ex-nuptial boom' (*Sydney Morning Herald* 1996), 'Third of births in U.S. to unmarried women – study' (Reuter 1996), 'EU survey has Britain third on the list for illegitimacy' (Jury 1994) and – a distinctively Australian touch – 'A nation of bastards. One in three babies born out of wedlock' (Luff and Barnsley 1997). Ex-nuptial birth statistics are considered an essential prerequisite for any sensible public discussion of the issue (which usually means, more negatively, the 'problem' or the worrying social trend) of increasing proportions of sole-parent families.

Conversely, a decline, as reported for the United States in 1996, is hailed as 'good news' about the country's social fabric. President Clinton told Americans in a national radio address that when the teen birth-rate drops for four years in a row, and out-of-wedlock births decline for the first time in a generation, they can be sure that 'The American family is getting stronger and we are making responsibility a way of life. Our economy and our society are on the right track' (White House 1996b). Reducing numbers rather than changing behaviour is now the primary goal of social policy. Thus Clinton suggested that America would be a better country if it could cut its teen pregnancy rate in half (White House 1996a). The state's priority is to identify a significant group of disadvantaged children (and their mothers) so that they can be helped, thereby contributing to the overall social and economic betterment of the nation.

No matter who uses them, or for what political purpose, contemporary illegitimacy statistics have trailing behind them the shreds of the middle-class moral and reformist project which gave birth to them in the nineteenth century. Given the long-standing social validation given to marriage as an institution, simply drawing a line between nuptial and ex-nuptial births inevitably, if unintentionally, sets up the ex-nuptial category as abnormal and undesirable by comparison with its more highly valued opposite. Nuptial births are the norm, not only because they represent the statistical majority but because western bourgeois society has always expected and preferred children to be born within wedlock. The marital two-parent norm has historically been equated with social improvement. If the category 'ex-nuptial birth' has a utilitarian value for those concerned with the welfare of sole parents and their children, it also perpetuates a moral dualism that, post-1970s euphemisms notwithstanding, brands a birth that takes place outside of marriage as by definition 'lesser' and more problematic than its marital equivalent. Social scientists, statisticians and the governments they serve may need to weigh up the advantages and disadvantages of retaining an anachronistic category more suited to the era of moral arithmetic than to the chaotic and complex world of the twenty-first century.

Contemporary western societies are more tolerant of sex outside marriage, non-marital births are no longer a statistical oddity, and paternity acknowledgement and long-term cohabitation is increasing while marriage rates are falling. Do these trends indicate that in the future social scientists might stop counting ex-nuptial births? It seems unlikely. The inherent methodological problems of illegitimacy and other moral statistics did not deter nineteenth-century scholars of society from attempting to quantify various forms of bad working-class behaviour. The appeal lay partly in illegitimacy's association with what middle-class observers saw as the repulsive yet fascinating sexual habits of working-class men and women. For all their problems, the impulse to collect, arrange and interpret illegitimacy statistics proved irresistible.

The pleasures of dealing scientifically with illegitimacy were, I would suggest, as much intellectual as sexual. Nineteenth-century social scientists were intrigued by the statistical regularity with which illegitimate births took place in comparison to legitimate births. In a non-scientific context, premarital sexual intercourse and the birth of illegitimate children were intimate, random and unpredictable human events. The magic of statistics revealed that 'in fact' the ratio of illegitimate to legitimate births was relatively fixed. On the other hand, while illegitimacy statistics held the promise of providing concrete answers to abstract moral questions on informed scholarly examination they yielded few obvious or indisputable truths, if not blatant contradictions. It was deliciously impossible to draw from statistics any firm conclusions about the causes of illegitimacy, or why the proportions of illegitimate and legitimate births varied so widely across the cities, counties and nations of the western world. Illegitimacy statistics were, on the one hand, deadly serious, on the other, titillating and tantalising – a winning combination that may explain why they continue to fascinate social scientists all over the world.

CHAPTER 3

Reproducing at the Nation's Expense

The vital statistics that emerged out of Europe in the early nineteenth century enabled certain scientific arguments to be made about the rightness of 'natural' social arrangements, including marriage and the family. More particularly, French Revolutionary statistics supported the ideas of the Reverend Thomas Robert Malthus, the first theorist writing in the English language to present illegitimacy as a problem for society. The return of Malthusian interpretations of illegitimacy in the second half of the twentieth century, and their impact on welfare debates in the 1990s, suggests the need for a closer look at Malthus' *An Essay on the Principle of Population* (first published 1798 and substantially revised in later editions; the 1986 version is a reprint of the 1803 and 1826 editions).

Mathematics, Malthus' main subject of study while he was at Cambridge University in the 1780s (Winch 1987, p. 11), provided the empirical underpinnings of the *Essay*. The *Essay* was a treatise built around the difference between the geometric rate of increase in the population and the arithmetic rate of increase in food supply. Without its arithmetical formulas and population statistics, Malthus' unconventional thesis would not have been taken so seriously by either his supporters or critics. As Foucault states in *The Order of Things*, 'the recourse to mathematics, in one form or another, has always been the simplest way of providing positive knowledge about man with a scientific style, form and justification' (Foucault 1973, p. 351).

Malthus' *Essay* is considered a pioneering work of population theory. It marked a major turning point in eighteenth-century ideas about the relationship between population size and the pursuit of the wealth and happiness of the people. Before Malthus, population scholars generally adhered to the mercantilist view that all governments needed 'men and money', and that an expanding population would contribute to a nation's power and economic progress. It was not uncommon for European governments to attempt to stimulate increases in their population by encouraging marriage, rewarding the formation of large families or discouraging celibacy. Hospitals for foundlings were established and illegitimacy treated with greater leniency for the same reason (Smith 1951, p. 10). To solve the problem of the depopulation of Iceland in the eighteenth century, for example, the King of Denmark decreed that 'no disgrace should fall on any maiden who had as many as six children' (Stangeland 1904, p. 128). Holding a similar belief that the new French Republic needed as many subjects as possible, the early Revolutionary Government of France removed the legal disabilities attached to illegitimate birth.

Arguing instead that population growth was detrimental to national wellbeing, Malthus' *Essay* reversed many of the assumptions that had dominated political thinking about the population from the sixteenth to the eighteenth century. Malthus' explicit intention was to counter some of the utopian social theories emerging out of the Revolution by responding directly to William Godwin and the Marquis de Condorcet, writers well known for their optimistic support of the doctrine of human perfectibility and the 'reign of reason' in human affairs. Malthus disputed the principle of unlimited human improvement. Where Godwin had argued that social misery was the product of human institutions that could be reformed, Malthus' view was that misery was an inevitable outcome of the forces of nature. Commentators point out that in this respect the *Essay* was only one among many counter-revolutionary tracts written at the time (Winch 1987, p. 16).

In the opinion of one twentieth-century critic what Malthus contributed was 'a scientific pessimism, which, gloomy and fatalistic as it was towards the hopes of the working classes, absolved the ruling classes from the need to make "futile" efforts on their behalf' (Smith 1951, p. 34). The political context of Revolution and the intellectual context of the Enlightenment out of which the *Essay* was born produced an unusually powerful and durable truth about the 'natural' laws governing the relationship between population growth, public assistance and national misery.

Illegitimacy was a minor theme in Malthus' work, and in that of his followers and critics, as any reading of the extensive body of Malthusian literature makes clear. Illegitimate births are explicitly referred to on barely a dozen pages of a long book. Nevertheless, the *Essay* has made a major contribution to the idea that the state cannot afford to support illegitimacy. Unlike his predecessors in political economy Malthus imagined 'the population' as an entity that embraced illegitimate as

well as legitimate births. It was the first scientific treatise in English to
use statistics of illegitimate birth to construct a vision of illegitimate
children as a dangerously prolific and unstable component of the
population.

Malthus used the figures published in 1800 by French
Revolutionary statistician Jacques Peuchet. Malthus became interested
in illegitimacy some time between the publication of the first edition
of *An Essay On the Principle of Population* in 1798 and the second revised
and much-expanded version of 1803. In the interim Malthus
supported his controversial arguments in the first edition by collecting
more 'facts' from various parts of the world for the second. It is
possible he obtained a copy of Peuchet's statistical essay during a visit
to France just before the second edition was published. Many of
Malthus' comments on the French illegitimacy figures appear in foot-
notes, the longest one appended to the chapter on 'The checks to
population in France', written in haste on his return to London at the
end of 1802 (James 1979, pp. 72, 92–3). Assessing the impact of the
Revolution on the French population, Malthus expressed concern that
the proportion of illegitimate births had risen from $1/47$th to $1/11$th of
the whole number of births. He proposed that these figures indicated
a net increase in the population (pp. 219–20). Under normal conditions this 'extraordinary' increase in illegitimate births would be
absorbed by high levels of mortality as infants were abandoned to
foundling hospitals. However, sources of funding for the hospitals
dried up during the Revolution and nurses could not be paid. Because
the hospitals reduced their support when the economic condition of
agricultural labourers was improving and illegitimate births increasing,
Malthus speculated that a greater number of babies than usual were
reared at home and were therefore more likely to have survived
(p. 227). Historical evidence of exceptionally high rates of infant
mortality in Revolutionary France, as we saw in chapter 1, suggests that
Malthus was far too generous in his calculation of the size of the illegitimate population.

As no comparable figures were available for Britain, Malthus could
only guess that the proportion of illegitimate births in England was less
than the one in forty-seven in pre-Revolutionary France (Malthus
[1803] 1986, p. 282). Whether French or English, illegitimate births
were, for Malthus, an inflationary influence on the population.
Undesirable population growth occurred among the lower classes. The
poor imprudently produced too many babies who, when they grew up,
lowered wages, exerted pressure on food supplies, drained the state of
limited resources and thereby increased social unhappiness. In
Malthus' view, the numbers of superfluous poor illegitimate children

produced by the political upheavals in France could only be bad for the state. Malthus invented the now familiar formula that high or rising illegitimate birth-rates have undesirable consequences for national wellbeing.

Illegitimacy has a negative meaning in the *Essay* and in much of the social inquiry that Malthus has influenced since. Its rhetorical power derives from the way in which Malthus intersects illegitimacy with conventional early nineteenth-century notions of sexual difference, sexual morality, marriage and family. Illegitimacy was undesirable not only because it increased the population but also because it was associated with immorality and the absence of parental affection. Misery would only be kept in check, according to Malthus, by reducing the number of children born to married male labourers who had the means to support them. Malthus advocated moral restraint – delaying marriage, thereby reducing the number of children born – as the best means of regulating population growth. However, moral restraint would only be effective if deferring marriage did not produce more 'vice' in the form of prostitution, adultery, promiscuous intercourse and 'improper arts to conceal the consequences of irregular connections'; that is, contraceptive measures ([1803] 1986, p. 16). High rates of illegitimacy were transparent proof that the labouring classes were failing to exercise moral restraint.

Underlying Malthus' theory of moral restraint was his assumption that men and women had different natures, capacities and social functions in relation to the population. Women, he claimed, were the ones who actually exercised moral virtue ([1803] 1986, p. 315). Men's role was to refrain from any act prompted by the desire for immediate sexual gratification until they were in a position to maintain their family and become responsible and reliable breadwinners. In the meantime, they should acquire not only savings but 'habits of sobriety, industry and economy' (p. 475). The ideal Malthusian marriage thus comprised a moral wife and a prudent husband.

In Malthus' opinion, society's age-old disapproval of illegitimate births proved that the institution of marriage was one of the fundamental laws of society. Because women could not be reliable breadwinners, the children of an illicit union were necessarily dependent on society for their survival. To prevent this 'inconvenience' to the community, Malthus argues, women came to attract a greater disgrace for a breach of chastity than men. Like the 1791 *Encyclopaedia Britannica*, Malthus acknowledged the unfairness of a custom that punished the woman and not the man for transgressing the marriage law. Nevertheless, the illegitimacy rule and therefore the institution of marriage appeared to be a law of nature.

Malthus' program placed a high premium on chastity for both men and women ([1803] 1986, p. 476). Sexual passion could never have a civilising effect where it was gratified early and universally (pp. 469–70). Promiscuous intercourse degraded women's character, weakened the best human affections and, if no 'improper arts' were used, burdened society with as many illegitimate children as those born within marriage. Under a regime of moral restraint passion would be repressed for a time, only to 'afterwards burn with a brighter, purer, and steadier flame' (p. 476). Sexual passion was beneficial to society when it took place in the context of love between husband and wife, parent and child: 'The evening meal, the warm house, and the comfortable fireside, would lose half their interest, if we were to exclude the idea of some object of affection, with whom they were to be shared' (p. 469). For Malthus, chastity had 'the most real and solid foundation in nature and reason'.

To discourage imprudent parenting Malthus proposed the gradual abolition of the Poor Laws. The *Essay* was published at a time of mounting concern about growing numbers of able-bodied labourers requiring public relief and the consequent increase in Poor Law expenditure (Winch 1987, p. 9). Joseph Townsend had argued in his 1786 *Dissertation on the Poor Laws* that though 'beautiful in theory' the Poor Laws 'promote the evils they mean to remedy, and aggravate the distress they were intended to relieve' ([1786] 1817, p. 2). In Malthus' view, the Poor Laws counteracted England's natural advantages by draining national resources and creating 'wide-spreading tyranny, dependence, indolence and unhappiness' (Mathus [1803] 1986, p. 515). Most importantly, the provision of public relief eroded men's natural desire to support their families and encouraged them to desert the women and children who depended on them.

To save the rising generation from a 'miserable and helpless dependence upon the government and the rich' Malthus' controversial proposal was that no child should receive parish assistance. The illegitimate child's right to parish assistance was especially dubious:

> after the proper notice had been given, they should on no account whatever be allowed to have any claim to parish assistance. If the parents desert their child, they ought to be made answerable for the crime. The infant is, comparatively speaking, of no value to the society, as others will immediately supply its place. Its principal value is on account of its being the object of one of the most delightful passions in human nature – parental affection. But if this value be disregarded by those who are alone in a capacity to feel it, the society cannot be called upon to put itself in their place; and has no further business in its protection than in the case of its murder or intentional ill treatment to follow the general rules in punishing such crimes; which rules for the interests of morality, it is bound to pursue,

whether the object, in the particular instance, be of value to the state or not. (Mathus [1803] 1986, p. 517.)

Malthus argued that most illegitimate children taken into the care of the parish died anyway. Under his plan the death of an illegitimate child would be considered 'the necessary consequence of the conduct of its parents' ([1803] 1986, p. 517). Forcing the father of an illegitimate child to marry the mother would not solve the problem, because such marriages were destined to burden society with a family of paupers. Malthus believed that poor men and women would refrain from immoral behaviour and men would support their children, whether legitimate or illegitimate, if they knew that they might otherwise starve to death (p. 519). The sins of the fathers had to be visited upon the children (p. 520).

Malthus scholar Donald Winch aptly describes the *Essay* as a 'science of morals' (1987, p. 99): on the one hand, Malthus was a man of science holding an Enlightenment belief in the application to social affairs of general laws like those established by Newton; on the other, he was a theologian and man of religion – in daily life a Church of England curate – who unquestioningly accepted Christian ideas of sin, vice, virtue and morality. There was no conflict between Malthus the Christian moral philosopher and Malthus the scientist (Winch 1987, p. 37). Scientifically, illegitimacy was a consequence of the principle that the passion between the sexes will always produce more babies. Society condemned it because it transgressed the natural law of marriage. Morally, illegitimacy was wrong because it denoted lack of chastity and restraint and because illegitimate children were denied parental affection and guaranteed support.

Malthus' *Essay* prompted a spate of impassioned responses. Not all of his respondents mentioned illegitimacy, and those who did refer to it tended to do so briefly or parenthetically in the course of wrestling with the 'bigger' questions of population growth and its relationship to pauperism. Contributions to the Malthusian debate were variously framed by legal, philanthropic, utopian, humanitarian, Christian or economic discourse. Malthus' *Essay* provided a rallying point for the expression of a range of views on society's responsibility towards the illegitimate child.

The majority of Malthus' critics argued that his proposal for the gradual abolition of the Poor Laws was inhumane and unchristian. Malthus' original protagonist, William Godwin (1820, pp. 550–2), professed an angry incomprehension that anyone could be so heartless as to deny the right of the poor, the helpless and the deserted to support. The problem of the seduction of helpless females by the 'unfeeling monsters' of the higher classes would be solved, according to John McIniscon (1825, p. 211), if everyone simply adhered to Christian principles. William Hazlitt accused Malthus of effectively advocating infanticide. Malthus wanted to promote the growth of affection between individual parents and their children, yet it was only 'by extinguishing every spark of humanity in the breasts of the community towards the children of others that the ties of parental affection can ever exist in full force' (Hazlitt, 1807, p. 336).

Michael Thomas Sadler disagreed with Malthus' provocative claim that the illegitimate child was of no use to society. Sadler used statistics to prove that Malthus had greatly underestimated the demographic significance of illegitimate births, arguing that in countries where delayed marriage was common, illegitimate children were necessary to the preservation of the species (Sadler 1830, p. 159). Because Nature refused to be thwarted, Sadler argued, moral restraint would only result in the growth of an illegitimate – and therefore miserable – population. Sadler shared Malthus' perception that illegitimacy was potentially ruinous to social happiness.

Several writers took issue with Malthus' argument that publicly funded charitable institutions exacerbated the problems they were intended to solve by encouraging vice, indolence and poverty. Foundling hospitals presented these critics with some philosophical difficulties, however. James Grahame, a Scottish lawyer and prolific writer on a range of social questions, granted that of all charitable establishments, foundling hospitals were guilty as Malthus had charged. They did multiply the number of illegitimate births; but he concluded that it would be 'foolish and inhuman to abolish the remedy altogether' (Grahame [1816] 1994, p. 231). American lawyer and diplomat Alexander Everett agreed that legal provision for the aged, the infirm and the destitute was absolutely necessary. Foundling hospitals did 'in a slight degree' encourage vice. But almost every act of benevolence had some indirect and undesirable consequences, and the innocent child should not be made to suffer for the faults of its parents (Everett [1826] 1994, pp. 105–8).

It was probably criticisms such as these that caused Malthus to modify his position on the value of the illegitimate child in the 1826 edition of the *Essay*. The illegitimate infant became of 'little' rather than 'no' value to society. Malthus conceded that rather than the illegitimate child having no claim to assistance whatsoever it might be supported by private charity. The criticisms levelled at Malthus and his own change of mind suggests that, from its moment of birth, the problem of how society ought to deal with the illegitimate child was inherently controversial and possibly unsolvable.

The Malthusian controversy crystallised a random set of informal personal, philanthropic and religious perspectives on illegitimacy into a more rational and scientific way of speaking about immoral sexual and reproductive behaviour. After Malthus, illegitimacy was no longer just a problem for the individual, the family or the parish. Malthus and those who engaged with his theories presented it as having serious consequences for the region, the nation and, wider still, for western civilised society. Malthus' incorporation of illegitimate births into the problem of population growth placed illegitimacy at the heart of the question of how the nation ought to reproduce itself.

The debate that followed the publication of *An Essay* brought old concerns about the care of the illegitimate poor into the newer, more scientific, ambit of population economics. In the process scholars elaborated on Malthus' rather sketchy notion of illegitimacy as an intolerable expense for the nation. Thus George Ensor argued that foundling hospitals not only encouraged illicit intercourse and pregnancy and contributed to the premature death of children, as Malthus had argued, but just as importantly drained national resources:

> The woman who erred and suffered the penalty of rearing the fruit of her transgression would probably have ceased to sin; but relieve her of her child, and she seduces or is again seduced. Thus it happens that two or three lewd mothers and their consuming brood waste the means of a virtuous family. Suppose the children die; all that was expended on them is lost. If some be reared, what is the profit? (Ensor 1818, pp. 166–7.)

The child of the 'lewd mother' was, Ensor implied, less entitled to support than the child of a 'virtuous' one. Support was wasted on illegitimate infants who, if they survived, were feeble and sickly, likely to become vagabonds and generally produced little profit to society. In fact, because the mother was prevented from earning while she was pregnant the illegitimate child 'costs so much before he is born' (Ensor 1818, p. 168).

The English edition of Adolphe Quetelet's 1842 *Treatise On Man* reinforced the Malthusian doctrine on illegitimacy. Quetelet described the ratio of illegitimate births in some states as 'exceedingly great' and in others as 'increasing' or 'unfavourable'. Following Malthus, Quetelet argued that the production of illegitimate children was socially detrimental, since it increased the number of individuals who became a burden on the state. Besides, these individuals generally possessed a 'feeble organisation' and failed to survive. They never compensated for the sacrifices that society had made for them (Quetelet [1842] 1969, p. 22).

The publisher of the English edition of the *Treatise* added a long and somewhat critical footnote pointing out that Quetelet's discussion did not refer to the 'causes' of 'illegitimacy'. Quoting from Sir Edmund Head's report on the Law of Bastardy included in the Sixth Annual Report of the Poor Law Commissioners of 1840, the English publisher linked illegitimacy to other perceived social problems: delayed marriages because of lack of prospects; legislation allowing the retrospective legitimation of children on the subsequent marriage of the parents, as in Scotland; the demand for wet-nurses among the higher class of mothers in towns; and the existence of foundling hospitals, as in Sweden (Quetelet [1842] 1969, p. 23).

Quetelet wrote about 'illegitimate births' not 'illegitimacy'. The English commentator's use of the noun indicates it was acquiring the status of a definable social problem. Where Malthus and Quetelet characterised illegitimacy primarily as a problem of scarce economic resources, Quetelet's publisher characterised it as deviant but potentially understandable social behaviour. While some social observers continued to accept Malthus' proposition that illegitimate children were too expensive for the state to support, by 1840 the growth of scientific ways of talking about the problem had shifted the focus away from radical social policy that would cut public expenditure in an attempt to stop illegitimate reproduction. Instead, intellectual activity focused on the need to rationally explain the genesis of illegitimacy as a social phenomenon.

Quetelet's work marked the point at which Malthus' authority started to recede, at least in the English language. When, after mid-century, demographic evidence suggested that England's population was not expanding as Malthus had predicted but was declining, the status of his theory of illegitimacy waned. Malthus' social program was clearly at odds with the various social reform programs aimed at improving the condition of the working class that got underway in the second half of the nineteenth century. Malthus' proposal that poor, illegitimate children be left to starve not surprisingly horrified British anti-infanticide reformers and doctors like William Burke Ryan (1862, p. 47).

By the 1870s the educated public of Britain and the colonies was generally sceptical of Malthus' prediction of the dire social consequences of over-population. Instead, it was believed that in the interests of national prosperity, social wellbeing and the advancement of the British race the English peoples both 'at home' and in the dominions must urgently increase their numbers and thereby improve the condition of their working classes. Eminent British statist William Farr argued, for example, that 'new and multiplying industries in towns call for men', especially in the American, South African and Australian colonies (Farr 1877, p. 577).

The anti-Malthusian climate extended to Australia where the need to increase the legitimate population was considered urgent. Australian medical expert Walter Balls-Headley argued, for example, that it was against Nature and contrary to evolutionary principles for married women to delay having children (Balls-Headley 1894, p. 12). Malthus was deemed guilty by association with the neo-Malthusian movement. Sex reformers like Annie Besant modified Malthus' doctrines to argue that the over-population problem would be solved if birth control methods were practised within marriage. Octavius Charles Beale, a leading figure in the move to stop the decline in the Australian birth-rate and an outspoken critic of birth control, devoted several pages of his book *Racial Decay* to a scathing attack on Malthus' proposal that Nature be left to dispose of 'superfluous babies' and the encouragement his work offered to 'the apostles of sexual abnormality' (Beale 1910, pp. 32–9). By World War I social scientists in Britain and the United States were congratulating themselves on their modern enlightened approach to social problems. Malthus' 'drastic' views on illegitimate children were considered distinctly old-fashioned (Bisset-Smith 1918, pp. 165–8).

Malthus re-entered the public stage as an indistinct background figure in the groundswell of public opinion against state-supported illegitimacy that began in the late 1950s. This opposition was most noticeable in the United States. City officials and taxpayers began to worry about financing the care of what statistics showed to be a sharply rising number of illegitimate children through the Aid to Dependent Children (ADC) federal welfare program (*US News and World Report* 1959). Allegations of widespread fraud within the ADC program began to surface. By the 1960s the tide of public opinion had started to turn against what were coming to be called 'welfare mothers' (Gross 1960).

Liberal social scientists defended unmarried mothers (Morrison 1965; Goode 1967). But conservatives like American scholar Shirley M. Hartley suggested that 'the amazing rise of illegitimacy in Great Britain' was the result of the combined effects of an increased emphasis on youth, freedom and individuality, and a welfare state which removed the need for rational planning. Hartley explained that she had decided to focus on birth statistics for England and Wales because Britain, 'as the home of Malthus', had a long history of open discussion on the importance of population control (Hartley 1967, p. 535). The availability of 'cradle to grave security' under the English social welfare system reduced people's motivation to prevent conception and rewarded the less responsible at the expense of the more responsible. Hartley, like most mid-twentieth-century analysts, accepted the principle that society had a duty to support the unmarried mother and her child, but she agreed with Malthus that state assistance encouraged undesirable forms of reproduction.

The Malthusian critique of illegitimacy receded again as feminist support for single parenthood grew in the 1970s and 1980s. The dominant concern within liberal and feminist-influenced social inquiry was not that welfare encouraged illegitimacy but that single mothers and children reliant on welfare suffered from discrimination and social and economic disadvantage. Fears of out-of-control welfare expenditure and its links to increasing poverty and a rapidly rising illegitimacy rate returned in the 1990s, particularly in the United States. A spate of articles citing damning social scientific evidence of the negative welfare–illegitimacy connection appeared in major American newspapers: 'The scourge of illegitimacy: stop the subsidy' (Krauthammer 1994), 'Illegitimacy: an unprecedented catastrophe' (Broder 1994), and 'Working to make welfare a chore' (Besharov 1994).

Malthusian anxieties about the over-production of economically dependent citizens surface constantly in contemporary welfare debates. Middle-class single mothers who can afford to give their children adequate financial and emotional support are seen as much less of a problem for society than 'reckless' working-class single mothers who seek assistance from the state. The plain message of welfare reformers – 'don't have babies you can't support!' (Nathan 1996, p. 16) – is aimed at the working class. A large part of the problem is the unacceptable social behaviour of the poor, especially mothers who are, says sociologist Lawrence Mead, impulsive, immature and uncommitted (Mead 1996, p. 38). Charles Murray looks forward to a time when 'the concepts of "gentleman" and "lady" once again become governing norms for behavior' (Murray 1995, p. 132).

Contraception and abortion have, of course, become more widely practised since Malthus' time, and few social scientists would now argue that illegitimate pregnancies invariably inflate the population. Anti-welfare campaigners, like Malthus, advocate chastity. Government-supported teen abstinence programs attempt to control young people's premarital sexual activity and to get the message through to them that 'It's wrong to be pregnant or father a child unless you are married and ready to take on the responsibilities of parenthood' (Holland 1997).

Social conservatives claim that the expansion of the American welfare state is directly responsible for rising illegitimacy rates and therefore for social disintegration. Murray, like Malthus, characterises illegitimacy as an insupportable burden on the state. Illegitimate children are simply too costly. Both acknowledge that welfare support may in the short term help alleviate poverty and other social problems, but in the long run has undesirable social consequences. Poor relief, in

Malthus' view, was no remedy but rather an irritant to pauperism. In Murray's more modern terms, welfare discourages integrity, responsibility, self-determination, personal accountability and 'the human need' to be absorbed in pushing yourself to realise your capacities' (Murray 1989, p. 82). Murray predicts that if state aid was withdrawn, young, disadvantaged parents would be discouraged from socially inappropriate sexual behaviour, leaving illegitimate children to be supported privately by their mother's parents, boyfriends, siblings, neighbours, church or philanthropic organisations (1994b, p. 63). Murray, Douglas Besharov and other major architects of welfare reform in the United States follow in the footsteps of Malthus, the 'father' of the New Poor Law of 1834 that stopped outdoor relief to the able-bodied poor and removed all material aid outside the workhouse for mothers of illegitimate children (Ducrocq 1986, p. 35).

Anti-welfare conservatives would not deny that, promiscuous, demoralised and improvident though many of them are, the inner-city poor lead wretched lives. Neither would Malthus. Malthus believed that certain immutable laws governed the relationship between population growth and subsistence, implying that nothing the state or 'society' could do, including providing welfare assistance, would ever solve a social inequality that was natural. In addition to being ruinous to the poor, degrading to the rich, unnatural, and antichristian, Malthus' *Essay* suggested that the Poor Laws were useless. The poor had to help themselves (Smith 1951, p. 300).

A late twentieth-century version of Malthus' theory that social inequality was based in Nature appeared in *The Bell Curve* (1994) by Richard Herrnstein and Charles Murray. The authors argue that cognitive ability is genetically determined, and that the difference in IQ levels between the middle and working classes, and between whites and blacks, is innate and fixed. Ameliorative social policy aimed at redressing economic and social inequalities is therefore a waste of public money. If the poverty of the American poor is a natural, not a cultural phenomenon, current welfare programs are as useless as Malthus believed the English Poor Laws to be. Malthus believed the poor had illegitimate babies because they lacked 'foresight'; Herrenstein and Murray believe that single mothers are less intelligent than married ones.

Clinton's campaign to 'end welfare as we know it' plays on fears of over-population among the poor. Anti-welfare measures rely on the image of a rising underclass tide that will swamp and obliterate civilised society and implicitly refer to the Malthusian principle that unregulated population growth creates unbearable pressure on finite resources (in today's context, urban facilities, schools, housing, energy, transportation systems). After visiting the Chicago housing projects, a poor black community with notoriously high levels of single-parent households, Housing Secretary Henry Cisneros warned Clinton that 'With meagre public resources coming in, what people would do in desperation, I don't know' (Gibbs 1994, p. 33). One of the principal Malthusian legacies to modern thought is exactly this 'irrational fear of a full world' (Smith 1951, p. 330).

As it was nearly two centuries ago, the relationship between social science and the politics of welfare is an unstable one. Intense debate currently surrounds the question of whether or not welfare subsidises illegitimacy. At least one statistical report to the US Congress on out-of-wedlock childbearing, by Kristin A. Moore of Child Trends Inc., concluded that 'research to date indicates that welfare is at most a small part of the explanation' (United States Department of Health and Human Services 1995, p. 28). The Chairman of the Senate Committee on Finance, Bob Packwood, on the other hand, opened the committee's 1995 hearing on teen parents and welfare reform with the remark: 'If there is anything this Committee has heard about in its welfare hearings, it is teenage pregnancy, teenage pregnancy, teenage pregnancy, and the relation between teenage pregnancy and the likelihood of being on welfare for a long period of time' (United States Senate, Committee on Finance 1995, p. 1). Douglas Besharov, a population scholar attached to the conservative American Enterprise Institute was able to provide the committee with statistical evidence that never-married women were three times more likely than divorced women to be on welfare for ten years or more (United States Senate, Committee on Finance 1995, p. 4).

It was the evidence of expert witnesses like Besharov that ultimately won the day for conservative forces. The 1996 Personal Responsibility and Work Opportunity Reconciliation Act ended guaranteed federal aid to poor families, placed time limits on access to welfare benefits, and transferred the responsibility for administering welfare and employment programs to the States. In most cases welfare assistance is cut off after a maximum of two years. Single mothers are required, through various work incentive schemes, to re-enter the workforce. After 180-odd years as an anachronistic oddity, Malthus' prediction that a welfare state spells social disaster again rings true for many Americans. Others object to what they see as punitive, ineffective or ill-conceived welfare 'reform' measures. David Ellwood, Professor of Public Policy at Harvard, for example, described the legislation as 'an election-fuelled tragedy in the making' (Ellwood 1996). Katha Pollitt was critical of the nineteenth-century ideological tone of legislation that assumed that 'impoverishing the poor will bring about a reign of virtue and industry' (Pollitt 1996). Today's liberal scholars continue the long-running controversy sparked by Malthus' ideas in his own times.

In Britain and Australia there has been a similar reversal of the optimism and expansion that characterised the first five or six decades of the modern welfare state. In Britain, rumblings of complaint about expense to the state of single mothers on welfare emerged shortly after the *Sunday Times* invited Charles Murray to visit and comment on the emerging British underclass in 1989. Over the last five years or so there have been sporadic outbreaks of anti-single-mother sentiment, particularly from Conservative Party politicians. British newspapers reported that the Conservative Government was considering cutting social security benefits to lone mothers (Brindle 1993), withholding benefits from mothers who refuse to cooperate with the Child Support Agency (Brindle 1996) and amending the law to encourage young single mothers to give up their babies for adoption (Smithers 1996).

Until 1996 there was little support in Britain for any serious dismantling of the welfare state on the American scale. But there is a growing consensus among conservatives that welfare is both expensive and responsible for encouraging the wrong kind of social behaviour. The *Spectator* commended Clinton for ending 'the iniquitous system which makes the breeding of illegitimate children profitable (Johnson 1996). Although the Labour Government elected in 1997 claims it has a more compassionate approach to the problem of single parenthood than its Conservative opponents, Prime Minister Tony Blair is considering instituting welfare reform similar to that implemented in the United States in 1996. His social security minister Frank Field has argued that Britain's biggest welfare bill comes not from the jobless but from the numbers of single parents, and that the welfare system is responsible for the recent 'dramatic increase' in the nation's proportion of out-of-wedlock births (Johnston 1997).

In contrast to the United States where the problem is mostly framed as one of increasing levels of cash assistance, a central focus of welfare criticism in Britain has been single mothers' privileged access to scarce public housing. In the most notorious incident, in 1992 Conservative politician Peter Lilley accused teenagers of getting pregnant just so that they could get to the head of the housing queue, a charge repeated by his colleague John Redwood in 1995. Some commentators argue that Murray is right, and that instead of being punished as she used to be, the unmarried mother is rewarded today with state benefits and a roof over her head (Jones 1993). The core problem is the same in Britain and America: welfare benefits produce immoral behaviour (mostly attributed to women) while draining the nation of scarce public revenue. Within this rhetoric 'the nation' stands implicitly for the law–abiding, socially responsible and morally upright subject, the ideal male citizen who produces and consumes within his means. The conservative *Spectator* (1993), proposing in a leading article that adoption was a solution to welfare overspending, claimed that 'the unmarried mother has been increasingly encouraged to think that it is her right to bring up her child at someone else's expense'.

As *Guardian* columnist Francis Wheen pointed out in 1994, the views of Charles Murray on the evils of out-of-wedlock births 'chime in harmoniously' with those of Conservative politicians like Peter Lilley. Murray tailored his analysis of the American underclass and welfare system to fit the British context, arguing that the problem in both countries is that providing money to single women enables many of them to do 'what they would naturally like to do' (1990, p. 29). Increases in benefits in Britain in the 1970s and the passage in 1977 of the Homeless Persons Act (which allowed pregnant women and single mothers to get accommodation immediately, without having to wait in the queue for council housing) lifted a large portion of low-income young women above the threshold where having and keeping a baby became economically feasible (Murray 1990, p. 30). Murray's 'bleak' message is that in Britain, as in America, 'no matter how much money we spend on our cleverest social interventions' babies will continue to be born to the teenage mothers of the rising underclass. Illegitimacy's contribution to social deterioration simply is not amenable to 'social engineering' (Murray 1990, pp. 33–4).

In recent years conservative social scientists have added a new twist to the Malthusian critique of state-supported illegitimacy. Patricia Morgan, a sociologist attached to the London-based Institute of Economic Affairs, argues that the problem is more serious than rising levels of income support and housing privileges for lone parents. As a result of various government taxation concessions the single-parent family is actually better off economically than the two-parent family. The two-parent family is often poorer than the single-parent family, yet social policy effectively penalises the two-parent family by making it bear the burden of taxation (Morgan 1995, ch. 1). The argument that under existing social policies marriage attracts an economic penalty has survived the transition to New Labour (Daley, J. 1997) and has been taken up by conservatives in the United States (Besharov and Sullivan, 1996).

Conservative Australians' views on welfare are closer to those of their British and European cousins than they are to the more radical American 'end of welfare as we know it' camp. Until the 1996 federal election that brought the (conservative) Liberal–National Party Coalition to power the right of sole parents to government support appeared unquestioned. Australians generally believe themselves to be more accepting than Americans of the idea that the government has the ultimate responsibility to take care of all its citizens (Hewett 1996). Nevertheless, attacks on single mothers on welfare feature regularly on popular television, talkback shows and radio current affairs programs, and the idea that at least some single mothers abuse the welfare system is common among women in what market researchers call 'middle Australia' (Consumer Contact 1992, p. 79). High-profile public intellectuals like Padraic McGuinness (1995; 1996) and Bettina Arndt (1993; 1996) have repeatedly argued in the press that Australia needs to rethink single parents' automatic right to government assistance. The almost commonplace observation that the rise of single parenthood in Australia coincides with the introduction in 1973 of the Supporting Mother's Benefit (for example, Arndt 1993) strongly suggests an unhealthy causal relationship.

Reports that single mothers are having 'babies for profit' have resurfaced amidst signs that the Howard Government intends steering Australian social policy towards support for the two-parent traditional family (Kingston 1996). The Lyons Forum, a secretive Christian pro-family association that functions as a covert political faction within the Coalition Government, appears to support more stringent controls of payments to single mothers on the grounds that state welfare assistance encourages young women to have ex-nuptial children (Davidson 1997, p. 2).

Much of the Australian anti-welfare rhetoric is imported directly from the United States. Some commentators argue that the unmistakable trend towards replacing welfare with work incentive schemes and the apparent success of Clinton's welfare reform measures will inevitably have an effect on Australian social policy (Hewitt 1997). The ideas of American conservative critics are distributed in Australia through organisations like the Australian Family Association, the Centre for Independent Studies and the Institute for Public Affairs. The Centre for Independent Studies, for example, invited Charles Murray to offer his comments on 'The American experience with the welfare state' at one of its conferences (Murray 1989).

Like their American colleagues, Australian conservatives have a Malthusian preoccupation with immorality's contribution to social deterioration. Judgements about 'right' and 'wrong' forms of state intervention and 'good' and 'bad' forms of social behaviour implicitly inform conservative political and economic analyses. Although conservative arguments are typically framed with reference to the specifics of the Australian political context, Australian academics agree with Murray that welfare payments have inflated the population of dependants and contributed to family breakdown in Australia (Moran and Chisholm 1994; Swan and Bernstam 1988). The claim that couples who stay together subsidise couples who split up implies that the welfare state is rewarding morally questionable behaviour (Tapper 1993–4, p. 26). Barry Maley opposes state intervention in general, and welfare assistance in particular, because it contributes to social demoralisation (Popenoe et al. 1994, p. 81). Dr Claire Ibister of the Australian Family Association criticises taxation and social security payments that 'favour the uncommitted sexual relationships' (1990, p. 8).

Anti-welfare conservatives do not lack sympathy for, or necessarily want to punish, struggling single parents. Few would argue that all aid to poor mothers and their children should be stopped. Apart from any personal reluctance to act harshly towards suffering women and children, the social sciences have characteristically embraced a certain degree of humanitarian sentiment. Malthus himself considered that it was unjust to punish 'so natural a fault' as an unmarried woman's lapse from virtue, and pointed out that it was the mother who was 'driven from society for an offence which men commit nearly with impunity' (Malthus [1803] 1986, p. 337). He eventually conceded that the illegitimate child was entitled at least to charitable support, if not money from the government. Today, few would deny the state's responsibility to assist the unfortunate and 'genuinely needy' individual but the notion that 'society' cannot afford, economically or philosophically, to support illegitimacy (as distinct from illegitimate children) still lingers.

Some of today's conservative social scientists explicitly argue that Malthus' insights can be directly applied to contemporary welfare policy analysis (Bernstam and Swan 1989; Morgan 1995, p. 147). Generally, however, Malthus' influence is more subtle. Malthusian principles are embedded within the body of thought inhabitants of western cultures draw on to say what needs to be said. Malthus' ideas have seeped into the western vocabulary of thought about population and welfare problems, carrying with them the shadows of an earlier set of taken-for-granted assumptions about gender, class, sexuality and marriage. Malthus' ghostly archival presence helps explain why changes in welfare policy can still be supported today by moral rationales.

In one crucial respect, today's illegitimacy-prone class differs from its Malthusian predecessor. In place of Malthus' wars, famines and plagues, respectable citizens are, we are told, faced with rising levels of violence and crime, family breakdown, juvenile homelessness, suicide, delinquency, and chronic welfare dependency (for example, Tapper 1993–4, p. 24). Malthus' improvident white labouring classes have been transformed into a predominantly black 'underclass'. In the United States it is primarily poor African–American teenagers who are perceived to be uncontrollably breeding a new generation of lawless paupers destined to drain the state's coffers. Australian and British social scientists and journalists have produced less racialised but just as frightening national versions of an underclass only one step removed from the spectre of the American black ghetto. Social inquiry, as the next chapter argues, has firmly shackled the concept of racial inferiority to that of illegitimacy.

CHAPTER 4

Illegitimate Genes and Racial Inferiority

Social scientists universally report much higher rates of out-of-wedlock birth among African–Americans than among the white population. In the United States, therefore, the illegitimacy problem is invariably perceived as a racial issue. Conservative social scientists have reinforced the widespread public perception that illegitimacy is innately associated with the 'different' behaviour of black Americans. Charles Murray's *Losing Ground* (1984, p. 130) noted that black illegitimacy rates were considerably higher, and since the 1950s had been increasing at a faster rate, than white. Murray (1993) proposed that a young black woman's decision to have a child out of wedlock is influenced by a black culture characterised by 'a broader definition of family and a generally lower level of stigma associated with illegitimacy'. Murray claimed that 'Something in black culture tolerates or encourages births out of wedlock at higher rates than apply to white culture in any given year' (1994a, p. 55). This feature, previously unique to the black population, appears to be spreading to the white population according to Murray. The consequent social deterioration in lower-class communities 'may be as devastating for whites in the 1990s as it was for blacks in the 1960s' (1994a, p. 54).

Murray's vague reference to 'whatever-it-is about black culture' (1994a, p. 56) that is spreading to whites gestures towards a historically determined set of repressed fears and anxieties about the 'otherness' of non-white races. Middle-class North Americans (even conservative ones) are generally too polite to say in public that illegitimacy is a black thing. If commentators do make the connection they are quick to mention the poverty, lack of employment opportunities and general structural disadvantages that characterise many urban black communities. Arguments like Murray's nevertheless subtly convey the idea that black men and women have different notions of what constitutes acceptable family structure, sexual morality and parenting practices. These racial differences are a social problem because conservative discourses present them as a problem for American society as a whole.

African–American (Dickerson 1995; Omolade 1994), liberal (Zucchino 1997) and feminist (Sidel 1996; Phoenix 1993) writers point out that the current attack on single parenthood draws on well-established racist myths, misconceptions and stereotypes. Historian Rickie Solinger (1992) has shown that this tendency to racialise unmarried motherhood, and to view African–American unmarried mothers as inherently inferior to their white counterparts, goes back at least to the postwar period. Experts and other public figures viewed all unmarried mothers as a social problem. However, in white women, unwed pregnancy was seen as a treatable neurosis, leaving the 'biological stain of illegitimacy' affixed to black unwed mothers (1992, p. 9).

I want to suggest in this chapter an alternative way of critiquing the assumed relationship between racial inferiority and illegitimacy. Academic studies of the significance of illegitimacy to black cultures overwhelmingly refer to the United States, and there is now a vast and complex literature analysing black motherhood and the history of the black family. Scholars from other countries with a long history of racial conflict, such as South Africa, have also addressed the intersection of race and illegitimacy (Burman and Preston-Whyte 1992; Burman and van der Spuy 1996). Experts in other nations have paid little or no attention to the ways in which the single-parenthood problem intersect with racial questions. What I would like to do here, as a white Australian, is offer some speculations on how British and Australian social inquiry might nevertheless have contributed to the idea that high illegitimacy rates are conceptually inseparable from racial inferiority.

My claim that non-US cultures have historically linked race and illegitimacy may seem odd, given that race barely figures at all today in British or Australian accounts of single parenthood. An obvious answer lies in demographic statistics. According to sociologist Ann Phoenix, one of the few British scholars who has explored this silence, almost no statistical information is available on the relationship between race and lone parenthood in Britain, due in part to political opposition to collection of race statistics. In addition, the black British population, predominantly Asian and African–Caribbean, is smaller (roughly 5 per cent) and of more recent origin than the United States' African–American population (about 12 per cent of the total population). Rates of intermarriage are low in the United States and relatively high in Britain (and in Australia), consequently there are no national statistics on the incidence of teenage motherhood among young black women in Britain (Phoenix 1993, pp. 76–9).

Phoenix questions the automatic presumption of racial difference in both the United States and Britain. She suggests that socially constructed illegitimacy is racialised by the existence of race statistics which are themselves the product of a given culture's historical preoccupation with racial difference. In contrast to Britain, in the United States illegitimacy statistics were differentiated by race from the moment of their first official appearance in the 1920s.

Phoenix's suggestion that without statistics race–illegitimacy problems are barely thinkable is borne out by equivalent Australian discourses. Australia, like Britain, has not been home to significant numbers of inhabitants of African descent. The Aboriginal and Torres Strait Islander population has, by comparison, always been much smaller in size. Aboriginal people were typically dispersed in outback areas rather than visible in the cities, and were not officially counted in 'reckoning the population' of Australia until a Constitutional amendment was approved by a referendum in 1967. Reliable figures were available for the first time in 1971, the first census to ask respondents to indicate the race to which they considered themselves to belong. Official statistics indicate that indigenous people currently constitute less than 2 per cent of the Australian population.

The non-white single mother of Australia is barely visible in statistical discourse. The 'single-parent Aboriginal and Torres Strait Islander family' and the 'Aboriginal sole parent' have emerged only in the last decade as distinct social types, and then less as a result of sociological curiosity than as a consequence of methodological refinement. 1986 census data made it possible to calculate that 33 per cent of all Aboriginal or Torres Strait Islander families were one-parent families, more than double the rate for all other Australian families (Australian Bureau of Statistics 1991, p. 12). Australians now know that in 1995, 74 per cent of all Aboriginal and Torres Strait Islander children were born ex-nuptially, compared with 27 per cent of all Australian children (Australian Bureau of Statistics 1997, p. 64).

Perhaps because of the slow growth of this statistical data, Australian social scientists have shown minimal interest in the racial aspects of sole parenthood. A handful of studies examine ethnic differences in the experience of single parenthood (Jordens 1993; Cass et al. 1992) and the specific problems faced by Aboriginal single mothers (Daly 1992; Jonas et al. 1992). Most Australians probably know, or would guess, that significant numbers of Aboriginal women give birth to ex-nuptial children but in both social inquiry and public debate about single parenthood racial difference is barely an issue. The Australian single mother and pregnant teenager are, by default, assumed to be white. Single parenthood is seen as a white problem and race is considered either marginal or simply not germane to the problem of rising rates of ex-nuptial births.

The discursive separation of race and illegitimacy in Australian public debate is evident in the controversy surrounding the 'stolen children'. The 'stolen children' or 'stolen generations' were the victims of the assimilationist policies of Australian State governments which, until their demise in the 1960s and 1970s, dictated that certain Aboriginal and Torres Strait Islander children be removed forcibly from their natural parents and communities and 'for their own good' placed in orphanages, children's homes, missions or in the homes of white adoptive or foster parents (Read 1984). The suffering caused by these welfare practices to large numbers of Aboriginal and Torres Strait Islander people was recently the subject of a national inquiry conducted by the Human Rights and Equal Opportunity Commission (1997). Many of the stolen children, categorised in the racist terminology of the time as 'half-caste', 'quadroon', 'octoroon', 'mixed blood' or 'lighter caste', were born to parents who were not married (often to an Aboriginal mother and white father), and were therefore considered, according to white cultural norms, 'illegitimate' (Link-Up NSW and Wilson 1997).

Understandably, any discrimination the stolen generations might have experienced as a consequence of the social stigma attached to ex-nuptial births has attracted much less public attention than the physical and sexual abuse, emotional pain, loss of family ties and personal identity, and ongoing psychological trauma caused by racist attitudes and colonialist practices. Although the illegitimacy of the stolen children is sometimes mentioned as a salient fact in the removal policy, the problem has been constructed overwhelmingly as one of the government's mistreatment of Aboriginal children on the basis of perceived racial status and its attempted genocide of the Aboriginal race. In direct contrast to the United States, in Australia the race problem is radically divorced from the illegitimacy problem.

Australian and British social scientists have not always been so reluctant to view illegitimacy in racial terms; neither did they consider themselves to be unduly hampered by the lack of appropriate statistics, at least in the nineteenth century. The scientific notion of illegitimate reproduction grew out of the seedbed of eighteenth- and early nineteenth-century constructions of racial inferiority. It was widely believed that the non-white races lacked sexual morals, disregarded marriage and bred prolifically and indiscriminately. Dominated by unruly sexual passions and insensitive to civilised standards of moral propriety, the racial 'others' of the early nineteenth-century population debate represented the depths to which western society might descend should it fail to control population growth among the poor. Malthus observed that in 'savage life', and even in (unspecified) 'southern countries', sexual impulses were almost immediately indulged and passion degraded to 'mere animal desire'. Sexual passion would contribute to social happiness, according to Malthus, only when it took the form of 'virtuous love'; that is, when it was restrained and regulated by Northern European conventions of acceptable sexual and marital behaviour ([1803] 1986, pp. 469–70). The illegitimacy problem was, from the moment of its birth, indelibly branded with racial politics.

Some of Malthus' followers explicitly associated undesirable population growth with 'the indolence, poverty, and demoralisation' of indigenous peoples (Quetelet [1842] 1969, p. 22). Adolphe Quetelet cited the example of the people of Guanaxato in Mexico. An observer had noted:

> the sad concurrence of excessive mortality, fecundity, and poverty, in Mexico, [and] attributes it to the banana, which almost ensures them an adequate quantity of food; others charge the raging heat of the climate, which begets an insurmountable aversion to labour, and leaves the inhabitants of this indolent region in a manner insensible to every other desire but that which impels the sexes towards each other. Hence the myriads of children, the greater part of whom do not live to be weaned, or only appear on the registers to give place immediately to others ... [Quetelet, [1842] 1969, p. 22.)

Quetelet's reference to the absence of maternal sentiment and excessive infant mortality among the banana-dependent people suggests he may have had illegitimacy in mind. The story about the Guanaxato appears under the heading 'The influence of morality' and is immediately followed by his discussion of European illegitimacy statistics.

The blatantly racist idea that indigenous peoples were like animals and therefore morally inferior to Europeans became less acceptable as social inquiry assumed an increasingly self-conscious 'objectivity' in the second half of the nineteenth century. The educated inhabitants of Britain and its colonies typically believed that the British people, and people of British descent, belonged to an inherently superior race. When they used the term 'race' they meant a specific human population – the British – defined by certain inherited predispositions, behaviours and national characteristics, a people joined by 'blood' rather than by the accident of environment. This 'unique' racial strength of the British people could be traced back centuries, to the various invasions of the Danes, the Anglo-Saxons and the Celts.

The British Registrar-General observed in his fourteenth Annual Report that unmarried women living in the southern counties of England (that is, the descendants of the old Saxon population) had few illegitimate children, while illegitimacy rates in the counties corresponding to the ancient Danish population were excessive (Lumley 1862, p. 235). W. G. Lumley argued, on the other hand, that the mixing of the races over the last ten or twelve centuries made any possible influence difficult to determine (Lumley 1862, p. 235). Lumley's contemporary, George Seton, believed that 'blood' may have some influence on national and individual characteristics, but that 'the effect of *circumstances* is probably much more potent' (Seton 1860, p. 7). William Lecky, author of the *History of European Morals*, argued that the immorality of a nation could not be judged by its statistics of illegitimate births (Lecky [1877] 1892, p. 144). Nevertheless, the suggestion that the regional distribution of illegitimacy in the British Isles might correlate with patterns of ancient racial invasions proved attractive to social scientists as late as the 1920s (Brownlee 1926, p. 181).

Albert Leffingwell's *Illegitimacy* (1892) lent weight to the idea that genetic make-up determines a people's propensity to illegitimacy. According to Leffingwell, heredity and ancestry, 'the predisposition that lies wrapped in organization, and which is passed onward by inheritance', were the most potent causes of human conduct. Racially specific tendencies towards vice or virtue crystallised as fixed elements of character and physique, and were passed on from one generation to another:

> Suppose, for instance, that a thousand years ago, upon part of the English coast – not then England – there descends a horde of piratical adventurers. They delight in blood and warfare; they toss the captive infants from spear to spear; they have no regard for chastity – indeed, they have little reverence for any religious constraints whatever. They take possession of the land, enslave the conquered, and become gradually, after a few generations, fixed to the soil. Now it is quite within the bounds of possibility that from the first conquest, bastardy may have been regarded among the people of such a tribe with much greater lenience than by another and more civilized tribe … That something like this has happened is at least probable. One tribe of our common ancestors were [sic] pirates, and piracy was never provocative of domestic virtue. (Leffingwell 1892, pp. 57–9.)

The result, a thousand years later, was an especially high rate of illegitimate births among the descendants of the tribe. Leffingwell's illustration is a dramatic, and to contemporary eyes, extremely racist representation of 'primitive' culture. Its rhetorical purpose, however, was to counter the popular idea that high rates of illegitimacy implied low moral standards. Leffingwell's alternative, ostensibly more 'scientific' hypothesis, claimed that a particular race's attitude to bastardy was not a moral flaw or deficiency, but was transmitted from one generation to another.

The non-white races especially demonstrated this 'hereditary proclivity' to immorality:

> The negro, transplanted from his native barbarism to America, Christianized, educated, and given the rights and privileges of citizenship, retains as a race, it would seem, nearly all the vicious and lascivious propensities of his forefathers in the jungles of Africa. The rate of illegitimacy prevailing in the American capital is three times that of London; but this is almost entirely due to the coloured population. (Leffingwell 1892, p. 64.)

Malthus and other early nineteenth-century social scientists had argued that the 'primitive races' had inferior moral sensibilities and were by their nature more prone to illegitimacy. Leffingwell also represented non-whites as 'other' but by suggesting the influence of 'ancestral vices and virtues' he appeared to be offering a scientific explanation and justification, rather than a moral judgement. The modern 'negro' could not help behaving the way he did because he was a victim of his ancestry. Leffingwell's still undeniably racist reformulation was influenced by rationalism and a paternalist impulse to defend the less fortunate.

As Leffingwell was exploring the influence of racial inheritance on illegitimacy rates, many of his colleagues in Australia and Britain applied themselves to the problem of the decline of the white birthrate. Unlike the statisticians and politicians of the French Revolution who had believed that illegitimate children boosted the size and strength of the national population, nineteenth-century British and Australian population experts viewed illegitimate births as either irrelevant to, or as a bad influence on, the size of the legitimate birth-rate. A high or rising illegitimacy rate indicated that all was not well with the vitality of 'the race'. The term 'the race' used in late nineteenth-century social–scientific discourse appeared to embrace the entire human species, but implicitly and specifically it meant men and women of English origin. The future of the race was of supreme importance to Walter Balls-Headley, Australian doctor, social commentator and author of *The Evolution of the Diseases of Women*: 'The ideal of marriage is the formation of unity, a perfect whole, a complete sexual body able and willing, healthily and happily, to perpetuate the race' (Balls-Headley 1894, p. 8). Balls-Headley believed that modern civilisation – including the trends towards women's greater emancipation, education and tight-fitting dresses – had made woman less physiologically fitted for the tasks of marriage and childbearing that were her evolutionary destiny. Young men were equally to blame because they seemed to prefer prostitution to matrimony. As a result, normal relations between the sexes were corrupted and women were failing to marry, or marrying too late, thus bearing fewer legitimate children (Balls-Headley 1894, ch. 2). Among the demographic evidence Balls-Headley provided in support of his thesis was an increase in the illegitimacy rates of all the Australian colonies. In Victoria in 1872, for example, 2.99 of every 100 births were illegitimate; by 1892 this figure had increased to 5.59 illegitimate births per 100 (Balls-Headley 1894, p. 18). A rise in the illegitimate birth-rate was a clear sign that the normal evolutionary course of the white race had gone awry.

Balls-Headley's contemporary, New South Wales statistician Timothy Coghlan, disagreed that the proportion of illegitimate births was rising. In his detailed statistical essay on *The Decline of the Birth-Rate of New South Wales and Other Phenomena of Child-Birth* (1903) Coghlan used what he considered to be a more accurate calculation that showed that the illegitimacy rate was *not* increasing, as it was popularly believed to be 'according to the ordinary mode of reckoning', but had remained virtually unchanged for decades (1903, p. 11). The apparent reason for the stability in New South Wales illegitimacy rates between 1861 and 1901 was disturbing. Like their married sisters, single women seemed to have learned 'the art of applying artificial checks to conception' (Coghlan 1903, p. 68). Coghlan produced official statistics that told a gloomy story of a rapid drop in national 'fecundity' since the mid-1870s. In Coghlan's opinion, and that of the Royal Commission that followed, Australian women were patently failing in their national duty to reproduce legitimately.

The Royal Commission on the Decline of the Birth-Rate and on the Mortality of Infants in New South Wales did not express disapproval of illegitimate births *per se*; rather, the Commissioners were concerned with illegitimate deaths. They pointed out that, on medical evidence, illegitimate infants were more likely to die than their legitimate brothers and sisters. In a section discussing the problem of infantile mortality the report noted that while many causes of death applied equally to legitimate and illegitimate babies, there were several 'additional' causes of death in the case of illegitimate infants: maternal indifference and the social and economic disabilities of mothers; mothers' defective management of their homes; the secret adoption of infants for monetary gain; the early separation of infants from their mothers; and the prevalence of infanticide and foeticide (New South Wales Legislative Assembly 1904, p. 39). High illegitimacy rates constituted a problem for national progress primarily because they brought with them a higher incidence of infanticide and infant mortality.

Racial imperatives informed these calls to decrease illegitimate and increase legitimate reproduction. The happy vision of Australia as a bright new country and an ideal land in which 'the people would prove fruitful and multiply' was rapidly fading (Coghlan 1903, p. 3). Coghlan warned that unless the decline in the marital birth-rate was halted the people of Australia would never take their place among the great nations of the world (Coghlan 1903, p. 69). The Commissioners referred explicitly to the need to preserve 'this fair heritage of the British race' and maintain a 'White Australia' in the face of Japanese and Russian rivalry for supremacy in the Western Pacific (New South Wales Legislative Assembly 1904, pp. 53–4).

As indigenous inhabitants were ignored in the birth-rate debate and in national population counts, the category of 'Australian people' clearly meant white Australians. Aboriginal people were not only completely discounted from any calculation of national wealth but their existence, like that of white illegitimate children, was implicitly positioned as potentially disruptive of social progress and an obstacle to the pursuit of a wholesome, healthy and prosperous white population. At the same time as Australian governments were representing the birth of white illegitimate children as a problem for population growth, they represented Aboriginal children as a problem because they needed 'civilising' and 'training' in the ways of European culture. The Aborigines Protection Act of 1909 gave the New South Wales Government complete power, including the power of removal, over all Aboriginal children deemed to be in need of care and control. Children whom officials assumed were not 'full-bloods' but part-European were the main focus of Aboriginal Protection Board activities because the Board believed 'the only chance these children have is to be taken away from their present environment and properly trained' (Link-Up NSW and Wilson 1997, p. 52).

The continued existence of what officials deemed to be 'destitute' and 'neglected' children represented a serious blot on Australia's social welfare record and hindered its progress towards prosperous enlightened nationhood. If 'half-caste' children were to be 'rescued' from their Aboriginal surroundings and reclaimed for the white population, they had to be radically and permanently separated from their own families and communities and forcibly placed in white homes or institutions. In the context of population policy, therefore, government efforts to Europeanise Aboriginal children and those to reduce the white illegitimacy rate were part of a common project. Both strategies were aimed at increasing the numbers and quality of the legitimate white population of Australia. Both government strategies were heavily supported by social scientists: anthropologists, welfare officials, statisticians, doctors and other experts on social questions.

By the time the British Government held a similar inquiry into the decline of its birth-rate in 1918, public and official attitudes towards illegitimacy had begun to change. Politicians, welfare workers and journalists expressed concern during World War I for the situation of 'war babies', children born as a result of typically fleeting sexual encounters between unmarried English women and soldiers. One American observer informed readers of the *New Republic* in 1915 that public opinion on support for war babies in Britain ranged from opposition on the grounds that it encouraged immorality, to calls to abolish illegitimacy altogether because every baby was a welcome addition to 'the grievously depleted human stock'. Fathered by men seen to be doing their duty for the Empire, war babies also inspired sentimental patriotism. As Charlotte Haldane, author of *Motherhood and its Enemies*, observed a decade later, the idealisation of the putative fathers of war babies – 'those brave boys' – tended to counteract the perceived moral lapses of their mothers (Haldane 1927, p. 90).

The war baby debate made possible a re-evaluation of illegitimacy's contribution to 'the race'. The unprecedented and urgent need of Britain and its European allies to replenish their white populations in the wake of the war's human losses gave the illegitimate child an increased social value and placed sexual immorality in a different perspective. 'If ever there was a time when infant lives are valuable', wrote T. W. Naylor Barlow, Medical Officer of Health for the English borough of Wallasey, 'surely it is now, when one regards the awful waste of life as the result of the war' (1916, p. 236). George Bisset-Smith, HM Examiner of Registrations, claimed at the end of the war that leaders in health matters had recognised that the health of children represented the real wealth of the nation and that the child was 'the one essential national asset' (Bisset-Smith 1918, p. 357).

The ubiquitous wartime rhetorics of life, death and national survival proved useful to a group of mostly female reformers who around World War I began to argue for social and legislative changes in favour of the unmarried mother and her child. C. Gasquoine Hartley (Mrs W. M. Gallichan, described as 'author of *The Truth About Women, The Position of Woman in Primitive Society*, etc. etc.') wrote in the *Nineteenth Century* magazine that the immense loss of life as a consequence of war had forced the nation to consider the need to preserve the new generation 'even to its last and meanest members'. England could not afford to be wasteful of the lives of little children (1921, p. 511). Mary Skrine (1917) argued in the *Spectator* that illegitimate children, 'these sad little black lambs of our national fold', were still the children of England, 'the

Greater Mother'. In times of war all babies were 'the most valuable thing in the world'.

Australian women were equally angry about the injustices experienced by unmarried mothers and equally adept at borrowing emotive wartime propaganda to make their point. Tullie Wollaston's sixpenny pamphlet *Compulsory Marriage* (1917) proposing that men be forced to marry the women they seduced and support the children they fathered was permeated by imperialist war rhetoric. Wollaston argued that in times of war people gained a new appreciation of the value of human life, and that this sensibility ought to be extended to the young woman and her illegitimate baby betrayed and abandoned by 'dastardly skulkers' no better than army deserters (1917, p. 6). The case of the poor gullible 17-year-old girl forced to poison her baby and hanged for murder was, she suggested, no different to the war atrocities committed by the Germans against Belgian women and children (p. 10). Just as Germany faced defeat because she lacked compassion, God would surely sap the strength of Australian women 'if for ever we turn away our cold hearts from the mute appeal of the innocent and helpless' (p. 23).

Reformers and welfare workers observed that the war had encouraged the growth of a new enlightened sympathy based on actual knowledge of human nature and social conditions. War brought 'a welcome tendency to face facts' (Wakefield 1919, p. 4). The prewar preoccupation with moral questions was replaced by a more 'strictly anthropological' approach (Lundberg 1918). As women entered the workforce in large numbers, foster mothers and wet-nurses for illegitimate babies became harder to find. The British Government stepped in to provide welfare support enabling unmarried mothers and babies to stay together, thereby hopefully increasing the illegitimate infant's chances of survival (Barnes 1917, p. 556). Homes were provided in which the unmarried mother could give birth to and then nurse her child, and nurseries set up for the children of women working in munitions factories and other wartime employment (Haldane 1927, p. 90). Bisset-Smith (1918) argued that it was this government assistance to unmarried pregnant women and the mothers of illegitimate children fathered by soldiers that had generated greater sympathy for the plight of the unmarried mother. The National Council for the Unmarried Mother and Her Child was established in Britain in 1918 to pursue legislative reform, secure accommodation for mothers and babies that would allow them to stay together for breastfeeding, and provide practical welfare assistance to individual unmarried mothers (Dixon 1981, pp. 2–3).

The wartime visibility of the unmarried mother and her child in public debate and social policy coincided with the growth of the social welfare professions. From the second decade of the twentieth century, child welfare experts and social workers in the United States and Britain, many of them women, assumed responsibility for the care of the unmarried mother and her child. As historian Regina Kunzel has noted of the movement in the United States, social workers 'energetically took to the task of transforming benevolence into a profession' (1993, p. 37). In Britain, too, women brought a self-consciously scientific and non-moralistic language to work previously done by philanthropic and religious organisations. There was, according to Annie Barnes, growing dissatisfaction with the old methods and attitudes characteristic of rescue work. Instead of the old regime of 'locked doors, laundry work and Bible classes', social workers were trying to keep mother and child together in an effort to save infant life, whether legitimate or illegitimate (1917, p. 557). Supporters of the unmarried mother and her child prided themselves on adopting a rational approach and an 'intelligent insight into causes and effects' (Hartley 1914, p. 89).

As a result of all these wartime changes – the controversy surrounding war babies, government welfare measures, the professionalisation of welfare work, a pervasive rhetoric about the sanctity of life – the illegitimacy problem achieved an unprecedentedly high public profile, not only in Britain, but also in Australia and the United States. Many of these wartime discussions of illegitimacy were inflected by the desire to pursue racial vigour and preserve the strength of the Empire. As C. Gasquoine Hartley (1914, p. 81) argued, ignoring the health and welfare of the illegitimate would have serious consequences for the race, and for the state. Statisticians were just as preoccupied with racial questions. Sir Bernard Mallet, Registrar-General of Births, Deaths and Marriages for England and Wales, examined a range of vital statistics, including illegitimacy rates, in order to assess what impact the war had had on the health and wellbeing of the British people. Mallett noted the 'surprising result' that the war appeared to have had little effect on illegitimacy rates (Mallet 1918, p. 13). Ascertaining such demographic facts was, he believed, necessary to determine precisely what damage had been inflicted on the British population, and how best to repair it. At stake was 'the whole great question of racial advance or decline' on which the fate of Britain depended (Mallet 1918, p. 1).

Questions of imperial strength were just as prominent in studies conducted by Australian health experts. J. S. Purdy, Medical Officer of Health for Sydney, was convinced that lowering the infant mortality rate and improving children's health was the key to both national prosperity and maintaining British supremacy. White Australians were proud to be descendants of the British people and believed the fate of their own population was closely tied to that of 'our Empire'. There was no point in winning a world war if by the end of the century Australia had not consolidated its victory

> by a world plan of social campaign and a peace programme of which one of the main features must be the rearing of a virile race, embodying the mental, moral and physical qualities which, under God's blessing, have enabled one nation thus far to sow far and wide the seeds of a higher civilization. (Purdy 1922, p. 296.)

Purdy included illegitimate children in his vision of a future virile race. The illegitimate infantile mortality rate in New South Wales had dropped substantially since 1900 as a result of the increasing concern shown for the 'unwanted child' by the New South Wales Government (1922, pp. 291–2).

In Britain, meanwhile, experts concerned about the decline of the birth-rate reconsidered the value to the nation of white illegitimate babies. The central political issue at stake in the British Government inquiry into the birth-rate begun in 1918 remained the maintenance of imperial power over what it proudly estimated to be one-quarter of the whole earth (Great Britain 1920, p. lxxiii). With a reduced birth-rate and inadequate manpower, in any future conflict Britons risked becoming slaves to another nation. British stock in the Dominions would decline and Britain would lose control over the native races who inhabited them, some of whom had 'race ambitions' (Great Britain 1920, p. lxxiii).

Where late nineteenth-century debates about the decline of the birth-rate in white populations had focused on quantity, twentieth-century population theories tended to concentrate on quality. A re-evaluation of the illegitimate child as a potential citizen promised a solution to the problem of racial decline. The British Commission noted that there was still a widespread public perception that illegitimacy should not be encouraged, but the decline in legitimate births in Britain since 1914 persuaded some experts that the illegitimate child could make up for the deficiency of births in wedlock (Great Britain 1920, p. lx). Mrs Bramwell Booth of the Salvation Army saw no reason why there should be any difference between the legitimate and illegitimate child in terms of its value to the nation (Great Britain 1920, p. 52). Newton Crane of the National Council for the Unmarried Mother and Her Child described illegitimate children as 'the capital of the State' (Great Britain 1920, p. 161).

With such great dangers facing the Empire, the Commissioners concluded that the British Government could not 'acquiesce in the destruction of children, legitimate or illegitimate' (1920, p. lxxi).

Contemporaries outside government agreed that, given that the birth-rate was falling, 'the racial significance' of illegitimacy had to be acknowledged ('Lens' 1920, p. 639). The idea that, in view of impending threats to white civilisation, unmarried mothers and their children ought to be accorded more social value resurfaced in Britain in debates about post-World War II reconstruction (Willoughby et al. 1942, p. 196) and in postwar Australian population theory (Wallace 1946, pp. 116–18, 327). Child welfare legislation passed in 1923 extended the right to a boarding-out allowance – state financial assistance initially designed to support women with dependent children (widows and deserted wives) – to white women whose children were illegitimate (Link-Up NSW and Wilson 1997, p. 68). No such reward for producing racially desirable citizens was offered to Aboriginal women.

In most pro-natalist discourses, talking about 'race' was simply a matter of distinguishing white from black (or Anglo-Saxons or Northern Europeans or British inhabitants of the Empire from 'the rest'). The white race was assumed to be homogeneous. In eugenic discourse, by contrast, the white race was imagined as an internally differentiated organism. When American, British or Australian eugenicists spoke of 'the race' what they imagined was a white population comprised of different individuals and social groups. These various racial 'types' occupied a genetically fixed place in a social hierarchy ranging from inferior to superior. Through various 'racial hygiene' or 'social hygiene' measures, eugenicists aimed to improve progressively the genetic quality of the race, or a nation's racial stock, by encouraging the reproduction of 'fit' members of society and discouraging that of the unfit. English sex analyst Havelock Ellis explained that social hygiene combined sanitary and eugenic reform in the service of the purification of the race (1912, p. vi). In practice what most eugenicists tried to do was 'to promote parenthood amongst the higher types, and to check fertility in inherently inferior homes' (Darwin 1918, p. 2).

With their emphasis on the need to encourage 'good' forms of reproduction and discourage 'bad', eugenicists contributed a new negative meaning to illegitimacy to those that already existed between about 1910 and 1930. Some social observers, like unmarried-mother supporter C. Gasquoine Hartley, believed that eugenics offered useful scientific backing for the political movement to help the illegitimate child (1914, p. 78). Generally, however, eugenicists opposed what they saw as the dangerously liberal views of pro-natalists, child-welfare advocates and supporters of the unmarried mother. Most eugenicists were strong upholders of monogamy and marriage (of the right or 'higher types', naturally). Major Leonard Darwin, member of the Royal Statistical Society, a contributor to the *Eugenics Review* and an expert witness at the British National Birth-Rate Commission, granted that society ought to treat the illegitimate mother more humanely than it did but, in his opinion, non-marital unions were temporary and ill-considered, and as a result illegitimate children inferior in civic worth. Reducing their number could only benefit the race (1918, p. 11).

A minority of eugenicists did approve of unmarried motherhood, but only for women of the higher social classes. Swedish reformer, social philosopher and 'freedom of love' champion Ellen Key (her work was translated into English and published in New York and London), argued in *Love and Marriage* (1911) that, provided they loved each other, young people ought to be able to become parents. From the individual woman's point of view, and from that of the race, any kind of motherhood was better than none. However, in Key's opinion, some single women were more fit to reproduce than others. She approved of the woman who possessed 'all the riches of her own and her lover's nature to leave through the child as a heritage to the race' (1911, p. 190). Those who did not love, or refused to associate with, the child's father risked injuring that child and forfeited the right to motherhood (1911, p. 176). Key was critical of unlawful unions which produced a 'weak and unwelcome child' (1911, pp. 127–8).

Key's anti-working-class sentiments emerged more clearly in *The Renaissance of Motherhood* (1914). Key was pleased that old notions of sexual morality were being revised and unmarried mothers increasingly accepted by society. She was outraged, however, by 'all the miserable progeny which, married as well as unmarried, mothers cast upon society' (1914, p. 73).

> What can be more immoral than to ask the strong and healthy members of society to burden themselves with increasingly heavy taxes in order to support the vicious human offscum, and, moreover, allow this class to propagate its kind? The bygone custom of putting children to death showed a much higher morality from the point of view of social ethics. (Key 1914, pp. 73–4.)

Key had some difficulty reconciling the competing objectives of eugenic reform and women's emancipation. The individual woman's right to 'self-assertion in love' had to be balanced by society's right to 'limit this self-assertion on behalf of the welfare of the race' (Key 1914, p. 77). Ultimately, racial and class imperatives proved paramount. The quality of the race would only be improved if the 'worst elements' were not allowed to multiply in an uncontrolled manner while 'the women best fitted for motherhood are unable or unwilling to fill the high office' (1914, p. 81). Key, one of the most progressive thinkers and ardent supporters of unmarried motherhood of her time, nevertheless firmly associated working-class illegitimacy with white racial decline.

Perhaps because she assumed that all unmarried mothers came from a working-class background, Australian eugenicist Marion Piddington implied that unmarried mothers were, by definition, unfit to reproduce. Marion Piddington was an outspoken, somewhat idiosyncratic public figure whose work, like Key's, revealed a mix of eugenic, socialist and feminist sympathies. Piddington also advocated a rational approach to sex matters but, unlike Key, was strongly attached to the ideal of monogamous heterosexual marriage. Between 1916 and the 1930s Piddington campaigned widely for married women's rights to sexual and reproductive freedom, and especially for the need for child sex education (Curthoys 1989).

The prose in Piddington's pamphlet on *The Unmarried Mother and Her Child* (1923) is less elegant and more polemical than Key's carefully argued social philosophy, but no less passionate. In order to achieve what she saw as the central objectives of social reform – strengthening marriage and instituting a single standard of morality – Piddington argued that society had to be saved from the dysgenic effects of a high rate of ex-nuptial unions. This would be achieved through the widespread sex training of the young, and by removing the disabilities and social stigma attached to illegitimacy (1923, p. 1). Piddington accused members of her own sex of continuing to stigmatise the unmarried mother. She urged all women to take a pen, write the word 'illegitimate', 'then draw through that accursed expression the blackest line that pen can make' (1923, p. 8).

Like Wollaston (1917), Piddington pointed out that the abandoned girl and her child needed sympathy and practical assistance, not blame (1923, p. 9). But Piddington's support for the unmarried mother was shaped as much by eugenics as by feminism or philanthropy. She claimed that if society took good care of the individual 'in whatever plight', the problem of the unmarried mother would disappear, thereby advancing the progress of the race (1923, p. 11). Key had accommodated the conflicting demands of feminism and eugenics by arguing that only 'fit' unmarried women should be mothers. Piddington's solution was to say that individual unmarried mothers (fit or unfit) deserved society's assistance, but that collectively ex-nuptial unions were bad for the race and ought to be discouraged.

Although Piddington appears to have been less concerned than Key with the reproduction of bourgeois values, her pamphlet strongly suggests that 'irregular matings' and the 'individual, social and racial curse' of haphazard procreation outside marriage (1923, p. 3) were working-class predilections. Deserted mothers were no different to the thousands rendered homeless or friendless by some serious disability (p. 9). Irregular matings, which in Piddington's definition included prostitution, encouraged the spread of venereal diseases and added degenerate and profoundly damaged children to the race (pp. 12–13). The unmarried mother gave birth to a deficient child who, if female, herself became an eugenically unfit mother who gave birth to an even more deficient child, and so on, in an endless downward spiral (p. 15).

There is no indication that Piddington perceived the unmarried mother and her child to be anything other than a white problem. Despite her compassion for women suffering as a result of what she considered to be an outmoded and socially detrimental moral distinction, Piddington held firmly to the idea common wherever eugenic discourse took hold that illegitimacy was a debilitating influence on white racial strength. American population experts were just as keen to discourage illegitimacy because it was associated with the inferior classes and contributed to disease and defectiveness (Reuter 1923, pp. 159–60). For that considerable proportion of social scientists who enthusiastically embraced eugenic theories in the interwar period, the continued reproduction of illegitimate children represented the worst kind of white racial pollution.

Given the amount and discursive breadth of scholarship that has at least since the mid-nineteenth century presented as a firm scientific fact the idea that illegitimacy contributes to racial inferiority, it is not surprising that race lurks not far beneath the surface of current constructions of single parenthood. In British and Australian discourses what has been repressed – those who have been erased from the writing of history, the indigenous and the weak and morally degenerate – returns to haunt the present. Social scientists no longer refer blithely to the inherent racial superiority of the inhabitants of the British Empire. Neither is it appropriate in the 1990s to imply that ex-nuptial children are genetically inferior to those born within marriage. Nevertheless, some contemporary conservative social science perpetuates the notion that illegitimate reproduction is undesirable for racial (or, put more palatably, 'national') reasons (Murray 1993; 1994a; 1994b).

In Australia, the conservative tendency to correlate racial strength and legitimacy occurs rarely and more obliquely than in the United States. Barry Maley, Senior Fellow at the Centre for Independent Studies, has expressed concern at the decline in the (legitimate) fertility rates of the 'developed countries' of the world, including Australia. Maley assumes that it is preferable for the Australian (presumably white) population to maintain itself without resorting to (presumably Asian) immigration (Maley 1992, pp. 21–2). White babies are the prime 'national resource'. Although the number of single-parent families has risen rapidly since the 1960s the increase in ex-nuptial births 'goes nowhere near compensating for the decline in nuptial births' (1992,

p. 23). Maley attributes the decline in marital fertility to legal and moral changes affecting the status of the family, the entry of married women into the workforce, and a welfare state that transfers money from two-parent families to 'broken families'. Australian Government policies, he concludes, 'discourage the formation of native-born families' (1992, p. 22). In order to sustain the quality of the white population, legitimate births must be favoured over illegitimate.

In debates that centre specifically on single parenthood in Britain and Australia, race is barely mentioned. As Ann Phoenix (1996, p. 183) observes, the absence of discourses of black pathology in recent conservative attacks on lone motherhood outside the United States requires explanation. Demography provides only part of the answer. More significant, she argues, has been the long-standing discursive construction of black families as outsiders in the British nation. High rates of black lone motherhood are constructed as a threat from outside the British nation; high rates of white lone motherhood are constructed as a threat from within. It is the insiders, 'whose belonging to the nation cannot be challenged', who become the targets in campaigns to reduce welfare support for lone mothers. The omission of lone black mothers still renders them pathological since it indicates that they are not genuinely British (1996, pp. 187–9). Phoenix's theory applies equally well to Australia where, like families of African–Caribbean descent, Aboriginal families have always been constructed as outside the Australian nation. Aboriginal single mothers escape censure for being single mothers, only to attract it, even more ferociously, for not being real (that is, white) Australians.

The historical texts I have discussed in this chapter offer further support for Phoenix's theory. Although contemporary representations of single mothers appear to be racialised almost exclusively in the United States, the idea that some categories of person are, by virtue of their heredity, physically stronger and morally superior and hence better fitted to reproduce than others has been central to social–scientific endeavour in Britain and Australia, as well as in Europe and the United States. Social scientists have struggled to define the relationship between illegitimate births and racial characteristics for at least two hundred years. Social inquiry in Britain and Australia has been preoccupied with what has appeared to be the greater propensity to produce illegitimate children of some populations – mostly non-Anglo-Saxon but also white though 'genetically-flawed' communities – and whether racial difference might explain different degrees of sexual morality.

The racialised character of the illegitimacy problem is more deep-seated, more widely dispersed and more complicated than is indicated by United States accounts focusing exclusively on African–Americans, Hispanic–Americans, Asian–Americans and other black minorities. Countering the racial myths, stereotypes and scapegoating mechanisms thrown up by the illegitimacy debate is critically important. These racial knowledges are, however, much more than surface ideological phenomena and they extend beyond the national boundaries of the United States. Race literally saturates, indeed forms the substance of, western understandings of illegitimacy. The discursive embrace of racial inferiority and illegitimate reproduction is tight and enduring.

CHAPTER 5

The Immorality of the White Working Class

In their special report on 'The white underclass', *US News and World Report* social investigators David Whitman and Dorian Friedman et al. (1994) present a white slum life characterised by idleness, poverty, neglect, sexual deviance and family dysfunction:

> From city to city, white underclass neighbourhoods look much the same. Most do not contain high-rise housing projects of chocka-block [sic] tenements. Instead, the streets look innocuously decrepit, filled with row houses with peeling paint and an occasional abandoned house. On warm nights, groups of men can sometimes be seen drinking on street corners or in parks, congregating in taverns or kibitzing on front stoops. An occasional prostitute may wander by to solicit her johns. Inside the row houses, young mothers, sometimes joined by their parents, pursue lives of cigarettes, television and Nintendo. The apartment walls often sport cheap reproductions of portraits of Jesus or Leonardo da Vinci's *Last Supper*. (Whitman and Friedman et al. 1994, p. 44.)

Whitman and Friedman et al. define the 'white underclass' as white neighbourhoods in which a high proportion of residents live in poverty and in which there are high rates of female-headed families. Pointing out that poor blacks face more extensive and entrenched forms of discrimination, especially in housing, they question the prediction of some social scientists that the white underclass will soon eclipse its black counterpart and do not support the move to end welfare payments. But they do agree that social acceptance of out-of-wedlock childbearing is the primary factor in the formation of the white underclass (Whitman and Friedman et al. 1994, p. 53).

In this and numerous other accounts of major social dysfunction, illegitimacy is the primary catalyst in social deterioration. This chapter investigates social inquiry's habit of viewing illegitimacy among the white population as a symptom of social and moral decay, and its implication that those whites who conceive or give birth to illegitimate children are morally and socially deficient. Conservative social science reinforces the idea that illegitimacy is causally related to low socio-economic status in general and (though less overtly stated) to the behavioural deficiencies of poor people in particular. The social problem of rising illegitimacy rates has come to mean a problem with working-class culture.

America appears to be hopelessly enmeshed within a catastrophic process of urban social disintegration: rising levels of violence, racial tensions, vandalism, failed businesses, property neglect and the general spread of 'no-go' areas in which white middle-class people fear for their personal safety. Journalists describe this process as the 'social meltdown in the inner cities' (Gibbs, *Time* cover story, 1994, p. 27), 'the unravelling of American society' (*Chicago Tribune* 23 July 1994, p. 18), and 'the crisis of public order' (*Detroit News and Free Press* 15 July 1995, p. 5). The liberal dream of the 1960s has turned into a social nightmare (Magnet 1993).

Where liberals are likely to attribute the decline of inner-city neighbourhoods to economic and other structural factors, the primary cause of social chaos in conservative discourse is family breakdown, and especially illegitimacy. American social critics note with alarm that high illegitimacy rates have in recent decades become a 'white thing' (Eberstadt 1996, p. 22). 'The ominous rise in illegitimacy' costs America dearly, according to the *Reader's Digest* (1994), repeating Daniel Patrick Moynihan's apocalyptic vision of 'crime, violence, unrest, disorder – most particularly the furious, unrestrained lashing out at the whole social structure'. The feature draws on Charles Murray's analysis of illegitimacy's disastrous impact on the social fabric in a frequently reprinted *Wall Street Journal* article. In it Murray points out that the national illegitimacy rate is now about 4 percentage points higher than the black illegitimacy rate was when Moynihan made his sobering prediction in 1965. On the basis of the white illegitimacy statistics, Murray says, one would expect the inner-city culture to be '"Lord of the Flies" writ large'. It is not – yet. American society must act now to prevent the descent into chaos, for it will not survive an epidemic of illegitimacy among whites (Murray 1994b).

Daniel Moynihan, currently a Democrat Senator for New York, is still a powerful presence in debates about welfare, poverty and the family. In his much-cited 1993 article 'Defining deviancy down' Moynihan adopts Emile Durkheim's idea that societies define what is acceptable by articulating what is deviant or criminal behaviour. Choosing the examples of mental health, single-parent families and crime, Moynihan argues that in recent decades deviancy has been redefined in a way that normalises conduct previously stigmatised. As a consequence 'We are getting used to a lot of behavior that is not good for us' (1993, p. 30). The liberal position on social deviancy also comes under attack from Robert Bork. For Bork, a legal scholar, the root problem of America's unprecedented slide into social decay is modern liberalism's insistence on the individual's right to self-gratification, and an egalitarian ideology that inhibits judgement and the will to punish (Bork 1996, p. 154).

Rising crime rates offer rhetorically spectacular and empirically concrete measures of social deterioration. The genesis of criminal activity is firmly linked to illegitimate families (Lamb 1995). As Patrick F. Fagan, a Fellow in Family and Cultural Studies at the Heritage Foundation (1996, p. 36) puts it, a wealth of evidence in the literature of criminology and sociology suggests that the breakdown of family is 'the real root cause of crime in the U.S.' Both historian Gertrude Himmelfarb and sociologist Charles Murray suggest a strong causal relationship between the two sets of social statistics. They present graphs showing almost identical gradients in crime and illegitimacy rates from 1950 to 1990. The crime and illegitimacy graphs are placed either right next to, or directly underneath, each other, giving the impression that they are equivalent measures of social breakdown (Murray et al. 1990, p. 36; Himmelfarb 1994–5, pp. 16–17).

According to conservative analysts, when boys grow up without the benefit of a father's authority they are likely to develop behavioural problems and drift into all sorts of anti-social activity, from car-stealing and petty theft to drug-dealing, rape and murder. The absence of a father impedes his son's ability to control aggression (Bork 1996, p. 157). The problem is exacerbated by a welfare system that encourages the formation of single-parent families. The illegitimate criminal teenager will get his girlfriend pregnant with no thought of marrying her (Fagan 1996, p. 38). David Popenoe cites social–scientific evidence showing that girls from single-parent families are more likely to become teenage mothers themselves, while boys are more likely to be 'delinquent and violent, and to become involved with the criminal justice system' (Popenoe 1996a, p. 26).

Both crime and illegitimacy are interpreted as the consequences of immorality. Crime rates would go down if only parents encouraged the moral development of their offspring (Fagan 1996, p. 38). Himmelfarb, like her nineteenth-century predecessors, chooses to describe both crime and illegitimacy rates as 'moral statistics' (1994–5, pp. 14–16); exactly in what ways crime and illegitimacy are moral equivalents is rarely explained. Moral conservatives assume a causal circle in which a lack of morals leads to illegitimacy; illegitimacy results in poverty and fatherlessness; poverty and fatherlessness encourage crime; crime destroys communities and makes them moral-absent places. The coincidence of rising illegitimacy and crime rates does not necessarily indicate that the former causes the latter, but it does strongly suggest to some commentators a 'general cultural decline' that began in the 1960s (Bork 1996, p. 156).

American social conservatives characteristically designate those communities riven by crime, illegitimacy and welfare dependence as 'the underclass'. Herbert Gans argues that 'the underclass' is only the most recent of a series of labels that social scientists and other professionals have given to able-bodied non-working poor people who have been deemed unworthy. The underclass is derived from the notion of the 'undeserving poor' that emerged in Britain during debates over the 1834 Poor Law. Gunnar Myrdal, the Swedish social scientist who wrote in 1944 a landmark study of race relations, *The American Dilemma*, is credited with coining the term 'underclass' in 1963. Gans argues that Myrdal's 'underclass' was a morally neutral economic term used to describe the victims of de-industrialisation (Gans 1995, p. 27). The 'culture of poverty' concept that originated in the 1960s with the work of anthropologist Oscar Lewis suggested that the poor were unable to escape poverty's debilitating effects because socioeconomic deprivation had bred certain values, attitudes and behaviours – idleness, hopelessness, resentment, racial hostility – that militated against individual social betterment. Slum children absorbed its basic values and were unable to take advantage of any opportunities for advancement. The influence of 'culture of poverty' thinking can be seen in the recent work of Lawrence Mead, in whose view the poor are 'dutiful but defeated' and would work more regularly if the government enforced the work norm (Mead 1992, p. 24).

As it has come to be used in the 1980s and 1990s, the term 'the underclass' is a behavioural, and therefore arguably derogatory, label for the poor. The current sociological concept of an underclass designates the permanent non-working poor of the slum areas of large cities. Until the early 1990s the underclass was understood to be comprised primarily of African–Americans, Hispanic–Americans and other non-whites. Now conservatives fear that the same symptoms of social malaise are spreading to their own race. In order to distinguish the general problem of (white) social deterioration from the problem of (black) racial disadvantage, conservative social scientists speak increasingly of the 'white underclass'.

As Gans suggests, the concept of an underclass is a highly contested one, and social scientists hold a range of opinions about its existence, extent, character and implications. Some positively embrace the term, many (including politicians and journalists) use it uncritically, others modify or refine it or, like Gans, completely reject it. Whether or not there is such a thing, and whether or not it comes in white, the idea of an underclass frames conservative understandings of the disturbing nexus between crime, welfare dependency, racial division, unemployment, family breakdown and poverty. It is the contemporary face of the class issue.

Charles Murray has done more than any other social scientist to popularise and add a moral twist to the underclass theory. Murray continues the 'culture of poverty' way of thinking about the poor by seeing them as being trapped by their own flawed value systems. But his version of the underclass attracts more public attention than most because he hitches the problem of the underclass securely to the problem of illegitimacy. Illegitimacy in his view is 'the best predictor of an underclass in the making' (Murray et al. 1990, p. 4). If the problem of the growing underclass is to be solved illegitimacy needs to be targeted, he claims, not because it is immoral or undermines the sanctity of marriage but because 'communities need fathers'. Murray does not explicitly criticise the sexual morals of unmarried mothers, but he does say that fatherlessness is wrong and two-parent families are right. As Andrew Blaikie points out, for Murray and his followers the root of the problem is not the cultural acceptance of unemployment, inadequate state assistance or other economic factors, but unmarried motherhood (Blaikie 1996, p. 118).

Even if social scientists do not explicitly embrace the underclass concept, they almost universally connect single parenthood to low socio-economic status. Some social scientists point to the presence of high proportions of single-parent households as an indicator of neighbourhoods that are relatively poor, while others (notably feminists) argue that entering single parenthood is likely to lower a family's income level. Rising rates of single parenthood are a major contributor to what has come to be known as 'the feminisation of poverty'. Some mention of the effects of poverty is almost mandatory in accounts of single parenthood, no matter what the political perspective.

Many writers position single parenthood as the primary cause of, or most significant context for, poverty. Lawrence Mead, for example, notes that poor, female-headed families accounted for 37 per cent of all poor people in 1989 (Mead 1992, p. 53). Sociology textbooks routinely state that single-parent families experience 'financial hardships' (Haralambos et al. 1996, p. 432), and it is commonplace for social scientists to make statements such as teenage girls from 'poor homes with low job prospects' are those most likely to become unwed mothers

(Fletcher 1997, p. 5). Lone parenthood is now seen as the main cause of poverty in Australia (Seccombe 1997), and even in European countries like Denmark, where 'single mothers are downright unremarkable', there is a growing concern that single motherhood brings with it poverty and crime (Bogert 1997, p. 42).

The idea that high rates of illegitimacy are socially destructive appears to be a universally applicable truth. However, if we track backwards the social–scientific narrative of illegitimacy's relationship to class, this universality becomes highly questionable. I want to tell the story backwards for two reasons. First, I want to show how meaning is made by an almost imperceptible process of discursive sedimentation. Going forward in time piles up the layers of truth one on top of the other from the bottom, or origin, onwards in an inevitable progression towards a well-known 'now'. Going backwards peels away the layers of truth, beginning with what is familiar and taken for granted, and exposing those truths, gaps and fault lines on which the current meanings depend but which remain subterranean. Writing history backwards arrives at what is strange. Secondly, I want to show how western intellectual cultures manufacture apparently universal social phenomena out of what are initially quite specific social observations. Going backwards we encounter some bumpy and unfamiliar terrain and arrive at unexpectedly particular destinations. The route social science took between the past and the present was not inevitable and preordained but only one of a number of possible alternatives.

Both 'class' and 'poverty' are specific discursive products of modern sociological thinking. Their pattern of interaction with illegitimacy (also a discursive product) has been uneven, and social scientists have not always seen economic factors as central to the illegitimacy problem. When social scientists spoke about illegitimacy between about 1940 and 1980 they referred frequently, but not as often as they do now, to poverty (the state or condition of being poor in terms of goods and money, and the cultural environment of those who are thus deprived). The idea that it is mostly working-class women who bear children out of wedlock has similarly advanced and receded within social–scientific thought over the past two centuries.

Before Murray's 'underclass' concept brought the working-class nature of illegitimacy back into the realm of acceptable academic discourse, class-based analyses of abnormal social-reproductive behaviour were generally out of favour. Social scientists of the 1970s and 1980s replaced what they saw as the comparatively crude, unscientific and rather *passé* language of 'working class' and 'middle class' with more neutral terms such as 'socioeconomic status'. This was partly due to the political squeamishness that came to surround anything vaguely resembling Marxist terminology. More significantly, sociologists increasingly acknowledged the complexity and messiness of the social world. As Shirley Foster Hartley, Professor of Sociology at California State University, concluded in her important textbook on illegitimacy, sociologists are rarely able to look at the effects of change in one variable while the 'other things remain equal' (1975, p. 258). Sociologists found it almost impossible to separate the effects on illegitimacy rates of social class from those related to other variables such as education, race, occupation, religion and income.

Evidence that both middle-class and working-class girls became unwed mothers contributed to the sociological uncertainty about the significance of social class. It was accepted in the 1960s that middle-class girls and women were just as likely to become illegitimately pregnant as those from the lower social strata. Robert Roberts observed that 'illegitimacy has invaded our middle-class high schools and colleges, the white collar occupations, and the adult population with a force which has not been known before' (Roberts 1966, p. 4). Part of the evidence for this shift came from psychoanalysis, part from the sociological analysis of the new cultural norms that appeared to be shaping sexual and reproductive behaviour among American youth. In his influential 1961 book *Unmarried Mothers*, Clark Vincent noted that since the 1920s accounts of illegitimacy had been based on the records of social agencies, charitable institutions, psychiatric social workers or the courts; that is, they excluded from analysis those unmarried mothers who were not institutionalised, emotionally well-adjusted or not in need of financial assistance. Studies based on the multiple sample sources available by the late 1950s provided tentative evidence that 'within given age and social groups such mothers were fairly representative of the general population of unmarried females with respect to education, intelligence, and socioeconomic status' (Vincent 1961, p. 88).

Before the 1960s illegitimacy was firmly associated with the low income and distinctive habits, lifestyles and attitudes of the working classes. Barbara Thompson, an almoner at Aberdeen Maternity Hospital, carried out a social study of the records of all women having illegitimate children in Aberdeen between 1949 and 1952. Her most striking finding was that both illegitimacy and pre-nuptial conception occurred predominantly in the lower social classes (Thompson 1956). Pointing to the influence of insecure family life, poor and overcrowded homes, lack of constructive recreational aims and outlets, lack of general planning ability and permissive attitudes towards extra-marital relations, Thompson argued that 'illegitimacy, like delinquency, thrives when social values, cultural as well as material, are low' (1956, p. 86).

The connection between illegitimacy and the 'less moral' behaviours and attitudes of those people situated towards the lower end of the social spectrum was even clearer in the 1930s, when the *Encyclopedia of the Social Sciences* (1932) included drunkenness, immorality, delinquency and prostitution in the list of factors contributing to illegitimacy. The *Encyclopaedia* briefly mentioned poverty as a cause of illegitimacy but gave far more weight to 'the character of home life and of parents'. George Mangold's major sociological study of children born out of wedlock in the United States (1921) devoted over forty pages to 'the causes and conditions underlying illegitimacy' without making any specific mention of poverty.

It was not so much that social scientists and welfare workers considered poverty inconsequential, but rather that in the first half of the twentieth century they remained unconvinced of the primacy of economic over moral or genetic factors. As the Reverend E. G. D. Freeman explained in an address to a School for Neighbourhood Workers on 'Illegitimacy, immorality and poverty', in dozens of cases seen by social workers in Toronto: 'the family history will begin with some form of immorality and take you through a history of venereal disease and illegitimacy to a resultant condition of feeblemindedness and poverty, and this resultant condition will perpetuate itself and become the prolific source of endless Social problems' (Freeman 1919, p. 335).

When experts did pay attention to class it was in the form of occupation. The 1930 *Encyclopaedia of the Social Sciences* drew on the work of Charlotte Lowe, a psychologist with the Minnesota State Board of Control. Lowe found that among the unmarried mothers she studied the most common forms of amusement were attending public dances, going for automobile rides and going to parties and movies. Of a total of 288 cases, 203 belonged to occupational 'class E'; that is, they were engaged in 'mechanical work without supervision', such as factory work or waitressing. Most of their fathers were farmers or unskilled labourers (Lowe 1927, pp. 788–91).

The socioeconomic classification system used by Lowe and others in the 1920s developed out of a less formal but still scientific interest in the contribution of poor physical environment to working-class sex behaviour problems. Percy Gamble Kammerer's *The Unmarried Mother* (1918) analysed 500 case studies of women employed predominantly in domestic service and factory work. Kammerer's study revealed, among other factors, the influence of bad environment (a category that included 'contaminating employment conditions', 'vicious neighbourhoods' and girls being 'away from home influence without protection'), bad companions and – 'by far the most important factor' – bad home conditions. The girl who came from a home where quarrelling, abuse, alcoholism or immorality was common was most likely to become an unmarried mother ([1918] 1969, p. 291). Kammerer found that overcrowded housing and tenement living led to a loss of modesty and diminished adult supervision that exposed many girls to early sex experience and thereby to the risk of giving birth to an illegitimate child (pp. 293–4).

Part of the problem of bad home environment was that young working-class men and women suffered what Kammerer called 'recreational disadvantages'. The Juvenile Protective Association of Chicago was one of many early twentieth-century social reform organisations that attempted to dissuade young people, many of them with immigrant parents, from going to saloons, dance halls, theatres, amusement parks and other commercial forms of amusement. Louise de Koven Bowen (1914) argued that working-class leisure pursuits contributed to illegitimacy in her study of 163 bastardy cases that came before the Court of Domestic Relations in Chicago. Because of the lack of decent places where young men and women could meet – school social centres, settlements and girls' clubs, for example – practically all of the young people involved in her study 'seemed to have carried on much of their courtship on the city streets' (Bowen 1914, p. 15). Young men in particular needed moral substitutes for the 'barbaric and morbid expression of their energies' to which city life lured them (p. 24).

Well into the twentieth century social investigators assumed that what a person did, and with whom, said more about their moral standards than their income level. It was not so much the poverty of the domestic servants, factory employees and agricultural labourers that was responsible for illegitimacy, proposed John Ryan, a contributor on illegitimacy to the *Catholic Encyclopedia*, but rather 'certain associations and modes of living connected with the occupation' (Ryan 1910, pp. 650–1). Ryan believed that poverty was a factor only 'within certain limits' and that its influence was almost impossible to verify because it was so interwoven with other factors. Robert J. Parr, Director of the (British) National Society for the Prevention of Cruelty to Children, was also reluctant to single out economic deprivation as a causal factor in the suffering of illegitimate children in Ireland, drawing attention to the 'triple disadvantages of shame, poverty and physical risk' (Parr 1909, p. 13).

Further back still, poverty was explicitly ruled out as a cause of immoral sexual behaviour. It was perfectly evident, according to a characteristically confident Albert Leffingwell, the acknowledged pre-World War I authority on illegitimacy, that 'poverty of itself does not predispose to vice or to looseness of morals' (1892, p. 25). Largely because of the professional respect accorded Leffingwell's pioneering work on the subject, especially in Britain, poverty was barely mentioned as one of the 'scientifically proven' causes of illegitimacy until the 1920s. The 1910 edition of the *Encyclopaedia Britannica* provided a statistical table showing that the illegitimacy rate in the well-to-do parts of London (Kensington, for example) was considerably higher than in notoriously poor areas such as Stepney, Bethnal Green and Whitechapel. The figures 'clearly disprove[d]' the theory that poverty caused illegitimacy.

The concept of poverty may have meant little to nineteenth-century investigators of illegitimacy, but being a member of the working class did. Lynnette Finch (1993) has shown that throughout the nineteenth century officials and other members of the respectable middle classes read the character of the working classes of Britain and Australia through the grid of sexuality. She argues that the working class, as a distinct, observable social phenomenon, was a product of the sexual discourses articulated by medical experts, social investigators and government administrators. Like incest, abortion, masturbation, prostitution and infanticide, illegitimacy was viewed as a peculiarly working-class sexual pathology that offered clear evidence of a different set of sexual practices that was potentially dangerous to civilised society. One of the 'key measuring gauges of morality', high rates of illegitimate births, proved that the working class – and the sexual behaviour of working-class women in particular – needed to be closely monitored and regulated by their social superiors (Finch 1993, pp. 26, 92).

It was the morality of the rural poor, specifically, that most concerned nineteenth-century European social investigators. Using a crude form of social questionnaire, William Cramond, a Scottish schoolmaster, analysed 123 replies to a circular letter sent to clergymen, proprietors, factors (stewards or bailiffs), farm servants and the chairmen of Parochial Boards and other public officials in Banffshire, Scotland. Of the ten principal causes mentioned by correspondents those most often referred to were 'the circumstances and conduct of farm servants and their upbringing' (85 mentions), 'the low moral tone prevalent in the country' (60), and 'the relation between masters and mistresses towards their servants', that is, that the former did not properly supervise the latter (46). Cramond included the following representative comment from an Established Church minister:

> The class in which I have found [illegitimacy] to be most prevalent is that of farm servants, male and female. They mix together so much without any restraining supervision, indulge so much in obscene language, that their moral feelings get blunted, and immoral conduct is the result. Those in bothies wander at night, prowl about the sleeping apartments of the thoughtless and giddy, or the fallen, female servants. (Cramond 1888, p. 43.)

Cramond's study is not strictly quantitative and is far less 'scientific' in tone than, say, Charlotte Lowe's 1927 article on the social background of unmarried mothers. However, he does attempt to define a moral problem with some empirical precision.

Before Cramond's survey, social investigators relied on uncorroborated impressions of the low social background of women who became illegitimately pregnant. The *Nation*'s London correspondent was of the opinion, for example, that English farm servants rarely got married until their pregnancy was well advanced, and in general 'the standard of morality was low amongst English peasant girls' (*Nation* 1865, p. 270). George Seton's theory of illegitimacy (1860) similarly consisted of a series of unsubstantiated speculations about the principal causes of the 'Social Evil'. Some of Seton's twenty causes are economic: low wages and the scarcity of employment, for example. The majority point to the demoralising effects of working-class culture. Seton was particularly concerned with the dangers of unsupervised social interaction between young working-class men and women engaged in rural labour. Promiscuous mingling was encouraged by crowded unsegregated living accommodation, the 'bothy' system (a bothy was a house provided for groups of unmarried farm labourers of both sexes), the employment of women in agriculture, the presence of (male) itinerant railway labouring gangs, market fairs where labour was hired or the 'secret and stealthy way' in which courtship was carried on 'in the darkness and silence of night'. Seton noted the lax moral habits typical of country working-class men and women evident in drunkenness, the love of dress and extravagance among domestic servants, Scotsmen's dirty and untidy habits, and the transmission of licentious behaviour from one generation of women to another.

Even when Seton was not focused exclusively on the immoral activities of the poor he saw class everywhere. He criticised the middle and upper classes for failing to provide the poor with sufficient religious education and 'mental cultivation'. The wealthy lacked a proper Christian sympathy for the poor and many women of high social position treated female unchastity with unnecessary severity. Some problems could be attributed to men of every rank of society: the public acceptance of the idea that a young man might 'sow his wild oats'; the neglect in boys' education of games, athletic sports and physical exercise; and men's reluctance to marry, creating 'a numerous fraternity of selfish bachelors' (Seton 1860, p. 21).

Norwegian social researcher, Eilert Sundt, held remarkably similar views on the relationship between working-class living arrangements and immorality. Sundt was the author of a series of government-funded reports on the sexual customs of rural Norway based on interviews he conducted in several farming communities between 1856 and 1866. He was confident that 'in the working class and among poor people, thoughtless coarseness and animal-like immorality are much more widespread' (Sundt [1856–66] 1993, p. 86). Sundt assumed that working-class sexual immorality, and the illegitimacy with which it was synonymous, was attributable to the living arrangements of rural labourers forced to sleep in barns or outhouses some distance from the farmer's house. After the working day was over young men and women workers could evade the virtuous influences of the domestic hearth and the control of their master and mistress, and were free to indulge in 'night courting' and other dangerous practices (p. 74).

English-speaking social scientists appear not to have referred to Sundt's work. Apart from the fact that Sundt's study was not translated into English until 1993, Norwegian farming communities were culturally very different to English villages. So it is intriguing that Sundt's insistence on the dangers of courtship, rural employment and inadequate housing is almost identical to accounts of illegitimacy written by mid-nineteenth-century British men of science. Member of parliament, John Strachan, was certain from his own experience as a physician that immorality and illegitimacy in Scotland was 'entirely confined to the working class' and that few working-class women preserved their chastity until marriage. Illegitimacy resulted from crowded accommodation, coarse language, the low moral tone of young working men and the late hours at which courting activities customarily took place. Strachan especially disapproved of the secrecy and mystery that accompanied courtship in the dark, and of the Scottish habit of 'going a-courting merely for amusement'. Where there was little opportunity for lust among the upper classes, in working-class youth, weakened by a previous 'indelicacy of thought and conduct', virtue was often overwhelmed by the temptations to which private courting exposed them (Strachan n.d. ?1859).

In England discussions of illegitimacy were often coloured by the Poor Law debates, but English investigators were just as preoccupied as their Scottish colleagues with the low moral tone of rural workers. J. C. Wilks presented a paper on 'Bastardy in the rural districts' to the National Association for the Promotion of Social Science in 1859. Wilks attributed bastardy to 'the healthy animalism of the country people, and the weakness of safeguards, moral principle, self-respect, and public opinion', much of it fostered by the Poor Law. The remedy was 'healthful amusements, an interest in the world of nature and of books, singing, taste in dress' and supervised courtship, instead of dancing 'in the large room at the not very respectable "Three Bells"' (Wilks 1859, pp. 733–4). Wilks' narrative reveals some distinctively English touches but it is hard to escape the conclusion that even at mid-century there existed in Europe a shared and pervasive climate of thought about the nature of working-class life and sexual habits. Whether in Norway, England or Scotland, it 'went without saying' that illegitimacy was caused by crowded housing.

I would argue that there are strong discursive connections between the American 'white underclass' debate and mid-nineteenth-century European accounts of working-class illegitimacy. National and temporal differences in the illegitimacy problem are not as great as one would imagine. In identifying the continuities between mid-nineteenth and late-twentieth-century social–scientific representations of illegitimacy, I am not discounting the possibility that contemporary modes of speaking about out-of-wedlock births might be unique. What I do want to do is suggest that social science has a history of telling truths about social problems. Over the last two hundred years social scientists have either strongly implied or openly claimed that their version of the illegitimacy problem was as accurate and as unbiased as it was possible to be. Each new generation of practitioners finds those versions of social reality distorted, incomplete or false, and rejects or modifies the old truth narrative in favour of a new and more accurate account. Historical investigations show, however, that today's accounts of the problem are steeped in, and depend conceptually and linguistically on, those of their predecessors. British ideas of the 1850s and British, Australian and American ideas of the 1990s are not as radically divorced as professional discourse would have us believe.

The picture of working-class culture painted by Seton and his colleagues exhibits a clear kinship with those of conservative analysts who are at this moment attributing high rates of white illegitimacy to the demoralisation of inner-city underclass neighbourhoods. The association of social decay with black city ghettoes gives the underclass concept a particularly strong currency in the American context. However, Charles Murray has successfully, if contentiously, exported the white underclass idea to Britain (Murray et al. 1990). Murray (1994c) argues that crime and drug use, unemployment among young men and lone motherhood are on the increase in England and Wales as they are in the United States. The increase in British births out of wedlock that drives all the other social problems occurs in the lower classes and is widening the cultural gap between the low-skilled working class and the upper-middle class. Murray predicts that the affluent, well-educated class ('the New Victorians') will move back to marriage, the two-parent family and traditional moral values. A large portion of what used to be the British working class, meanwhile, will descend into an American-style underclass, 'the New Rabble' (Murray 1994c).

Australian social scientists also debate the existence of an underclass, if less energetically (Nahan et al. 1993; Whiteford 1995). A cover story in the *Bulletin* classified the Australian underclass as street kids, people living in public housing, migrants, the unemployed, the poor and single mothers 'creating a breed of outlaw children who reject all help' (Crisp 1990, p. 48). Australian conservatives believe that the high crime rates and disorder of American cities is only a step away, and that unless something is done to solve the poverty caused by rising rates of out-of-wedlock births Australia will inevitably succumb to America's urban decay, 'culture of despair' and spreading underclass (Healey 1995, p. 26). The underclass rests not on race but on family breakdown (Santamaria 1995, p. 26).

In all three countries much of the concern focuses on the physical degradation of the places where the working class live. Instead of worrying about crowded tenement buildings or rural labourers' huts, social scientists in the United States today note that many teenage mothers are living in poor white neighbourhoods and project housing (for example, Whitman and Friedman et al. 1994). According to British sociologist and social theorist, Norman Dennis, and social psychologist, George Erdos, in Britain single parenthood and social disorder are associated with housing estates, especially in economically depressed areas of the north of England (Dennis and Erdos 1993, pp. 1–2). In Australia writers include in the underclass single mothers who inhabit 'inaccessible, sterile public housing suburbs or high-rise flats' (Crisp 1990, p. 48). These white underclass areas of the 1990s are little different to Kammerer's (1918) 'vicious neighbourhoods'.

Like nineteenth-century observations that young working-class people preferred meeting away from home in dark places, contemporary social inquiry finds that a dangerous street nightlife thrives in today's underclass communities. In the United States it is the sons of single mothers who are most likely to engage in street riots, kill or injure members of rival gangs, get involved in drug-related violence and steal and wreck cars (for example, Zinsmeister 1993, p. 45; Moynihan 1993, pp. 26–8). Young men gather ominously on street corners, in parks, outside taverns or on front porches (Whitman and Friedman et al. 1994, p. 44). In England young working-class men roam shopping centres, pedestrian precincts and bus stations; there is overwhelming evidence of a rise in street crimes such as hooliganism, car theft and vandalism, principally among young men (Dennis and Erdos 1993, p. 84).

Older concerns with the contribution of drunkenness to illegitimacy have developed into the perceived problem of 'teenage' or 'youth drinking' and other drug-related activities. The rate of drug use is reportedly several times higher among adolescents living apart from their fathers than it is among those who live with their fathers (Zinsmeister 1993, p. 45), while alcohol remains 'the scourge of the white underclass' (Whitman and Friedman et al. 1994, p. 48). Australian and experts from other countries frequently link high alcohol consumption in young women to sexual promiscuity, unsafe sex practices and teenage pregnancy (Cook 1994).

Popular culture, like the immoral 'commercial amusements' targeted eighty years ago by Bowen, is frequently blamed for the rise in illegitimacy and its criminal consequences. The undisciplined sons of single mothers have a great deal of unsupervised time on their hands and are free to spend many hours consuming the images of violence and sex presented by television, videos, movies, computer games and rap music (Bork 1996, p. 157). Mass culture, including 'gangsta rap', is vastly underrated as an engine of social breakdown according to social conservative Charles Krauthammer (1995, p. 17). William Beaver (1996) argues in the *Journal of Social, Political and Economic Studies* that 'the sheer volume of sexual messages' sent by television programs and advertisements helps shape a young person's sexual values and behaviour. Voluntary restraint by media organisations, a ratings system and the installation in television sets of chips allowing parents to exert control over their children's viewing will, he argues, play an important role in reducing illegitimacy.

Some anti-illegitimacy social scientists, particularly in the United States, see the reinstatement of religious values and practices as critical to the restoration of social order (Fagan 1996, p. 38; Browning 1996). In his analysis of the British underclass Murray (1994c) expressed a hope that among the upper-middle class there would be a revival of religion 'and of the intellectual respectability of concepts such as fidelity, courage, loyalty, self-restraint, moderation and other admirable human qualities that until lately have barely dared speak their names'. Three years later, after Murray and his supporters had persuaded the United States Government to dismantle the federal welfare system, Adam Meyerson (1997) claims that conservatives have won the argument that every child must grow up with a mother and a father. The next challenge is to convince the electorate of the importance of 'a revival of religious faith and observance'. Like George Seton, Don Browning (1996, p. 29), a self-described liberal Protestant theologian with an interest in illegitimacy, believes that the middle and upper classes ('the larger society') are partly to blame for the culture of out-of-wedlock births.

Contemporary social scientists single out Seton's 'numerous fraternity of selfish bachelors' as the principal cause of social breakdown. British scholars note the increasingly egoistic, nihilistic, thieving and loutish behaviour of young men dangerously 'liberated' from domesticity and their responsibilities to provide for a wife and children (Dennis and Erdos 1993, p. 5). It is not poverty, unemployment or the lack of housing that are pushing up the crime rate, Dennis argues, but feckless and sexually promiscuous unmarried fathers (*Daily Telegraph* 1997a, p. 12). Australian social investigators agree that juvenile crime is attributable to the spread of single parenthood (Hyde 1994; Maley et al. 1996, pp. 21–47; Tapper 1993). They report that the children of sole-parent families often feel 'acute anger, boredom, envy and exclusion'; they have no respect for private or public property and seek attention through dangerous games such as high-speed car chases (Nahan et al. 1993, p. 118). Such arguments, presented as scientifically verifiable contemporary truths, are clearly derivative of a much older moral rheroric. Yesterday's uncivilised peasants have become today's wild urban delinquents.

Those delinquents are generally assumed to be male. There is in today's underclass debate a tendency to differentiate the behaviour of the underclass's women from that of its men. The men of the white underclass are represented as idlers, inconsiderate studs and impregna-tors, and potential if not actual criminals; women as emotionally imma-ture and sexually irresponsible welfare cheats. In some ways this discourse is more obviously marked by sexual difference than its earlier equivalents. Although social scientists never entirely ignored the problem of the unmarried father, until the 1960s and 1970s they were unsure how to identify and study him and he remained a shadowy figure. For most of the twentieth century illegitimacy has been approached scientifically as the problem of the unmarried mother, that is, as a problem of female behaviour. Some nineteenth-century social inquiry was influenced by philanthropic and other sexualised discourses that represented women as the innocent or easily tempted victims of male seduction: Cramond's thoughtless, giddy or fallen female servants. Other accounts, possibly the majority, deemed working-class men and women to be equally immoral. Here, as in much of the contemporary underclass literature, the named problem is not the uncontrollable nature of female sexuality and reproductive capacity; more significant is the perceived innate predisposition of the undeserving poor of both sexes to act in ways that are selfish, unrestrained, immoral and socially destructive.

As an object of scientific inquiry illegitimacy has always been viewed through the lens of class, and has nearly always been associated specifically with the dangerous strangeness of the working class. It is not all that surprising, then, to find Charles Murray and others revis-iting the early twentieth-century reluctance to identify poverty as the prime cause, arguing instead that 'the prevalence of illegitimate births is drastically higher among the lower-class communities than among the upper-class ones' (1990, p. 7). More generally, within social research the tendency to attribute high illegitimacy rates to low social class persists. A recent Scottish study found, for example, that one in four pregnancies in one Edinburgh housing estate was conceived by teenagers, compared with only one in 250 in a middle-class suburb four miles away (Hannan, M. 1997). People in the wealthier harbour and city areas of Sydney are much less likely to be living in single-parent families than those in the poorer western suburbs (Lamont 1997).

This pervasive worry about the rising number of working-class babies, white as well as black, born out of wedlock suggests a crisis of the middle class. There is a growing perception on the part of the white middle class in Australia, Britain and the United States that its cultural norms are losing legitimacy. Sociologist William Goode, attempting in 1967 to explain a sudden upsurge in concern about illegitimacy, proposed that the socially advantaged no longer felt inviolate. They believed increasingly 'that those toward the bottom do not really believe that those above are superior in fundamental or essential ways' (Goode 1967, p. 271). Thirty years on, with statistics suggesting that for white women below the poverty line 44 per cent of births are illegitimate (Bork 1996, p. 158), middle-class standards of behaviour appear even closer to extinction.

Stanley Rothman, Professor of Government at Smith College, has warned of 'the decline of bourgeois America' (1996). Charles Krauthammer worries that, while the bar defining normality has been lowered for single mothers, criminals and the mentally ill, 'for the ordinary bourgeois, deviancy has been defined up' (Krauthammer 1993, p. 20). Myron Magnet wants to reinstitute 'the whole catalogue of antique-sounding bourgeois virtues' (1993, p. 19). At a 1995 National Summit on Young Children, President Clinton told Americans that if they were going to rescue their children's future they had to 'grow the middle class and shrink the underclass' (White House 1995b).

The crisis of middle-class authority is less pronounced outside the United States but some academics have called on the British and American middle classes to provide moral leadership and return to the 'hard virtues' if governments are not to preside impotently over 'a disorderly and decaying population' (Sullivan 1992, p. xiv). The *Bulletin* notes a 'crisis of confidence' among middle Australia (Bagnall 1996). Throughout the western industrialised world it appears that established certainties about the principles governing the economy, the labour market and entrepreneurship – the structures that have traditionally contributed to the material improvement and ideological dominance of the middle class – are dissolving. Conservatives could find no clearer measure of the waning power of bourgeois moral values and behavioural standards than rapidly rising rates of single parenthood.

Contemporary conservative social science represents the relationship between moral sense and social order as universal and timeless. This chapter has suggested that its statements are directly descended from a quite specific sociological orthodoxy, one which accepted as true the proposition that the unrespectable working class was, by nature and circumstance, disinclined to act morally or responsibly. The spread of white illegitimacy is, in today's underclass debate, a metaphor for a moral hell – a seething, chaotic, violent and licentious world inhabited by wildly copulating bodies and terrified abandoned children – an almost unrecognisable species of human life ruled by childish appetites and desires, into which respectable white society can topple with frightening ease.

CHAPTER 6

Illegitimate Infancy: A Deadly Risk

It is a bitterly cold January morning in Chicago. Marisol, a single, 18-year-old high-school senior, leaves for school. Soon after leaving home she begins to feel sick and returns to her second-floor apartment. Marisol is pregnant but has not told her parents because she is too afraid of what they might say. Realising that she is in labour Marisol spends the next three hours in the dining room, crying and praying, then goes into the bathroom where she gives birth, alone. She throws the baby out of the bathroom window into the alley below and goes to school. A neighbour finds and rescues the infant and Marisol is charged with aggravated battery of a child (*Canberra Times* 1995). A young, unmarried Englishwoman, Caroline Beale, is discovered trying to leave a New York airport with the body of her dead infant concealed in a plastic carrier bag stuffed into the waistband of her trousers (Wheelwright 1995). In Britain, a 16-year-old woman confesses to having secretly given birth to and killing a baby she said she did not know she was carrying (Grant 1993). In New Jersey, an 18-year-old student gives birth to a baby in a bathroom stall during her graduation prom. She wraps it in paper towels, places it in a wastebasket and returns to the dance (Lapham 1997, p. 39).

There is a growing perception that to be born out of wedlock exposes an infant to serious risk of death. Newpapers report that cases of infant neglect, abandonment and homicide are on the increase (Shirk 1991; Romero 1997). The majority of deaths, accidental or deliberate, occur to ex-nuptial infants born to young single mothers. The *Boston Globe* ran a story in 1994 headed 'Illegitimacy – a deadly risk for infants' (Jacoby 1994, p. 19). 'It is safer to be born poor than to be born out of wedlock', according to the *Chicago Tribune* (Chapman 1991, p. 3).

In this chapter I examine the historical-discursive process by which illegitimacy has come to mean a 'deadly risk'. My approach takes a different direction from the prevailing feminist scholarship on infanticide, much of which tends to focus on the melodramatic rhetoric, ideological distortions and sexist stereotypes that surround infanticide (Kirsta 1994; Laster 1989; Wilczynski 1994; Higginbotham 1989). Rather than viewing medical and social–scientific constructions of illegitimate death as false or inaccurate representations of the reality of women's lives, I assume that these discourses constitute reality. Social inquiry does not hide the truth, it produces it. Historical analysis suggests that current truths about illegitimate death are not so different from those manufactured in the more morality-conscious climate of the mid-nineteenth century.

Illegitimacy currently represents a serious problem for the health and medical professions. An article on health inequalities and the children of single mothers in the *British Medical Journal* cited a British Government study of perinatal and infant mortality. One of its key findings was that 'for babies born outside marriage and registered by the mother alone – a total of 8 per cent of all births in 1990 – the infant mortality rate was 13.1 (per 1000 live births), 80 per cent higher than that of babies born within marriage'. The children of lone mothers who are largely reliant on social security benefits 'have the worst mortality record of any social group' (Judge and Benzeval 1993). According to studies conducted internationally, infants born out of wedlock today are at considerably greater risk of death or physical harm than their legitimate counterparts. Rates of infant mortality are higher among births to unmarried mothers and higher among illegitimate children with one registered parent than among those with two (Hein et al. 1991; Gordon 1990). The incidence of Sudden Infant Death Syndrome, premature labour, still-birth, perinatal death, birth complications, low birthweight, low maternal weight gain and other 'adverse pregnancy outcomes' are all higher for teenage and ex-nuptial births (the two categories overlap significantly) (Zhang and Chan 1991; Adelson et al. 1992; Forsyth and Palmer 1990). Women who are illegitimately pregnant are more likely than their married counterparts to die or suffer health problems as a result of pregnancy or childbirth (Atrash et al. 1990; Jonas et al. 1992; Grimes 1994).

Researchers stress the strong correlation between infant homicide, low maternal age and unwed status (Cummings et al. 1994; Emerick et al. 1986). Infant homicide rates are higher where rates of births to teenage mothers are high (Winspinger et al. 1991), and child homicide rates are higher where rates of illegitimacy, births to teenage mothers and divorce are high (Gartner 1991). One Iowa study found that most neonaticides involved the birth of a live infant to an adolescent who had kept her pregnancy secret from family and friends (Saunders 1989). The children of Australian single mothers and those living in families with a step-parent are at greater risk of physical and sexual abuse and neglect than those who live with both biological parents (Sweet 1996). The injury rates from childhood accidents in Britain of children living in single-parent families are twice those of children in two-parent families (Roberts and Pless 1995).

The authors of these reports usually do not blame single mothers. Many medical experts sympathise with the young and financially struggling mother, pointing to economic and social disadvantage – poverty, poor housing conditions and social isolation – as a major part of the explanation (Roberts and Pless 1995, p. 925). Some researchers stress the adverse effects of sexual violence on women's reproductive health, including its relationship to unwanted and teenage pregnancies (Heise 1994). Others dispute the orthodox medical opinion that the youth or unwed status of mothers are *per se* physically dangerous to infants (Geronimus 1991, p. 446; Geronimus et al. 1994; Bennett 1992). The named problem in most of these studies is the lack of adequate social and economic support for single mothers.

Nevertheless, medical and public health constructions of illegitimacy tend to support the notion that rising rates of ex-nuptial births are bad for society. As Ann Phoenix argues, social researchers generally start from the assumption that teenage motherhood is problematic and highlight the negative findings. Once defined, the problem 'gains its own momentum' (Phoenix 1993, p. 81). The same process of problematisation occurs even in the highly people-oriented discourses of medicine and public health. Whether they want to or not, medicine's apparently natural, biological and sickly bodies participate in political debates about what constitutes proper or desirable reproductive behaviour.

A minority of experts explicitly link high rates of infant death to the immoral behaviour of unwed mothers. Usually this immorality is described as 'irresponsibility'. One study of infant mortality found that women who are young, unmarried, poorly educated and coping with their first pregnancy frequently fail to seek pre-natal care, even when it is readily accessible. In these cases even the provision of adequate support systems proved futile. The authors concluded that young women needed to be educated in 'responsible' parenthood, with the strong implication that illegitimate infants are placed at risk by the neglect or indifference of single mothers (Hein et al. 1990).

Nicholas Eberstadt, visiting fellow at the Harvard Center for Population Studies and a frequent contributor to journals with an anti-illegitimacy perspective, such as *American Enterprise*, has probably done more than any other expert to publicise the links between illegitimacy and high American infant mortality rates. Using what Linda Singer (1993) calls 'the rhetoric of epidemic' characteristic of post-AIDS culture, Eberstadt (1988; 1989; 1991a; 1991b; 1994) describes illegitimacy as a 'public health hazard' and one of the 'major killers of American children'. He finds that of all the biological and social factors, including race, that might account for America's embarrassingly high rate of infant mortality, the key lies in the relationship between illegitimacy and a lack of parental interest in pre-natal care.

> In 1987 illegitimate black babies were nearly four times as likely to have received no prenatal care as black babies born in wedlock. Illegitimate white infants were about five times as likely to have received no prenatal care as white babies born in wedlock. Although further research will be required to answer the question conclusively, it seems unlikely that social and economic factors alone could account for such disparities. (Eberstadt 1991a, p. 40.)

The basic problem, Eberstadt suggests, is a behavioural one. Low-income unmarried parents (such as those on government welfare programs) prefer to spend their available income on entertainment, alcohol and tobacco than on health care. High illegitimate infant death-rates are, at bottom, the result of the 'attitudes, inclinations and preferences of individual decisionmakers' (Eberstadt 1991a, p. 44); that is, we can assume, the immoral lifestyle choices of young, mostly black, single women.

Eberstadt's implicit criticism of government support for single mothers converges neatly with the claims of 'anti-welfare' social scientists like Charles Murray. Adding public health findings to sociological evidence leads to the potentially convincing proposition that state welfare policies which provide financial support for single mothers encourage immoral parental lifestyles and attitudes, which in turn produce behaviours that cause infant death. Medical discourse in general backs the common perception that illegitimate pregnancies and births are more likely to be socially and personally troublesome than those that occur within marriage. Conservative medical discourse adds a moral dimension to this argument. Because they represent single mothers (and fathers) as neglectful, selfish and disinterested in parenthood – as bad mothers and fathers – conservative medical experts corroborate the social–scientific position that illegitimacy is immoral. The National Secretary of the Australian Family Association draws on medical research to argue that 'the best thing you can give a child is its biological mother and father' (Muehlenberg 1993, p. 17); so does American columnist George Will in an article reproduced in the

Australian Financial Review: 'Negligent or otherwise incompetent parents', Will claims, 'are apt to be young and unmarried' (1993).

There are clear moral continuities in the idea that it is physically dangerous to be born out of wedlock and nineteenth-century accounts of infant mortality and illegitimate infanticide. These accounts appeared in medical, statistical, sociological, popular and anthropological journals published in Britain and Australia between 1850 and 1910. Before examining nineteenth-century discursive constructions of illegitimate infant death it is worth noting that the related medical problems of the unmarried mother and the pregnant teenager are much younger phenomena. It was not until the 1920s that the medical profession began to pay specific attention to the morbidity and mortality risks of unmarried mothers (for example, Purdy 1922, p. 291; Waite 1936; Allan 1928; New York Academy of Medicine [1933] 1987; Morris 1925). Cases in which girls or very young women had given birth were occasionally reported under headings such as 'Remarkable case of early maternity' (*Lancet* 1881, pp. 601–2), suggesting that teenage births were viewed in the nineteenth century as a medical curiosity. Social reformers referred to 'girl-mothers' and 'mothers of immature age' after the turn of the century (for example, Mackellar 1903, p. 14), but doctors were still talking about 'the pregnant child' in the 1940s (Danforth 1940, p. 590).

By the 1960s the teenage mother and the pregnant teenager became visible as a separate social category of person requiring specialised medical knowledge and intervention (for example, Osofsky 1968). In their important study of the 'invention' of teenage pregnancy in the United States, William Ray Arney and Bernard J. Bergen argue that around 1970 what used to be the moral problem of the unmarried mother turned into the scientific and technical problem of managing teenage pregnancy. Public health discourse gave the pregnant teenager a public face, presenting her as a deviation from the maternal norm, a client suffering from the problems of 'premature parenthood' (Arney and Bergen 1984, p. 14). Her medical care required management of an error not punishment of deviance. Instead of what Arney and Bergen present as a once-only turn-away from moral frameworks in the 1960s, I would argue that moral and scientific approaches to illegitimacy have been tightly harnessed to one another since the early nineteenth century, and continue to exist in an uneasy relationship.

Illegitimacy did not feature prominently in American medical or social science journals until around the turn of the nineteenth century. Some articles on infant mortality did refer to the 'illegitimate offspring of shame' (Reese 1857, p. 102). For most nineteenth-century American medical experts, however, abortion appeared to represent a much more serious problem than that of illegitimacy or infant homicide. Illegitimacy may also have been relatively invisible as a medical problem because American medical journals of the nineteenth century tended to be more technical than sociological in orientation. A more likely reason is that illegitimacy statistics were, much to the regret of some American doctors, simply unavailable (Chaille 1879, p. 306; Capp 1890).

The emergence of illegitimacy as a formal object of medical discourse in the second half of the nineteenth century was made possible by the development of vital statistics. As statistical inquiry grew into a profession in Britain and Australia, ways of counting illegitimate bodies, dead and alive, proliferated. Official statistics of both illegitimate births and infant mortality were published in Australia and Britain after the middle of the century. The first annual report of the New South Wales Registrar-General of 1857 included crude figures relating to 'deaths under 5 years of age'. In 1862 this category was referred to more scientifically as 'infantile mortality', but was still brief. The second half of the century witnessed a burgeoning official interest in, and the development of statistical techniques enabling the investigation of, illegitimate deaths. By the time Timothy Coghlan compiled his report on vital statistics in 1895, he was able to provide details of the ages of mothers of illegitimate children, the numbers of illegitimate children in city, suburbs and country districts, changes in the State's illegitimacy rate over the previous twenty years, the deaths of illegitimate infants in public institutions and a long tabulation of all the causes of death (including accident, negligence, infanticide and debility) of illegitimate children by age (New South Wales 1895). His *Statistician's Report on the Vital Statistics of New South Wales* included figures relating to the number of deaths in childbirth for single and married women, and the mortality rate for illegitimate infants (New South Wales 1900).

This increased statistical curiosity suggests that illegitimacy was perceived as having a causal relationship to infant mortality. In the minds of many Victorians, especially doctors, illegitimacy equalled death. From the 1880s British and Australian medical journals periodically included reports on the illegitimacy rates of different countries, suggesting that the number of illegitimate births was considered a matter of medical importance.

Medical journals rarely presented illegitimacy statistics as unadorned facts, however. They were moral weathervanes. The moral framework was especially noticeable when the statistics referred, as they typically did, to working-class communities or foreign cultures. W. M. Turnbull compared the proportions of illegitimate births in the Melbourne Lying-in Hospital to women of English, Irish, Scottish and Australian background. Noting that illegitimacy rates in Scotland were considerably higher than those for the Scottish women in Melbourne, Turnbull commented that 'it would therefore appear that the Scotch lasses have improved morally by their sojourn in Australia' (Turnbull 1864). Conversely, high illegitimacy rates in Antigua (72 per cent of the total) indicated that morals in that country were 'at a very low ebb' (*British Medical Journal* 1880a).

Moral judgements resided alongside an explicit attachment to the principles of dispassionate scientific inquiry. Medical writers complained about the absence of statistics and wanted to know the possible causes of illegitimacy. The *British Medical Journal* (1882) called for an investigation into a dramatic rise in the proportion of illegitimate births in Salford, including the birth of sixty illegitimate children in the workhouse. In an article commenting with approval on William Acton's pioneering 1859 study, the British *Lancet* supported the idea that illegitimacy was a social issue requiring social investigation:

> if the social investigator take up the inquiry precisely where the poet and moralist have left it, he will find a complete dearth of information. No one has ventured to let in the light upon those obscure and defaced stones of the social fabric which our conventions ignore, and our selfish delicacy thrusts out of sight. But at this day, when social science is prying into all the defects of our civilization, and seeks to discover at once the sufferings and the wants of hitherto unnoticed sections of the population, it were something more than negligent to omit the inspection of the social conditions affecting the welfare of a class into which some forty-four thousand persons are annually born. (*Lancet* 1860.)

Although the *Lancet* article provided some relevant statistical facts and marked out what it saw as a properly professional distance between social investigation and more conventional moral and literary models, it referred repeatedly to moral concepts and described illegitimacy as a vice and a sin. The article was called 'A way of help for the fallen'. Infanticide, the writer concluded, required social *and* moral remedies. The *Lancet* held a similar opinion in 1866, commenting that the mortality of illegitimate children was puzzling to both the moralist and the physician.

Moral, medical and social approaches to illegitimacy overlapped significantly. By the middle of the nineteenth century British medical reformers suspected that many aspects of their work were deeply embedded in broader social questions. According to Eileen Janes Yeo (1996, p. 96), between 1840 and 1880 doctors tried to establish the idea that medical men could make the most important contribution to sanitary science. Articles in medical publications routinely incorporated the findings of statisticians and social scientists. Among the members of the

(British) National Association for the Promotion of Social Science were a number of men with medical qualifications. The Committee of the Harveian Society on Infanticide, which presented its report in 1867, included in its membership John Brendon Curgenven (MRCS and member of the Infant Life Protection Society) and Edwin Lankester (Coroner for Central Middlesex), both prominent members of the National Association for the Promotion of Social Science. Curgenven had a special interest in the history of laws relating to illegitimacy and foundling institutions in Belgium and France (Curgenven 1871).

Doctors contributed a distinctively medical perspective on the problem, often representing illegitimacy as a moral disease infecting the social body. As John Strachan put in his 'Address upon illegitimacy to the working men of Scotland':

> A question that always forces itself on the consideration of the physician is whether the disease he is called upon to treat be curable or not? ... When called to a patient, having ascertained the nature of the disease, he next inquires into its cause or causes; and these, being discovered, often point clearly to the plan of treatment. There are many diseases, too, that, where you have discovered and removed their cause, will cure themselves. In the hope that we may be thus led to some remedy for this moral disease, let us endeavour to discover the causes which produce it. (Strachan n.d. ?1859, pp. 3–4.)

Much later, but using a similar metaphor, American physicians argued that illegitimacy required 'prophylactic' measures. Illegitimacy threatened the health of a society 'composed of interdependent parts performing functions essential to the life of the whole' (Davis 1904, p. 1135).

Doctors argued that their special expertise was essential to the administration of justice in cases of infant death. They considered themselves indispensable in issuing death certificates and helping the courts determine whether an illegitimate baby was born dead or alive. Medical journals often included reports of inquests into the deaths of illegitimate infants, like that of the 9-day-old daughter of Mary Barry, an unmarried woman living in Collingwood, a suburb of Melbourne, Australia. Barry took the infant to hospital after she noticed that it was having trouble breathing and that its stomach was swollen and discoloured. It died shortly afterwards. The cause of death, according to the medical witness, was congestion of the lungs, accelerated by pressure upon the abdomen such as would have been caused by the tightening of a bandage. Barry stated that she did not realise the bandage might have been too tight until the doctor at the hospital told her so. The jury found that there was insufficient evidence to show whether the tightening was done negligently or wilfully (*Australian Medical Journal* 1879). This and many other similar cases were reported in the medical press as disturbing evidence that the judicial system often failed to back up expert medical opinion.

The death of large numbers of infants born to working-class parents forced reformist doctors to reconceptualise infant mortality as a social as well as a medical problem. They noted that working-class mothers were often unable to take proper care of their infants. Medical members of the National Association for the Promotion of Social Science argued that the condition of the working classes, particularly women's employment in rural or factory work, tended to encourage poor nutrition, a lack of attention to health and infant neglect (Gairdner 1860; Husband 1864; Fraser 1860). Doctors pointed out the dangers of ignorant mothers in poor communities who did not know how to feed, clean or properly manage children (*British Medical Journal* 1880b). James Fraser, a Glasgow medical officer, observed that illegitimate infants in his city died from poor nutrition because the mother, forced to work, fed her child 'food in no way adapted to the active yet delicate assimilative organs of infancy', leading to indigestion, disease, and death (Fraser 1860, p. 653). The carelessness, laziness, lack of thrift, dirtiness, domestic neglect, drunkenness and lack of knowledge among men and women living in slum housing continued to be nominated as major causes of both legitimate and illegitimate infant deaths well into the twentieth century (Newman 1906, pp. 215–20).

Medical writers and social investigators were convinced that illegitimacy had an inflationary effect on infant mortality rates. By the middle of the nineteenth century it was an accepted, statistically supported, medical fact that death-rates were significantly higher among illegitimate infants than among legitimate. Medical men attributed high rates of mortality among illegitimate infants to the fact that, if they remained with their mother, they were more likely to be artificially fed than breastfed (for example, Litchfield 1899, p. 23), and, if not, to their neglect in so-called baby-farming establishments, infants' homes, lying-in hospitals and foundling institutions (for example, Routh 1858; *British Medical Journal* 1881; *Australasian Medical Gazette* 1886). In a typical paper presented to the Royal Statistical Society on 'The perils and protection of infant life' (1894), surgeon Hugh Jones reported statistics showing that three-fifths of all illegitimate children in Sheffield died in infancy. Listing a number of possible social and medical causes, Jones concluded that the shame attached to illegitimacy contributed to the neglect, 'frequently wilful and criminal', of infants (Jones 1894, p. 63).

Doctors were concerned that inadequate official oversight permitted women to conceal the deaths of illegitimate infants. In

Britain and Australia they campaigned for the compulsory registration of still-births by duly-qualified medical practitioners on the grounds that the absence of regulation allowed the criminal destruction of illegitimate children by unscrupulous midwives (*Lancet* 1866; Mullins 1892). Without the presence of a qualified medical man to issue a proper certificate as to the cause of death, an Australian article claimed, boxes and coffins came and went from private lying-in establishments late at night, 'and no one knows anything about them' (*Australasian Medical Gazette* 1886).

Of all the medical problems linked with illegitimacy, infanticide generated the most passion. Medical experts and social scientists joined contributors to popular journals of social inquiry in expressing horror at the inexplicable behaviour of white working-class mothers. William Acton described his table showing the number of infant deaths due to violent causes as 'a frightful list: no less than 846 babies are recorded officially, as hanged, strangled, poisoned, suffocated, and so forth, during the year 1856' (Acton 1859, p. 501). Infanticide was a crime 'of the most savage character' (*Dublin Review* 1858, p. 54), committed by 'unnatural' mothers whose notion of sin came from lenient legal sentences (Flowers 1875) or women 'insane' with shame and despair (Safford 1870, p. 210). 'Put the case as you may', Edwin Lankester told the National Association for the Promotion of Social Science, 'the suspected destruction of 1,000 infant lives annually by their mothers, in a country boasting of its civilisation and christianity, is a fearful blot' (Lankester 1867, p. 221).

Infanticide accounts revolved around a common narrative of the seduction, abandonment and despair of poverty-stricken women forced to end the lives of their babies in a fit of desperation. A typical story appeared in the *Nineteenth Century* magazine in 1877:

> On the 13th of December last, Mary Peterson Mahoney, a girl of eighteen, was brought to trial at Swansea for the murder of her newly born child; found guilty by the jury and sentenced to death. The prisoner was the daughter of Irish labouring people settled at Cardiff; her father and mother had died during her childhood, and the homeless girl was adopted by a poor neighbouring family, who brought her up until she was old enough to go into service. She could neither read nor write; but in her service she bore the character of an honest industrious girl; and it was the crime and treachery of another that brought her to ruin. Her seducer forsook her, enlisted in the army, and left the country. Taken unexpectedly with the pains of child-birth, desolate, terrified, and unhelped, she destroyed her child. The precautions which mark the concealment of premeditated crime were conspicuously absent, and as soon as the police visited the house, the poor girl confessed everything. (Fyffe 1877, p. 583.)

The author dramatises his argument against capital punishment by presenting a courtroom scene in which Mary Mahoney, driven mad on hearing the formal death sentence, tells the judge: 'Because I was poor and ignorant you were able to deceive me. My mind gave way because I thought that the law really meant what it said ...' (Fyffe 1877, pp. 584–5).

Observers were caught between a need to show sympathy for the 'poor girls' who committed infanticide, themselves victims of ignorance, male irresponsibility and social stigma, and their desire to protect the innocent child. Thomas W. Laqueur has argued that a 'narrative habit' that began to form in the eighteenth century made abandoned and murdered babies something to inspire compassion and motivate reform efforts. Humanitarian narratives of infanticide relied on images of the personal body 'as the common bond between those who suffer and those who would help and as the object of the scientific discourse through which the causal links between an evil, a victim, and a benefactor are forged' (Laqueur 1989, p. 177). An article on 'Infanticide and illegitimacy' in the journal *Meliora* illustrates the rhetorical power of this narrative habit:

> Perhaps the paragraph which most inevitably meets the eye of the reader of our daily press is the one which records with dismaying regularity how, on a certain day, floating in a canal, exposed by a river side, smothered in a ditch, left under a hedge-row, packed up in a railway parcel, or stowed away in a servant's box, the dead body of a newly-born infant was discovered by a policeman, by some casual passer-by, a railway official, a fellow-servant, or not infrequently by a dog. The medical man makes an examination, and pronounces either that it had been improperly and unskilfully delivered and had died in birth, or that, being born alive, it had met with death by strangulation, by external injuries, by cold, exposure, starvation, or neglect. The coroner and jury return a verdict of wilful murder against some person or persons unknown; the little corpse is committed to the ground by the sexton in the nearest churchyard, and so the matter ends. (*Meliora* 1863, pp. 323–4.)

Today, newspapers report that dead babies are found in trash cans and dumpsters. The effect of the narrative is the same. The bodies of infants who are not only the victims of murder but poor and illegitimately-born are victims several times over.

Professional and popular publications on infanticide revealed a chronic state of uncertainty about the causes of infanticide and its most likely solutions. Whether they wrote for an academic or non-academic audience, commentators referred to the statistics and published studies of doctors, statisticians and social scientists like Farr, Acton, Lankester, and Lumley. Despite this hard evidence, doctors, social commentators and social analysts found themselves mired within the same painful and apparently unresolvable dilemmas. Were the legal penalties for infanticide too harsh or too lenient? Did foundling hospitals reduce infanticide but thereby increase infant mortality and encourage immorality? Should unmarried mothers be employed as wet-nurses? How could the iniquitous practices of baby-farming and the evils of burial clubs be controlled? What was to be done about mothers who needed to return to work as soon as the baby was born? How could society force the father to contribute to the illegitimate infant's mainte-nance, thereby improving its chances of survival?

Infanticide provoked intense debate within the social–scientific establishment. Many social scientists found themselves in the difficult situation of attempting to rationalise not only an irrational event, but an immoral one. Herbert Safford disagreed with some of his colleagues that the legal punishment of 'these unfortunate women' should be harsher. It would be better to tackle the root cause of child-murder, which he considered to be the difficulty faced by servants and young women in 'light employments' in finding work while they were nursing their infant (Safford 1870, pp. 208–9). Safford's paper was followed by a long and lively discussion involving three other male paper-givers and eleven male and three female speakers from the floor.

The Harveian Society Committee on Infanticide also struggled to apply scientific principles and an objective collective mind to the problem. It pointed out that the conditions under which a single woman gave birth, especially her need to be delivered secretly and without adequate preparation and her need to continue working, explained the strong temptation to destroy the child and to hide its body (*Lancet* 1867, p. 61). The report combined a medical focus on the physical conditions of childbirth with a sociological sensitivity to the social and economic factors affecting working-class motherhood and contributing to illegitimacy. Whether the Committee succeeded in explaining why some women killed their infants, let alone preventing infanticide, remains an open question.

Popular writers were quick to expose the limitations of such experts. Periodical writers may not have been physicians or statisticians them-selves, but they wrote with the intellectual authority of men who consid-ered themselves well-read in the social–scientific literature of their day. Their imagined reader was the reasonable, sensible or thoughtful man who appreciated 'experience and sound reason' (Fyffe 1877, p. 594), 'practical good sense' (*Nation* 1865, p. 271), and 'the common sense of mankind' (*Dublin Review* 1858, p. 106).

From the sensible man's point of view, it was almost impossible for a medical witness to prove that no part of the infant was actually in the body of the mother when it was killed (*Dublin Review* 1858, p. 69).

Medical witnesses themselves, according to the *Nineteenth Century*, admitted that their tests were not infallible (Fyffe 1877, p. 586). Statistical evidence was treated with particular caution. The *Nation*'s London correspondent, commenting on 'Infanticide amongst the poor' in England, claimed that although statistical authorities could readily be found to explain that the percentage of illegitimate births and the rate of mortality among babies born out of wedlock were lower in England than in continental countries, 'we care very little about statistics' (1865, p. 270). *Meliora* was even more critical of the gaps and discrepancies in statistical discourse. After a long review of available statistics of infant mortality the author concluded 'we know absolutely nothing comprehensive or definite, and the result is simply a mass of contradictions' (1863, p. 330).

Journal writers were just as sceptical of the reform measures optimistically proposed by advocates of social progress. An *Economist* article on illegitimacy and infanticide reproduced in the *Journal of the Statistical Society of London* claimed that all programs for social or legislative change had grave drawbacks:

> It is very difficult to apply steady coercion while juries are so unwilling to convict, and while the public secretly feel its conscience shocked at the impunity conceded to the father while such a heavy penalty is exacted from the mother. It is equally difficult to relieve the mother of her babe without decreasing the restraints on licentiousness ... And lastly, a separate allowance for an illegitimate child, if granted out of the [poor] 'house', will in the end make large illegitimate families a source of profit, and restore the worst abuse of the old poor law. The single object, therefore, must be to discover some plan which, while diminishing the burden upon the mother, shall diminish no sexual restraint ... (*Journal of the Statistical Society of London* 1865, p. 423.)

The *Spectator* (1890) was even more pessimistic. The care of children could never be enforced by law 'upon parents, especially mothers, who have lost or never possessed the natural human instinct'.

Then as now, social inquiry had no definitive answer. Adherents of the rational approach to social and moral problems seemed unable to find a means of protecting innocent children and weak women without sanctioning illegitimacy and immorality, let alone explain why so many mothers committed murder. Even as an object of scientific inquiry, infanticide was surrounded by a deep sense of cultural unease and uncertainty.

This moral ambivalence surrounding white working-class infanticide was reinforced by colonialist discourses that represented infanticide as the ultimate expression of the ignorance, primitiveness and savagery of indigenous peoples. We need to remember, when considering the current unease that surrounds infant homicide, that infanticide has a long history as a highly racialised concept. The English masses, according to the *Spectator* (1890) in an effort to convey the awfulness of the crime, were no better 'those Hindoo tribes which for ages past have murdered half their female children'. British journalists joined an army of nineteenth-century religious men, philanthropists and ethnographers deeply concerned with the practice of (usually female) infanticide in various parts of the Empire, most frequently in India and China, but also among some Australian Aboriginal tribes.

Infanticide indicated heathenism. It betokened a society's ignorance or explicit rejection of Christian moral standards, and provided unambiguous evidence of the cultural backwardness of indigenous peoples. Hindu Indians and Aborigines alike were represented in early ethnographic accounts of infanticide as being so primitive, so lacking in moral sensibility, that they were incapable of understanding the wrong they were committing. 'The aboriginal mind does not seem to perceive the horrible idea of leaving an unfortunate baby to die miserably in a deserted camp, crawled over by ants and flies, and probably devoured by wild dogs' (Fison and Howitt [1880] 1967, p. 190).

Colonial observers did not invariably link infanticide in non-white populations to the marital status of the mother, as social scientists did in studies of white working-class women. But some did include illegitimate status in their lists of circumstances in which Aboriginal mothers might kill their babies shortly after birth. The term 'illegitimate' means a number of things in nineteenth-century ethnographic accounts of Aboriginal societies. Sometimes observers use it to refer to the children born of an improper alliance, that is, to parents who 'belonged to the same class, or were too nearly related to each other' (Fison and Howitt [1880] 1967, p. 358). Incestuous unions were sometimes described as producing children of illegitimate status. More usually, however, the term 'illegitimate' was used to describe children born outside of a marriage arrangement or to a young woman before marriage (Cowlishaw 1978, p. 264). Thus Brough Smyth, in his study of the Aborigines of Victoria, recounted the case of a Narrinyeri woman who killed her child because she (the mother) had been given in marriage to its father against her will (Smyth 1878, p. 52). Whereas social scientists attributed infanticide committed by white mothers solely to sexual activity outside of marriage, ethnographers linked it to the 'wrongness' of sexual relationships that transgressed racial taboos, rules of kinship, or tribal laws.

Some studies of Aboriginal society documented the killing of what anthropologists and government officials called 'half-caste' children – children born to one white parent (usually assumed to be a 'lower-class' man) and one Aboriginal parent (usually assumed to be an Aboriginal woman with or without an Aboriginal 'husband'). Among the Narrinyeri, according to Smyth, about one-half of the 'half-caste' infants 'fell victims to the jealousy of the husbands of the mothers' (1878, p. 52). It was generally taken for granted that the 'half-caste', being born outside of (white) lawful marriage, was technically illegitimate. However, British inhabitants of the colonies were less worried by the sexual irregularity implied by the birth of a 'half-caste' child than by the more visible evidence of racial miscegenation. The illegitimacy of the 'half-caste' was thus more a racial metaphor than a demographic fact. The so-called half-caste problem was primarily one of racial illegitimacy.

Ethnographic studies positioned indigenous illegitimacy and infanticide as the dark obverse of white middle-class European norms of legitimate family formation. Infanticide appeared in studies of Aboriginal societies, as it did in discussions of working-class white women, as a morally repugnant outcome of primitive living and improper sexual relations. However, ethnographers interpreted the behaviour of Aboriginal parents (usually but not always the mother) who killed their infants as logical, scientific and even 'natural', because Aborigines were considered to be closer to nature and to natural processes than 'civilised' peoples. Smyth argued that Aboriginal babies were killed as a means of limiting the population in obedience to an irrepressible law of Nature:

> The white mother kills her infant in the vain hope of preserving her social position – high or low – of concealing the error or crime which preceded the birth; the black woman simply, I believe, because she is not capable of supporting her offspring, in order to render impossible an increase of population which the food-resources of the tribe would be unable to meet. (Smyth 1878, pp. 54–5.)

Smyth's Malthusian theory of Aboriginal infanticide positioned Aboriginal mothers as Nature and their white counterparts as corrupted Culture.

Colonial discourses seeped into and lent rhetorical weight to social–scientific constructions of the illegitimate infanticide problem among the English working classes. Whether it took place in England or Aboriginal Australia, whether its victims were white or black babies, infanticide was wrong. Because white Australian women at least had the benefits of civilisation, Smyth argued that they were more immoral than Aboriginal women:

> Infanticide – the whites affect to believe – is a monstrous thing among savage and barbarous nations; but every newspaper one reads gives accounts of cases of infanticide, as practised by our own people, far more horrible than

any known to the Australians or Polynesians. Baby farming, the strangling of infants, the cruel destruction by mothers of their progeny by hiding them under fences, by laying them on cold door-steps, or throwing them into pits, are practices employed by those who enjoy the results of many centuries of civilization ... (Smyth 1878, pp. 54–5.)

Infanticide was only to be expected among savages who knew no better and, like animals, could only blindly follow the dictates of Nature. White Christian women, on the other hand, had no excuse. Infanticide was a manifestly savage and inhuman act.

What remained unspoken in accounts of both white and Aboriginal infanticide was the taken-for-granted equation between legitimacy and life and the invisible privileging of the middle-class, white, moral married mother. Illegitimacy, according to David Chidester, has a firm hold over the contemporary imagination because 'it is part of a single, complex, and pervasive cultural image, not only of the socially unacceptable, but also of the evil and dangerous' (1992, p. 146). This evil image depended on a Christian demonology, reinforced by nineteenth-century social science, that centred on orgies, incest, cannibalism and 'primitive promiscuity'. Infanticide sits easily in the Christian list of demonic practices. The actions of the woman who murders her infant, no matter how much she might deserve sympathy because of her youth, lack of education or poor economic circumstances, are aberrant, inexplicable, unnatural and almost unthinkable. *Harper's Magazine* essayist Lewis Lapham refers to the New Jersey schoolgirl who gave birth during a school dance as one of the most horrible instances of contemporary society's inability to construct a new moral order. The illegitimate infant, 'the product of desire, like Kleenex, is disposable. There is always a clean towel and another song' (1997, p. 39). The unmarried mother who allows her baby to die is excluded from humanity.

Not coincidentally, infanticide is at present the subject of lively investigation and debate among students of all kinds of animal populations from bumble bees to royal penguins and grizzly bears. Scientists believe primate infanticide to be of particular relevance to the study of human behaviour (for example, Fisher 1992, p. 75). Their interest may, as Donna Haraway suggests, be due in part to a fondness for dramas centring on violence and sex (1989, p. 311). The primatological study of infanticide contributes to a deep narrative tradition which allows the reinvention of Nature and the telling of important public stories. 'Primate social behaviour', Haraway tells us, 'is studied inescapably as part of the complex struggle in liberal Western democracies to name who is a mature, healthy citizen and why' (1991, p. 83). Clearly, young single mothers – especially those who are black – who neglect, abandon or kill their babies do not count as 'mature healthy citizens'. In this sense, contemporary studies of infanticide in animal populations have much in common with nineteenth-century anthropological, medical and sociological accounts of infanticide in human populations. The mother who kills her illegitimate child stands precariously on a thin line distinguishing animal from human behaviour.

In nominating medicine as one of the major manufacturers of the contemporary illegitimacy 'problem', I do not deny that medical knowledge and practices have had positive effects on the health and welfare of single married mothers and their children. All pregnant women, women giving birth and mothers of infants need access to the best possible health services and medical care, and perhaps only some members of the medical profession, at least in the twentieth century, have actually discriminated against single mothers.

What does need questioning is the medical version of ex-nuptial birth status as a transparently aberrant biological condition. Contemporary medical knowledge is, as this chapter has indicated, the product of multiple interactions that have taken place over the course of centuries between medicine and other cultural knowledges. Medical constructions of illegitimate infanticide and mortality have not stood alone but have acquired much of their potency through their intersection with moral, philanthropic, juridical, sociological, statistical and anthropological knowledges. The idea that illegitimacy means death has been part of western culture's belief system for at least 150 years.

The relationship between medical and non-medical knowledge works just as productively in the other direction. Social–scientific constructions of the problem of rising rates of out-of-wedlock births are parasitic upon, and powerfully legitimated by, medical narratives of the unhealthy or vulnerable illegitimate body. Medicine's particular contribution to the illegitimacy problem has been to pathologise the bodies, minds, actions and lifestyles of unwed mothers. Exposing the hidden moral and colonialist foundations of medical truths helps denaturalise them. The problem of single motherhood will not disappear until we dispute medicine's claim to speak with disinterested authority of the deadly dangers of illegitimacy.

CHAPTER 7

Offspring of Feeble and Neurotic Minds

In the first half of the nineteenth century illegitimacy meant feeble bodies, in the first half of the twentieth it meant feeble minds. This switch of focus from what happened outside the illegitimate body to what went on inside was revolutionary. Until the first few decades of the twentieth century it occurred to few social investigators that the illegitimacy problem might actually be in women's heads. The nineteenth-century scientific gaze was firmly fixed on deficiencies in the external environment – overcrowded housing, immoral peasant or amoral indigenous cultures, the lack of religious influences, poor education – as possible causes of illegitimacy. The rise of psychological and eugenic systems of thought in the second decade of the twentieth century did not overrule this long-established tradition, but the systems did allow social scientists to develop a dual focus on both the individual and society and on the interaction between them.

The eugenic constructions of illegitimacy that assumed prominence between about 1910 and 1930 built on the late nineteenth-century proposition that in some populations there was an inherited predisposition to high rates of illegitimacy (Leffingwell 1892). Eugenics promoted the idea that undesirable physical and mental characteristics, in particular 'feeblemindedness', were passed on genetically from one generation to the next. American, British and Australian social experts were all swept up in the intense eugenic focus on mental defectiveness as an obstacle to the social advancement of the white race.

According to eugenic theory, there was a close relationship between mental defectiveness and illegitimacy. It was accepted by a wide range of medical experts, psychologists, sociologists, child welfare and social workers and population theorists – even a contributor to the *Encyclopaedia of Religion and Ethics* (1914, p. 108) – that feebleminded women were a major source of illegitimate births. Feebleminded women, they argued, reproduced prolifically, typically giving birth to illegitimate children who were themselves likely to be feebleminded. The illegitimate and the feebleminded were thus responsible for perpetuating a degenerative cycle (for example, Piddington 1923). British physician Hugh Ashby, like many of his colleagues in the 1920s, was confident that 'Few facts are more sure or better known than that a great many of the illegitimate children are feeble-minded and born of feeble-minded women' (1922, p. 186).

It was the view of some eugenicists that the feebleminded girl was a problem not just because her mind was exceptionally weak but also because she was prone to immoral sexual conduct. They held that feebleminded girls had little power to resist sexual temptation and were unable to protect themselves from the predatory advances of evil-minded men. According to Australian doctor and child welfare reformer Sir Charles Mackellar (previously President of the 1904 New South Wales Commission on the Decline of the Birth-Rate and President of the State Children's Relief Board), 'The most sad and indeed horrible experience of my professional life was the sight of an unfortunate and very badly deformed idiot girl who was about to become a mother' (Mackellar and Welsh 1917, p. 6). The feebleminded unmarried mother presented a monstrous spectacle: immoral, undeveloped, uncontrolled and unthinking, an ugly affront to the bourgeois notion that mother-hood was a naturally virtuous, beautiful and sensible state.

The problem of the feebleminded unmarried mother received particular attention in the United States. By the 1920s American ideas about illegitimacy were strongly influenced by the experiences, practices and assumptions of social workers whose task it was to improve the welfare of unmarried mothers and their children. The language American experts used to explain the problem of the feebleminded unmarried mother was less overtly moralistic than Mackellar's. From about the time of World War I, professionally trained social workers and welfare agencies in the United States took the lead in moving away from older philanthropic models of aid for 'fallen women' towards scientifi-cally based and systematic interventions – known as 'casework' – with individual unmarried mothers. Social workers were encouraged to gather as much information as possible about their individual cases (Kunzel 1993). They sought data on the unmarried mother's social and family background, her personal relationships, her health and her mental state. Social work assessments often included a 'mental' or psychological examination of some sort (Watson 1918, p. 106).

It was just such case records, from private agencies in metropolitan Boston and one of the State boards in Massachusetts, which Percy

Gamble Kammerer analysed to produce his pioneering study *The Unmarried Mother* ([1918] 1969). Kammerer was an assistant minister of the Emmanuel Protestant Episcopal Church in Boston who described himself as having an interest in the 'psychotherapeutic treatment of functional nervous disorders' (Kammerer 1920). Kammerer estimated that mental examinations were conducted in 26 per cent of his 500 cases. Case 61, a 21-year-old woman who had arrived in Boston three years previously, had begun to 'associate with men of questionable reputation, frequenting dances and spending much time on the street'. Her examination included the application of the Binet test, which gave her a mental age of 9.6, and other tests for the presence of psychosis or congenital defects, visual memory, reasoning, judgement, apperception, attention and suggestibility. Case 61's 'arrangement of moral questions' was reported to be illogical and she was diagnosed as a defective delinquent (Kammerer [1918] 1969, p. 242).

Kammerer was particularly concerned with the accurate classification and precise definition of the nature of mental abnormality in unmarried mothers. The British Royal Commission on the Care and Control of the Feebleminded of 1913, on which Mackellar had extensively drawn, devised a typology of mental defectiveness comprised of lunatics, the mentally infirm, idiots, imbeciles, the feebleminded and moral imbeciles (Mackellar and Welsh 1917, p. 21). Kammerer was critical of unscientifically imprecise terms such as 'moral imbecile'. He adopted instead the definitions used by the American Association for the Study of the Feeble-minded, a more complicated system that specified a total of nineteen different types and sub-types of defectives. The 'mental abnormalities' category contained five sub-divisions: mental defect, mental dullness, constitutional inferiority, mental aberration (including psychoses and insanities) and mental peculiarities. The 'mental defect' sub-division was further divided into feebleminded, subnormal and defective only in some special ability (such as self-control). The feebleminded, in turn, were classified as idiots, imbeciles or morons (Kammerer [1918] 1969, pp. 236–7). Thus Case 62, a 19-year-old unmarried mother whose father was an alcoholic and whose brother and uncle were insane, came under the heading of 'special defect – self-control':

> At times she seemed obsessed with sex desires. She was a strong, precocious type, and her passions were continually overcoming her inhibitions. Finally she so gave vent to her sex feelings that she entirely disregarded community standards, and with heredity for an excuse gave herself over to extreme promiscuity. (Kammerer [1918] 1969, p. 245.)

Such cases indicated the social costs of mental abnormality. Like Mackellar, Kammerer wanted steps to be taken to control and segregate the mentally abnormal woman of childbearing age, an estimated 30 to 40 per cent of all the women he studied, who were 'incapable of self-control' ([1918] 1969, p. 317).

It was clear to Kammerer that there was a need for more knowledge of 'the whole range of subtle mental traits which directly affect behaviour' (Kammerer [1918] 1969, p. 264). Kammerer and other illegitimacy experts tended to assume that the mentally defective unmarried mother was located at one end of a broader continuum of female sexual and mental abnormality. When Alberta Guibord and Ida Parker diagnosed the intelligence status of eighty-two unmarried mothers they found them to be either normal, dull normal, borderline, feeble-minded or psychopathic (Guibord and Parker 1922, p. 73). Mentally, according to such experts, most unmarried mothers were not normal.

The precise proportions of unmarried mothers who were of 'inferior mentality' proved difficult to quantify. Perhaps because mental strength was inevitably a matter of subjective judgement, this particular measure of immorality was highly contested and not altogether successful. As Henry Schumacher, Director of the Cleveland Child Guidance Clinic, pointed out (1927, p. 775), estimates of the percentage of unmarried mothers who were feebleminded varied enormously, from as little as 7 to as much as 98 per cent. By the late 1920s child-welfare officials were of the opinion that early estimates were 'undoubtedly overstatements' (Lundberg 1926, p. 13). References to the feeblemindedness explanation of illegitimacy became more qualified and cautious in the 1930s and had virtually disappeared by the following decade.

As the idea of feeblemindedness receded the idea of IQ (Intelligence Quotient) gained in popularity. Assessing the intelligence of unmarried mothers in the form of their IQ rating was no less controversial but it did appear to be easier to measure. Measures of the IQ levels of unmarried mothers began to appear in the 1920s, predominantly in the American social welfare and psychological literature.

IQ test results painted an unflattering picture. In 1926 psychologist Charlotte Lowe conducted a study of the intelligence and social backgrounds of a group of 344 unmarried mothers on behalf of the Research Bureau of the State Board of Control of Minnesota. Lowe found that over 66 per cent had below-average IQ scores (Lowe 1927, p. 786). Others, like Enid Severy Smith, found a wide range of intellectual abilities suggesting the existence of 'a group of biologically normal, healthy, adolescent pregnant girls in the public schools' who ought not to be confused with 'older, less intelligent unmarried mothers, of lower social status' (Smith 1935, p. 86). The inclusion of IQ scores was a standard component of studies of the unmarried mother by the 1940s.

The ready acceptance of intelligence testing was a clear sign that psychological interpretations of the problem of illegitimacy were gaining ground. Illegitimacy experts did not always refer explicitly to Freudian theory, perhaps because most of the literature was designed to be of practical assistance to social workers untrained in psychological approaches. Nevertheless, from the second decade of the twentieth century its influence was clear. Early psychologically oriented accounts of illegitimacy stressed the need to acknowledge the universal existence of a sex drive, for example. Kammerer ([1918] 1969) included 'early sex experience', 'sexual suggestibility' and 'abnormal sexualism' in his list of environmental factors contributing to unmarried motherhood. Social workers suggested the need to pay attention to the 'mental hygiene' aspects of unmarried motherhood. The mental hygiene approach, according to Marion Kenworthy of the New York School of Social Work, viewed unmarried motherhood as a matter of 'social maladjustment'. Mental hygiene aimed to discover the motive behind every act and to take account of the role of personality factors. It was 'pure nonsense to tell a girl that she must not think of sex'. What the mental hygiene practitioner hoped for was 'the possibility of the management of these urges in a manner acceptable to social dictates' (Kenworthy 1921, p. 506).

Mental hygienists were often critical of the eugenics-inspired 'mental defectiveness' school of thought. Outlining his 'socio-psychiatric viewpoint' on the unmarried mother, Henry Schumacher disagreed with the prevailing assumption that a mentally defective woman was necessarily predisposed to indulge in an illicit sexual relationship. He described the 'feeblemindedness' explanation for illegitimacy as inadequate and methodologically dubious. A properly scientific approach would, instead, seek causes within the individual unmarried mother herself. Drawing on Freud's theories of repressed desire and the unconscious, Schumacher speculated that some women who were quite normal physiologically and intellectually engaged in illicit sex relationships 'to overcome or compensate for thwartings of desires or of activities in other directions'. Their promiscuity may be a form of unconscious protest (Schumacher 1927, pp. 778–9).

Psychological knowledge assumed equal importance in the work of the Children's Bureau of the United States Department of Labor, a federal agency with primary responsibility for the welfare of illegitimate children. By the 1920s it was widely believed that a large proportion of juvenile delinquents had been born out of wedlock (Lenroot 1921, p. 126). Psychological principles helped the Bureau's female officials define the relationship between illegitimacy and delinquency. American social scientists began to explore the sexual delinquency of the illegitimate mother. Annie Bingham, a psychiatrist attached to the New York Probation and Protective Association, included pregnant girls in her social analysis of sex delinquency in 500 female adolescents. She found that over 35 per cent of the group either were, or had at some time been, pregnant, and that 93 per cent of these pregnancies were illegitimate (Bingham 1922–3, p. 535). For Bingham and her colleagues, becoming pregnant out of wedlock was a physical symptom of irregular living and a general state of delinquency.

If delinquency meant 'atypical conduct that brings a person into conflict with accepted community standards of action', as Emma Lundberg explained, all unmarried mothers and fathers were, by definition, delinquent. Lundberg divided girls and women who became mothers out of wedlock into four distinct types: the mentally subnormal girl; the young, susceptible girl; the woman of good character deceived by false promises; and 'the really delinquent girl or woman, who knowingly chooses antisocial conduct, her illegitimate maternity being only an incidental evidence of repeated immorality' (Lundberg 1921, pp. 204–5). Delinquency, Lundberg found, was linked to the maladjustments of adolescence, inferior mentality and psychopathic traits, immorality fostered by bad environment, employment in unskilled occupations, broken homes and the absence of wholesome home influences (1921, p. 207). Lundberg's analysis of the unmarried mother happily combined eugenic, psychological and sociological theories. Or, as Lundberg herself put it, delinquency was produced by the combination of hereditary, temperamental and environmental factors.

To illustrate the complex interaction of psychological and social influences Lundberg described the case of twin daughters, born to an 'irresponsible almshouse inmate', who had been removed at birth, separated and placed in different foster homes. Although the twins knew nothing of each other's existence, both developed into troublesome and uncontrollable girls who, at the age of 17, were committed to the same reformatory for vagrancy. Both girls had been seriously immoral, both were classed as subnormal, both were epileptic and both were suffering from gonorrhoea. Lundberg suggests that their delinquency was the result of the same early experiences as illegitimate children, and that delinquency was transmitted from one generation to the next (1921, p. 208).

As Katharine Lenroot pointed out, delinquency and other 'conduct disorders' should be understood as the result of 'the interaction of complex forces', that is, as a product of society. The community must share with the individual the responsibility for social maladjustment. She approved of increasing state intervention in the lives of young delinquents in order, not to punish, but to protect them and to encourage socially desirable conduct through psychiatry and other non-institutional forms of treatment (Lenroot 1924, pp. 74–5). Although prostitution was classed as a form of sexual delinquency, social investigators believed that very few prostitutes became unmarried mothers. Only nineteen of the 306 New York prostitutes studied by delinquency researcher Alice Menken in 1922 were pregnant when they were placed on probation (Mencken 1922, pp. 99–100). The prevailing explanation was that prostitutes were more adept than 'normal' women at avoiding pregnancy (Thompson 1956, p. 84).

By the late 1930s unmarried mothers and their children were being subjected to a battery of intelligence, personality, educational achievement and attitudinal tests. As psychological techniques became more refined social investigators attempted to measure the 'emotional maturity' of illegitimate subjects (Nottingham 1937). Child psychologists like Florence Teagarden argued that the illegitimate child had fewer opportunities for emotional growth than their legitimate counterparts. Teagarden recalled that she had once worked with

> a delinquent girl who had been born out of wedlock. In fits of anger, the child's mother would snarl 'bastard' as if the child were in some way to blame for the whole unfortunate affair of her birth. It might be well for us to question whether *we* would have escaped delinquency if we had been reared under such circumstances. (Teagarden 1946, p. 245.)

Eustace Chesser claimed in his book *Unwanted Child* that modern psychological knowledge proved that 'children need for full emotional development a stable home and the love and care of two parents'. Children brought up in institutions, by contrast, suffered retarded emotional growth (Chesser 1947, p. 15). Two decades later, even religious authorities were convinced that if a child did not know his own father his emotional development would be seriously hampered (Church of England 1966, p. 9).

Researchers began to notice the emotional state of the unmarried mother for the first time in the 1940s. Social workers observed that Minnesota's requirement that unmarried mothers nurse their babies for three months before placing them for adoption caused considerable resentment and grief. During those three months an emotional relationship developed between mother and child which made separation difficult (Dahlgren 1940, pp. 2, 10). The unmarried mother, often hostile towards the father and rejected by her own family, was unable to develop 'emotional poise' (Teagarden 1946, p. 245). Miriam Powell found in her study of the case records of the Unmarried Mother Department of a New York child-guidance clinic that clients were 'emotionally maladjusted girls who had unhealthy emotional backgrounds and whose illegitimate pregnancies were a continuation of their earlier problems' (Powell 1949, p. 176).

Rickie Solinger (1992) has argued that the psychological explanation of unwed motherhood in this period applied specifically to white women. Some of the literature on the relationship between emotional maladjustment and illegitimacy was racially differentiated. Patricia Knapp and Sophie Cambria found that the emotional adjustment of Negro unmarried mothers bore no relationship to their reactions to illegitimacy. Their attitudes to illegitimacy were not, as commonly assumed, expressions of individual personality problems but were culturally determined (Knapp and Cambria 1947, p. 201). The notion that white unmarried mothers had typically been emotionally deprived as children was widely accepted by the 1960s (Webb 1961, p. 11).

Emotional deprivation was strongly linked to the institutional life experienced by many illegitimate children. Writers who routinely encountered troubled young women through the criminal justice system did not find it surprising that illegitimate children became rebels against social conventions and, more seriously, against its criminal laws. They were typically brought up in charitable or municipal institutions – a poor substitute, psychologists found, for a real home – and ended up in penal institutions because of the 'psychological trauma' caused by illegitimacy. Claud Mullins, an English magistrate with an interest in psychology, described his encounter with Mabel, a 17-year-old unmarried mother charged with theft. Mullins placed her on two years' probation, a condition of which was that she be placed in a home, where she was reported to be likeable but rude and involved in 'endless rows'. After Mabel left the home, and before her probationary period was up, she became pregnant a second time. Mullins noted sadly that the girl's Borstal Institution and women's prisons were full of Mabels (Mullins 1940, p. 27).

A troubled home life was seen as one of the main predisposing factors in unmarried motherhood. Experts in child welfare, social work and social medicine argued that unmarried mothers were likely to come from a broken home or from one in which there was some kind of problem with the parents. Of the thirty illegitimately pregnant girls studied by Miriam Powell as part of her social work thesis for Smith College, only one had parents who were both considered to be well-adjusted. Overall, they came from unhealthy emotional backgrounds (Powell 1949, p. 176). According to British medical researcher Barbara Thompson, both illegitimacy and delinquency were the products of insecure family life (Thompson 1956, p. 86).

In the 1940s social scientists began to listen to what psychologists were saying about the negative effects of father-absence. It was believed in the 1920s that the absence of the father or the mother or of both parents increased the rate of delinquency (Mangold 1921, p. 131). As the oedipal theory of development infiltrated delinquency studies the father–child relationship assumed priority. Claud Mullins accepted modern psychology's finding that the child's relationship with the father was the source of its attitudes towards authority. The father's role was to foster the development of 'the inborn impulses as may produce law-abiding citizens' (Mullins 1940, p. 13). The accepted view by 1950 was that poverty, unsatisfactory home atmosphere, a broken home and, above all, the lack of a father, 'the font of respect for authority', was responsible for illegitimate children's greater tendency to be delinquent (Stevenson 1950, pp. 131–2).

Another perceived cause of delinquency was the unmarried mother's lack of affection for, or rejection of, her illegitimate child during the crucial infant years when basic personality traits were formed. Internationally renowned expert on the crucial importance of maternal care, John Bowlby, argued that in western societies emotionally disturbed parents who had been deprived of maternal care when children themselves produced illegitimate children 'of a socially unacceptable kind'. One generation of deprived children provided the parents of the next generation with deprived children (Bowlby 1952, p. 95). Experts researching the unmarried mother and her child in the 1950s and 1960s were strongly influenced by Bowlby's work. British sociologist Virginia Wimperis, for example, repeated the claim that the severe emotional damage suffered by illegitimate children produced delinquent and anti-social behaviour (Wimperis 1960, pp. 296–8). Illegitimate children were particularly likely to be maladjusted if their mothers were unhappy, insecure, frustrated or resentful (1960, p. 301).

The view that the unmarried mother was suffering from some kind of emotional sickness reached its most extreme expression in psychoanalytic narratives of illegitimacy. In the 1940s psychiatrists and social workers began to notice that not all of their cases could be explained by social factors, that is, by the presence of a working-class environment or by mental defectiveness. Young women could be intelligent, academically successful, obedient, refined and come from a respectable family, yet inexplicably become illegitimately pregnant. Psychiatrists suggested that in such 'normal' white middle-class women a pregnancy must represent an hysterical dissociation state in which they were acting out an unresolved oedipus situation – an incest fantasy – by having sexual intercourse with a man who served as a 'phantom father' (Kasanin and Handschin 1941, p. 69). The actions of unmarried mothers could also be driven by adolescent fantasies of rape, prostitution or immaculate conception. According to Florence Clothier, unmarried motherhood in 'our' culture (that is, presumably, among white women) was a form of neurotic and delinquent behaviour representing a 'distorted and unrealistic way out of inner difficulties' (Clothier 1943, p. 548).

Helene Deutsch, the prominent European Freudian analyst, teacher and writer, suggested a more complex psychological portrait of white unmarried motherhood in her two-volume study *The Psychology of Women* (1945). As an unmarried 26-year-old medical student, Deutsch had become pregnant as a result of an affair with a married man, and had had an abortion. She married Felix Deutsch shortly afterwards in 1912 and gave birth to a son in 1917. Her relationship with her son proved to be difficult. Deutsch's biographers speculate that the privileged place she gave motherhood in *The Psychology of Women* was an attempt to compensate for what she saw as her own maternal deficiencies. She entered analysis with Freud in 1918 and by the time she and Felix moved to the United States in 1935 she had acquired a reputation as his foremost female disciple (Appignanesi and Forrester 1992, pp. 312–18). Like most psychoanalysts, Deutsch accepted the idea that the unmarried mother had a strong unconscious desire to complete the heterosexual family triangle, if necessary with the aid of a fantasy father. She offered a more complex psychological portrait of the unmarried mother, however, by pointing to other factors such as the conflict between a woman's compulsive immature wish for a child and social inhibitions, the female tendency to passive masochistic behaviour, the emotional stresses peculiar to adolescence, evidence of repetition in cases of multiple illegitimate pregnancies and, perhaps the most frequent theme of all, the flight from, and hate for, the mother.

Here Deutsch departed from Freud and from most psychoanalytic accounts of illegitimacy. Psychoanalysis typically positioned fathers as crucial to the healthy emotional development of the child. The absence of a father from death, divorce or desertion during a child's oedipal phase disturbed the oedipal triangle and could produce in children pathological symptoms such as insomnia, lack of appetite and 'importunate behavior' (Meiss 1952, p. 216; Neubauer 1960). Deutsch's account, by contrast, repeatedly emphasised women's tendency to over-identify with, or angrily reject, their mothers. In the case of Ida, for example, a 17-year-old governess and the daughter of a woman Deutsch described as a 'fanatically devout religious bigot':

> the rebellious struggle against her mother and her mother's moral commands and prohibitions acted as a powerful motive in the choice of her love object, her elopement, and her intercourse with her lover. A hateful protest against the mother often contains revenge tendencies, and when a young girl becomes promiscuous, a prostitute, or an unmarried mother, she often both fulfils a fantasy and punishes herself. (Deutsch 1945, p. 349.)

Deutsch's image of the unmarried mother – passive, self-punishing, and compulsive – is unflattering but not entirely unsympathetic. Her efforts to scientifically explain the complexities of behaviour that many of her contemporaries would dismiss as simply bad, neurotic or stupid suggest insight and (read in the light of her own pregnancy, and what she recalled as a conflicted relationship with her own mother) empathy.

Feminists have tended to be critical of Deutsch because she idealised motherhood and femininity and popularised the view that, by virtue of their biological make-up, women were innately and naturally passive. In her analysis of the unmarried mother Deutsch tempered this essentialism with a strong emphasis on the interaction of psychic and social forces. Before she trained as a psychiatrist Deutsch had been active in the Polish workers' movement, helping to organise and improve the conditions of women factory workers (Appignanesi and Forrester 1992, pp. 310–11). Her socialist sympathies may explain why she described illegitimate motherhood as a social problem that was judged differently in different societies. The poor emotional state of unmarried mothers was a reaction to the disgrace and shame with which illegitimacy was regarded in American society (Deutsch 1945, pp. 332–3). Deutsch urged social workers to consider both external reality and psychic forces in deciding, for example, whether an illegitimate child should be relinquished for adoption or should remain with the mother (1945, p. 392).

Leontine Young's *Out of Wedlock*, published later, directly addressed social workers facing these dilemmas daily. Young appears to have had no formal training in psychoanalysis – she was Professor of Casework at Ohio State University's School of Social Administration – and the publications she refers to come from the social-welfare, rather than the psychological, literature. Young's book provided a clear explanation in lay language of the psychoanalytic interpretation of illegitimacy. According to Young, an out-of-wedlock birth (a term that was just beginning to supplement 'illegitimate' in academic discourse) never 'just happens' – it is a woman's purposeful and deliberate, if unconscious, acting out of her compulsive wish to have a baby. The unmarried mother typically came from a home dominated by the mother, and having an out-of-wedlock baby was one of the few expressions of autonomy or revenge available to her. Less commonly, she was 'father-ridden'; that is, her actions were ruled by the fear, hatred and anger she felt towards a tyrannical father. Young considered that a minority of unmarried mothers were psychotic, psychopathic or 'socially disorganized'. When added to the plasticity and uncertainty of adolescence all unmarried mothers exhibited, to varying degrees, symptoms of emotional sickness and many were neurotic (Young 1954).

Like Deutsch, Young argued that society's rigid attitudes towards sexuality contributed to the unmarried mother's psychological disturbance. The more social disapproval she encountered, as in a strict middle-class home, the more disturbed she would be. Race and ethnicity also affected an unmarried mother's emotional wellbeing. The strict domineering father was, Young believed, more common in immigrant families, for example. Unlike most psychoanalysts, who assumed that the unmarried mother was white, Young claimed that the same psychological dynamics operated regardless of race. As in white culture, the degree of repression varied, and the personality structure and problems of the Negro unmarried mother coming from a severely circumscribed background would be identical with those of a white girl coming from the same kind of environment (Young 1954, pp. 121–2).

Young's primary objective was to convince social caseworkers that they needed to understand each unmarried mother's particular psychology, and to use that knowledge to help her 'plan and act more in accord with external reality' (Young 1954, p. 175). But she also had a clear political agenda, calling for more financial assistance, facilities and support for unmarried mothers. In a neat twist of the Malthusian argument that society cannot afford to pay for the illegitimate child, Young argued that:

> the price we pay today in hard cash for the consequences of some of these disregarded problems is many times the cost of a good preventive program. No one knows how many of the unprotected out-of-wedlock children are now in mental hospitals or prisons, are destroying their own children, are living out their days in hopeless dependence; but we know that there are large numbers of them. Not only are we paying for the consequences of their denied needs, but we have lost all the potential gifts and strength they might have contributed. (Young 1954, p. 239.)

Young did more than any other writer to popularise the psychological approach to illegitimacy and translate its ideas into social-work practice. Not only did *Out of Wedlock* achieve far more public notice than Helene Deutsch's study, the book was widely reviewed in social science periodicals and was one of the most frequently cited authorities on illegitimacy in Britain and the United States in the 1950s and 1960s. *Out of Wedlock* was one of two references listed at the end of the entry on illegitimacy in the 1964 edition of the *Encyclopaedia Britannica*. Although Australian social welfare and sociology publications on unmarried motherhood were still rare, Young's theories appear to have found ready acceptance among Australian professionals (Swain and Howe 1995, p. 141).

Some reviewers were, however, critical of the book's thesis and apparent inconsistencies in the argument. According to a review in the journal *Marriage and Family Living*, Young failed to provide convincing empirical data to substantiate her claims. She used no statistics whatsoever and relied instead on such imprecise terms as 'most of' or 'a few of' (Baber 1955, p. 379). Psychoanalytic approaches temporarily threatened the dominant sociological structural paradigm through which illegitimacy had been conventionally interpreted in the United States, Australia and Britain. By the 1970s psychoanalytic accounts had retreated to the margins of the academic study of illegitimacy, and sociology returned to occupy the centre.

The dominant theme in today's psychological literature, influenced by more liberal sexual attitudes and feminism, is not so much the distinctive (and deviant) psychology of the unmarried mother, but the psychological implications of sole-parenthood status on women and children. Studies focus on stress, 'role strain', wellbeing, coping skills, adjustment, social isolation, family dysfunction and other 'psychosocial variables' that impact on single-parent families. Feminists working in the mental health field argue that any therapeutic strategies must address the single mother's 'larger social context' and the effects of poverty, oppression and victimisation (Worrell 1988; Doherty 1995).

Contemporary psychologists thus retain Deutsch's and Young's psycho-sociological explanations of illegitimacy-related problems while repudiating their construction of unmarried mothers as, by definition, neurotic. Today's social scientists generally consider it morally inappropriate, or simply outdated, to talk about the problem of single parenthood in terms of individual mental incapacity, maladjustment or abnormality. Feminists in particular view psychological explanations for illegitimacy as characteristic of a less enlightened era of scientific thought that has, thankfully, disappeared (Solinger 1992; Kiely 1982).

In the last few years, however, particularly in the United States, conservative social scientists have tentatively revisited the association between illegitimacy and mental incompetence. The idea that unmarried mothers have low IQs made a surprise comeback in 1994 with the publication of Richard Herrnstein and Charles Murray's *The Bell Curve. Intelligence and Class Structure in American Life* and has since been confirmed by Murray (Holden 1997). A statistical analysis of the relationship between various social problems and individual intelligence levels, *The Bell Curve* attracted a storm of criticism, almost all of it directed at its claim to provide scientific proof of inherent racial and class differences in cognitive ability. Less controversial has been Herrnstein and Murray's equally provocative finding that white illegitimacy rates are strongly related to intelligence, even when class and income are taken into account. Low cognitive ability, they argue, is a much stronger predisposing factor for illegitimacy than low socioeconomic background (Herrnstein and Murray 1994, pp. 177–90). The relationship works thus:

> The smarter a woman is, the more likely that she deliberately decides to have a child and calculates the best time to do it. The less intelligent the woman is, the more likely that she does not think ahead from sex to procreation, does not remember to use birth control, does not carefully consider when and under what circumstances she should have a child. How intelligent a woman is may interact with her impulsiveness, and hence her ability to exert self-discipline and restraint on her partner in order to avoid pregnancy. (1994, p. 179.)

The same theory explains why the less intelligent a white mother is, the more likely it is that she will end up on welfare: 'For women without foresight and intelligence, it may seem like a good deal' (1994, p. 189).

At the centre of this scenario is a coherent, self-conscious and rational actor, someone who can plan ahead, rationalise, consider consequences, defer action and make sensible decisions, just like the ideal 'man of reason' who stands behind much classical political and economic theory. In contrast to early twentieth-century eugenicists, Herrnstein and Murray ignore the possibility that illegitimacy might be associated with low cognitive ability in men. The responsibility lies with women to 'restrain' their male partners. As the authors are fully aware, their causal model incorporates a moral judgement. Calling once again on the standards of the reasonable man, Herrnstein and Murray claim that no 'disinterested person' would consider conceiving a child outside of marriage 'to be in the best interest of all concerned, including the child's' (1994, p. 180). Their account assumes that having a child within wedlock is, by definition, a more intelligent act than having one outside it and perpetuates the notion that only unintelligent women have illegitimate babies.

The authors observe that racial differences in cognitive ability do not explain the differences between black, white and Latino illegitimacy rates (1994, p. 331). Elsewhere in their study, however, they find that African–Americans and Hispanic–Americans generally have lower levels of cognitive ability. As illegitimacy is strongly correlated with low IQ, this would suggest that according to *The Bell Curve* rationale African–American women are doubly likely to thoughtlessly give birth to out-of-wedlock children. Herrnstein and Murray argue that if American society wants to persuade 'poor single teenagers' (that is, implicitly, predominantly African–American single mothers) not to have babies the knowledge that 95 per cent of them are also below average in intelligence 'should prompt skepticism about strategies that rely on abstract and far-sighted calculations of self-interest' (1994, p. 387). Because intelligence is inherent to the individual and virtually unchangeable, providing poor teenage mothers with welfare assistance, educational programs or contraceptive advice will do little to reduce the illegitimacy rate. Murray's particular brand of social science provides another statistically backed reason why the state should remove all support for the illegitimate.

The view that personal qualities are fixed and innate, not to mention the idea that IQ is a measurable and immutable 'thing in the head' (Gould 1995, p. 21) is more contentious in the 1990s than ever before. It was not long before a more palatable version of some of *The Bell Curve*'s arguments appeared in the bestseller lists of Britain, Australia and the United States. *Emotional Intelligence. Why It Can Matter More Than IQ* (published in 1995 in the United States and in 1996 in Britain and Australia) was written by Daniel Goleman PhD, a behavioural and brain science writer for the *New York Times*.

Emotional Intelligence has a distinctively 1990s slant on the relationship between illegitimacy and the faulty female mind. It provides a good example of the way in which the automatic judgement that teenage pregnancy and motherhood are 'bad' permeates contemporary thinking about social problems, especially in the United States. The ideas in *Emotional Intelligence* have met with approval (for example, Edgar 1996). Yet the book exemplifies the subtle tendency of much social science to view women's proneness to extra-marital sexual activity and reproduction as a problem that exists in their minds. It also illustrates what is old and what is new about current thinking about illegitimacy.

Goleman argues that the concept of emotional intelligence offers a new way of making sense of the destructiveness of contemporary society: escalating random violence, family breakdown, teen suicide, eating disorders, substance abuse, child abuse and neglect, domestic conflict and other 'social pathologies'. According to Goleman, the individual perpetrators of anti-social behaviour are acting out the uncontrollable primitive emotional impulses of fear, hate, anxiety, resentment, grief and depression. Emotionally illiterate individuals lack or, more charitably, have not had the opportunity to fully develop those skills which would enable them to manage involuntary responses to threatening situations. The core emotional skills, according to Goleman, are empathy, impulse control, self-motivation, the ability to notice and correctly identify one's own emotional state, and a sensitivity to social dynamics (or 'social deftness').

Goleman claims that the extent of a child's emotional intelligence is a more accurate predictor of subsequent success in adult life – whether in career, relationship or health terms – than his or her cognitive ability, measured as IQ. Goleman includes an account of what he calls the 'marshmallow challenge'. In the 1960s Stanford University psychologist Walter Mischel put one marshmallow each in front of a series of 4-year-old children. He told each child that he had to leave the room for a little while to run an errand. They could eat the one marshmallow straight away if they wanted to; if, however, they were able to wait the fifteen or twenty minutes he was absent, they could have *two* marshmallows when he returned. Some went for the single marshmallow immediately; others found various ingenious ways of distracting themselves so that they would get the two-marshmallow reward. The study tracked down the same children twelve to fourteen years later as they were graduating from high school. Those children who had resisted the marshmallow temptation were, as adolescents, more socially competent, self-reliant, calm, stable, persistent, confident, dependable and able to defer gratification in pursuit of longer-term goals. The marshmallow-grabbers, by contrast, shied away from social contacts, were stubborn and indecisive, easily frustrated and prone to irritability and arguments. Now, as then, they were unable to put off gratification. The first group scored much higher than the second on standard tests of academic competency. The ability to delay gratification, Goleman argues, contributes to intellectual potential independently of a pupil's IQ. The experiment proves that emotional intelligence 'determines how well or how poorly people are able to use their other mental capacities' (Goleman 1996, pp. 80–3).

What distinguishes this book from other popular psychology texts and adds to its authority is its empirical anchor in recent brain research. Goleman refers to a new 'flood of neurobiological data' that allow for the first time glimpses of the brain at work while we think and feel, imagine and dream (1996, p. xi). He locates the primary mechanism governing the ability to stem impulsive actions and emotional responses in the physiological structures of the brain. *Emotional Intelligence* grounds a person's capacity to manage their emotions intelligently, and therefore their character, in their biological make-up. Social problems, like rising rates of teenage pregnancy, have their origins not in culture but in the head.

The emotional intelligence movement can be interpreted as one of the strategies by which modern societies teach individuals how to regulate and govern themselves as useful citizens. Under the EQ regime (the abbreviation is a media invention implying that emotional intelligence is equivalent to IQ) the individual takes responsibility for monitoring and managing their self in what Nikolas Rose calls 'a kind of alliance between personal objectives and ambitions and institutionally or socially prized goals or activities' (Rose 1989a, p. 10). Emotionally well-managed individuals who learn the right skills through parental instruction, school or therapy will become both productive citizen-subjects and autonomous selves. If, as Rose suggests, the mental sciences are 'techniques for the disciplining of human difference', the EQ idea enables the classification, labelling, measurement and management of individuals who are held to be responsible for the decline of contemporary society. From this Foucauldian perspective, emotional intelligence is a direct twentieth-century descendant of older psychological discourses aimed at achieving social objectives such as authority, tranquillity, sanity, virtue and efficiency (Rose 1989b, p. 121).

Despite its heavy scientific mantle, *Emotional Intelligence* is ultimately concerned with restoring traditional virtues. Goleman's prose frequently slides from social analysis to moral imperative. 'These are times', says Goleman:

> when the fabric of society seems to unravel at ever-greater speed, when self-ishness, violence, and a meanness of spirit seem to be rotting the goodness of our communal lives. Here the argument for emotional intelligence hinges on the link between sentiment, character, and moral instincts ... Those who are at the mercy of impulse – who lack self-control – suffer a moral deficiency. (Goleman 1996, p. xii.)

Although Goleman's unselfconscious use of the language of social decay and moral decline is characteristically American, the book's message that 'something's wrong with society' appeals to a much wider western culture of unease, especially in relation to sexuality and the family.

Goleman includes rising rates of divorce and teenage pregnancy in his repertoire of America's social ills. Families that either break-up or fail to form in the first place, as with the acts of rape and murder, are the disastrous consequences of emotional incompetence. *Emotional Intelligence* thus implicitly provides support for the 'remoralisation of society' project currently being pursued by social conservatives. The moral virtues that some critics want reinstituted bear a close resemblance to emotional intelligence skills. In EQ-talk, honesty has become self-awareness; compassion has become empathy; self-discipline has become impulse-control; perseverance has become self-motivation; and cooperation has become social sensitivity. The new terms come home shaking their Victorian moral tails behind them.

In other respects, EQ represents a distinctively late-twentieth-century twist on moral science. The principles of emotional intelligence are secular rather than religious and are heavily influenced by psychological understandings of individual behaviour. The book reflects the belief that the individual's responsibility to society is not as clear as it once was. Disciplinary institutions like the school, the factory, the prison, the military and even the family no longer occupy a central place in society. Their role in promoting the government of the self has become obscured in an apparently disordered, unstable and unpredictable postmodern world. The metaphors that dominate contemporary debates about the economy, society and the body centre on fluidity and flexibility. In a post-AIDS society apparent threats to marriage and the heterosexual norm are couched in the rhetorics of epidemic and organic decay. While Rose's global historical narrative helps make sense of EQ's moral genealogy and its embeddedness in western culture, it tends to gloss over what is specific about this particular manifestation of self-regulation techniques.

EQ terminology coincides particularly well with the contours of current political debates about racial and social disadvantage, for example. *Emotional Intelligence* considerably modifies the social analysis in *The Bell Curve*. Herrnstein and Murray represent IQ as genetically fixed and relatively impervious to experience or education. Goleman believes that emotional intelligence can be learned. A 'window of opportunity' remains open between infancy and adolescence, in which the still-developing neocortex can be reprogrammed and emotional relearning is possible (Goleman 1996, p. 223). In place of *The Bell Curve's* pessimistic scenario of a large, unchanging and widening gulf between the largely white, cognitive elite and the mostly black, cognitively deprived underclass, *Emotional Intelligence* allows the possibility of changing social competencies and therefore racial inequalities through the structured learning of emotional management skills. Compared with *The Bell Curve, Emotional Intelligence* offers a more acceptable theory of social inequality and a more optimistic solution.

The book's neurological angle adds a reassuringly biological dimension to an otherwise confusingly abstract set of moral issues. Like recent research that claims to have identified a 'gay gene', the brain studies that Goleman cites imply that there is a biological basis to 'immoral' behaviours, such as leaving a spouse, having sex before marriage or choosing not to live with the father of your child. Although Goleman doesn't actually advocate prefrontal lobotomies – they are a bad idea, he says, because they prevent the patient from experiencing emotions (Goleman 1996, p. 25) – his social program does assume that it is every individual's social responsibility to learn not to be emotionally dumb. Unlike structural solutions to perceived social deterioration – social policy initiatives, employment and training schemes, income redistribution, urban planning – emotional relearning programs target the inner life of the individual and therefore appear both cheaper and more likely to succeed. Or, in the face of increasing despair, at least worth a try.

No one, even those on the Right, seriously proposes going back to the nineteenth century, but conservatives like Himmelfarb (1995) do argue that we can learn from the past, importing and adapting its forgotten achievements to solve current social problems. In the particular intellectual and political climate of the United States of the 1990s, a theory based on psychological and neurological research that 'proves' empirically that emotional control is morally good for society is extremely attractive. EQ promises to reprogram the emotionally anarchic and immoral self into a citizen able to keep in check their own sexual and anti-social impulses.

Partly because of the publicity surrounding books like *The Bell Curve* and *Emotional Intelligence*, illegitimacy continues to be negatively linked to female emotional maladjustment and, to a lesser extent, to intellectual deficiency in women. British sociologist Patricia Morgan refers, for example, to aptitude and achievement scores and measures of educational attainment that indicate 'the low intelligence of many welfare mothers' in both the United States and in Britain (Morgan 1995, pp. 70–1). The assumption that young single mothers do not rate highly on IQ and EQ scales informs the persistent conservative concern with 'parental incompetence'. Douglas Besharov and Karen Gardiner have argued that teenagers are simply not ready for sexual relationships because they lack 'the requisite emotional and cognitive maturity' (Besharov and Gardiner 1993, p. 59).

Cautious versions of the mental explanation of illegitimacy also continue to resurface in British and American welfare debates. Single mothers are described in Britain as 'reckless' and 'feckless' (Roberts 1996). American social critics write euphemistically of the 'personal deficiencies', 'parental incompetence', 'defective character', 'low ability' and 'lack of cognitive maturity' of young women who have children out of wedlock (most of whom, incidentally, they assume are black) (Forum on 'illegitimacy and welfare reform', *Society* July/August 1996).

The idea that single mothers have 'low cognitive ability' has its roots in earlier preoccupations with mental defectiveness, intelligence testing and psychological measurement. *The Bell Curve* suggests that illegitimacy is still, in many ways, seen as a problem of female feeblemindedness. Goleman's characterisation of teenage pregnancy as a manifestation of low emotional intelligence has different antecedents in the post-World War II concern with emotional disturbance, delinquency and the distorted workings of the female unconscious. The use of brain science to justify a remoralisation progam may be fairly novel but the idea that illegitimacy and early parenthood are indicative of individual psychological maladjustment is not.

Social scientists claim they no longer embrace the ideas that led Kammerer to describe unmarried mothers as morons and Young to assess them as neurotic. Although the language is different and all such claims are highly contested, social inquiry still offers the means of providing empirical proof that single mothers are less intelligent and less emotionally mature than their married sisters. Its conservative practitioners represent the single mother as someone who 'by nature', or by virtue of her genetic or hormonal make-up, is unable to use her mind to control her body: a slave of sexual impulse. She is excluded from the compass of reasoning humanity.

CHAPTER 8

Fatherless Societies Go Primitive

In her book *Gone Primitive. Savage Intellects, Modern Lives* (1990), literary analyst Marianna Torgovnick explores the theme of primitivism in the work of major modern writers such as psychoanalyst Sigmund Freud, novelist Joseph Conrad, and anthropologists Bronislaw Malinowski and Margaret Mead. Torgovnick argues that the idea of the primitive constitutes a persistent strand in twentieth-century thought. Primitive societies function within contemporary western culture as a 'them' against which 'we' define 'our' modernity. We project on to primitive cultures our fears and our (mostly repressed) desires. Whether in the guise of nightmare or pleasant dream, the primitive defines the West's sense of self. It meets our need for coherent narratives of beginnings and endings and our wish to see human social organisation as infinitely varied but ultimately resilient. Torgovnick suggests we view the western impulse to record the traditions of primitive peoples as a way of 'handling, through displacement, the series of dislocations that we call modernity and postmodernity' (Torgovnick 1990, p. 245).

Torgovnick's thesis offers a useful vantage point from which to view the current attack on fatherless families. The unmarried father – or 'deadbeat dad' in American political rhetoric – is usually criticised for abandoning his female sexual partner and failing to provide adequate financial and emotional support for his ex-nuptial child. He is often represented as selfish, delinquent, irresponsible and wild. Unmarried fathers have become the standard-bearers of a new disorderly masculinity. Men's growing refusal to commit themselves to fatherhood and family life is, it appears, creating a new generation of poverty-stricken, unhappy and emotionally disturbed children, and therefore a host of social ills. According to conservative accounts of single parenthood, a society in which fatherlessness is endemic cannot cohere.

American conservatives assume that this new breed of unattached young men is comprised primarily of the uneducated, poor, black youths of the 'underclass'. Unconstrained by paternal responsibilities they habitually engage in anti-social behaviours ranging from illicit gang activity to sexual promiscuity. Dysfunctional families are producing violent youths who themselves produce violent communities (Fagan 1996, p. 38). American anthropologist David W. Murray describes neighbourhoods without fathers as 'seedbeds for predators' (1994, p. 10). Charles Murray fears that these savage male behaviours are contagious, arguing that the values of unsocialised male adolescents – physical violence, immediate gratification and predatory sex – are rapidly becoming the cultural norms of the black inner city (1994b, p. 61).

More concerned with class issues than with racial tensions, British critics of the fatherless society continue a long tradition of establishment disapproval of young working-class men. During the riots of the early 1990s, according to feminist critic Beatrix Campbell, the New Right 'ventured into the estates and saw the streets captured by thin, pale boys' (1993, p. 303). Conservative observers suggest that louts, yobbos and hooligans are those most likely to repudiate marriage and fatherhood. If men are not taught to cherish and protect women and if they do not know how to become dependable husbands and fathers, says the *Daily Telegraph*, their masculinity will inevitably find an outlet in crime. The virtue of manliness 'is what keeps our adolescents from savagery' (Hannan, D. 1997).

British social scientists are concerned with the social implications of the decline in paternal values and behaviours. Patricia Morgan suggests that low marriage rates are producing a warrior class of unattached and unpaternal men (1995, p. 143), while Labour MP and welfare reform campaigner Frank Field argues that disinherited males, forced through unemployment to become drifters, drug pushers or permanent adolescents, are at the core of a 'new barbarism' (1995, p. 6). The obnoxious English man who has emerged into public life in the last generation has been released from the expectation he will take life-long responsibility for a wife and children and has instead turned to a life ruled by egoism and nihilism (Dennis and Erdos 1993, pp. 4–5). This is the nightmare version of primitivism. Western society projects its fear of family disintegration and social chaos on to black and working-class young men. These unwed and unweddable fathers are imagined as a primitive subculture existing within, yet opposed to and ultimately threatening to undermine 'normal', white, middle-class domesticated society.

If this imagined community of male warriors represents the nightmare, what is the dream? Torgovnick suggests that in times of perceived social and moral crisis primitivism can also function as an exotic site of displacement. Pro-fatherhood rhetoric betrays just such an attachment to the primitive in its emphasis on the apparent timelessness of the nuclear two-parent family form. In this chapter I want to take a critical look at how social–scientific evidence, most notably evolutionary science and anthropology, 'proves' that the two-parent family is natural and that the continual presence of husbands and fathers in families is essential to social wellbeing. I focus in particular on the political uses to which anthropological knowledge about the family is put, and on the process by which a specific observation of a 'primitive' culture gets transformed into a universal truth about human culture.

The objective of the National Fatherhood Initiative, founded in the United States in 1994, is to 'reinstate fatherhood as a national priority' (Adler 1996, p. 61). The National Fatherhood Initiative belongs to a loose grouping of similar organisations that comprise an increasingly influential pro-fatherhood movement that is strongest and most militant in the United States but which (typically in the form of fathers' rights groups) has, since the late 1980s, acquired a political profile in Britain, Europe and Australia (Adler 1996; Chira 1994; Smart and Sevenhuijsen 1989; Healey 1995). The National Fatherhood Initiative's director is Wade F. Horn, formerly US Commissioner for Children, Youth and Families in the Bush administration. Horn claims that because fatherlessness has such disastrous effects on child wellbeing, 'fatherlessness is our most urgent social problem' (Horn 1995). The pro-fatherhood movement attempts to reinstate 'the father' as central in a culture that its members believe devalues and marginalises fatherhood. The mother–child bond has, they argue, been given undue emphasis, particularly within feminist discourse, and fathers are too often seen as superfluous to the task of rearing children and creating families. David Blankenhorn (1995) suggests that our cultural script of fatherhood has become impoverished and is now restricted to a series of negative stereotypes: 'the old father', 'the new father', 'the deadbeat dad', 'the visiting father', 'the sperm father', 'the stepfather and the nearby guy' and – trumping them all – 'the unnecessary father'.

The empirical backing for this political fight against fatherless families is provided by social inquiry. Journalistic accounts (Magnet 1992, 1993; Whitehead 1993; Bagnall 1994; Zinsmeister 1993) and scholarly studies (Blankenhorn 1995; Popenoe 1996b; McLanahan and Sandefur 1994) in all three countries cite social science research showing a correlation between father-absence and a disturbingly wide range of symptoms including psychiatric illness, behavioural problems, learning disabilities, school failure, drug and alcohol abuse, criminal activity, teenage childbearing, unemployment, street gang membership, poverty, welfare dependency, residence in public housing, early sexual activity, divorce and various character defects. As Barbara Dafoe Whitehead's widely-cited 40-page article 'Dan Quayle was right' (1993) claims: '*The social–science evidence is in*: though it may benefit the adults involved, the dissolution of intact two-parent families is harmful to large numbers of children'. Like Whitehead's essay, Diana Bagnall's 1994 article on absent fathers in the Australian *Bulletin* defers to social–scientific authority: 'The wheel has turned full circle, with *studies now showing* that children from one-parent families do suffer disadvantages compared with their two-parent brethren' (p. 29, my emphasis). Susan Bastick of the Australian Family Association points to studies showing that children raised by married parents fared better on any indicator than children brought up by de facto couples (Luff and Barnsley 1997, p. 2).

For anti-illegitimacy social scientists and fathers' rights advocates in the United States, some of this research proves that the parenting provided by fathers is different and complementary to that provided by mothers, and is therefore irreplaceable. In an article published in the Australian *IPA Review* Karl Zinsmeister, adjunct scholar at the American Enterprise Institute, draws on research conducted by psychologists and paediatricians to state that 'We know, *as a clinical finding*, that exclusive rearing by women restricts a child's environmental exploration and delays development of some kinds of external competence' (1993, p. 43, my emphasis). Across a wide range of cultures, Zinsmeister tells us, fathers play and stimulate while mothers soothe and caretake. It is fathers who cultivate children's self-respect, develop their internal control, teach them how to explore the external world and establish their sexual (that is, heterosexual) identity (1993, p. 44). Above all, fathers are more effective than mothers at the disciplinary tasks of parenthood. According to the National Fatherhood Initiative, by engaging their boys in 'rough-and-tumble play' fathers encourage their sons to develop internal control over aggression. By contrast, a father provides his daughter with the experience of having a relationship with a man 'who shows that the definition of love is "I care more about you than myself" ', thereby maximising her chances in later life of securing a responsible and committed male partner (Horn 1995).

Moderate versions of the argument that both a mother and a father are necessary to a child's full development appear in family research studies internationally. Don Edgar, ex-director of the Australian Institute of Family Studies, claims that 'Every child, boy or girl, needs parents of both sexes to learn about the human race and society' (Bagnall 1994, p. 30). There is almost universal acceptance in both professional circles and in the wider community of the principle that *ideally* every child should be brought up in a two-parent household.

The point being made by conservative critics is not just that children benefit from the presence of a father, but that they need a father in order to become a fully functioning, mature, happy and well-adjusted adult. It is assumed that a crucial aspect of that adjustment to adulthood is the formation of unambiguous gender (male or female) and sexual (heterosexual) identities. The presence of fathers is seen as necessary to reproduce the sexually differentiated social behaviours – in boys, controlled aggressive impulses and the drive to achieve in the public sphere; in girls, the desire to marry, have children and be a nurturer – upon which social cohesion depends.

Zinsmeister's reference to cross-cultural similarities in the physical postures typically adopted by fathers when approaching their infants (1993, p. 44) presents fathering behaviour as innate. The historical and anthropological record, even fossil evidence, shows that the mother–father–child household dates back to the beginnings of human existence. The two-parent family is humankind's 'universal child-rearing institution' (Zinsmeister 1993, p. 44). Here Zinsmeister is specifically countering feminist criticisms of the nuclear family form which suggest that it is a relatively recent historical phenomenon. Australian academic Alan Tapper cites the findings of biological anthropologist C. Owen Lovejoy that suggest that the nuclear family form dates back to the origins of man. 'An institution as old and as basic as this', Tapper claims, 'probably has something to be said in its favour' (Tapper 1990, p. 78).

Evidence of family function in past societies suggests that the differences between maternal and paternal behaviour have a solid foundation in Nature. In a chapter headed 'The essential father', sociologist David Popenoe refers to the findings of anthropology and evolutionary science to claim that the human male is 'endowed genetically with the capacity to be a social father in some form' (1996b, p. 165). Beginning with the branching-off of the human line from chimpanzees in Africa seven and a half million years ago, Popenoe traces the evolutionary adaptations that over several million years created a sexual division of labour in which males were hunters and protectors and females were gatherers and nurturers. Both took responsibility for feeding their young. Over time, these sexually differentiated practices left indelible biological marks, with the result that fathers developed a biological predisposition to pair-bond monogamously and to assist with child-rearing (1996b, p. 170).

Evolutionary science suggests that the fathering capacity built into the nature of men has been a source of evolutionary advantage, contributing to the survival of the species. As the human female began to walk upright, for example, she was forced to carry her infants in her arms instead of on her back, and therefore depended on a male who would protect her and collect food for her (Popenoe 1996b, p. 171). By the time that *Homo sapiens* appeared on earth some 120 000 years ago the fathering role had grown to encompass cultural transmission. Fathers taught their sons how to hunt for big game, for example. As hunting technologies improved and less time was taken up by hunting, fathers got involved in the direct care of their children (1996b, p. 178).

Granting that most of our knowledge of evolutionary history is 'highly conjectural', Popenoe turns to the more convincing anthropological evidence from 'living fossils' like the !Kung San. This research suggests that the !Kung San, or Bushmen, an isolated, seminomadic hunter–gatherer group living on the edge of the Kalahari desert, closely resemble the human societies of our evolutionary past. Anthropologists have found that !Kung San fathers are closely involved with their children and spend much of their non-hunting time with them. Young children frequently go to their fathers, 'touch them, talk to them, and request food from them, and such approaches are almost never rebuffed' (Katz and Konner 1981 cited in Popenoe 1996b, p. 179). Popenoe comments that these are exactly the kind of paternal behaviours 'highly recommended today by most paediatricians!'.

Popenoe's image of the gentle and involved !Kung San father functions as a 'natural' stabiliser in the context of a postmodern story of flux and flight. The primitive's lack of modern artifice provides a comfortingly ancient and solid anchor point in the midst of what Popenoe characterises as the most destructive social confusion. In his own society, Popenoe argues, the roles toward which men are 'biologically most inclined' – protector, provider, teacher and authority figure – are the very roles from which they have been removed (by, we assume, the feminist movement). Modern (feminist-influenced) societies ask instead that men assume a role that, historically, they have never had – the direct care of children – and that they do so with an increasingly lowered sense of paternity confidence (a consequence of the sexual revolution and women's independence) and often with children they positively know are not theirs (Popenoe 1996b, pp. 183–4). At the very time when fathers are so badly needed, 'the cultural ties necessary to hold them to fathering have withered' (1996b, p. 188).

Anthropological and evolutionary research on fatherhood in 'primitive' societies constitutes what Popenoe calls in the sub-title of his book 'compelling new evidence that fatherhood and marriage are indispensable for the good of children and society'. Not all his anthropological evidence is new, however. Popenoe bases his critique of contemporary society on a theory first articulated seventy years ago by Bronislaw Malinowski, 'the celebrated anthropologist'. Popenoe quotes

Malinowski's 'principle of legitimacy' which stated that it is a 'universal sociological law' that 'no child should be brought into the world without a man – and one man at that – assuming the role of sociological father, that is, guardian and protector ...' Popenoe claims that the principle has since been supported empirically and proves that 'Virtually every known society has distinguished between legitimate and illegitimate births and favored the former' (Popenoe 1996b, pp. 35–6). Contemporary societies thus flout one of the oldest and most fundamental laws of human social cooperation.

Despite its age, Malinowski's principle of legitimacy makes regular appearances in anti-illegitimacy discourses in Britain and especially the United States (for example, Zinsmeister 1993, p. 43). Malinowski's influence can be subtle. 'Poor suffering bastards', by anthropologist David W. Murray (a Bradley Scholar at the Heritage Foundation, previously of Brandeis University), draws on evidence from various non-western cultures to claim that, universally, marriage makes kinsmen out of strangers and creates the 'moral sentiments of commitment and formal responsibility' that constitute a society's essential cultural infrastructure. Individual marriages, says Murray, are the 'rivets of the social order' (Murray, D. 1994, p. 14). The importance that Murray places on the structural linkages between marriage, legitimacy and the social structure hints at Malinowski's subterranean presence. His influence is clear in the statement that most cultures 'try to ensure that every child have a pater, a father who assumes full responsibility for the child, even if he is not the biological genitor who actually sired the child' (1994, p. 10). Murray's cross-cultural analysis has proved a rich source of supporting evidence for those who argue that the current trend towards fatherlessness is unnatural and socially disastrous (for example, Morgan 1995; Raspberry 1994).

Patricia Morgan gives Malinowski's ideas pride of place. Her lengthy monograph on family breakdown is prefaced by two quotations placed side-by-side. The first is an extract from Malinowski's ([1927] 1953) *Sex and Repression in Savage Society* in which he states that in all cultures 'the human family must consist of a male as well as a female'; and the other a claim made in 1994 by Claire Rayner, popular broadcaster, that 'The only real family is the mother and her baby. Everyone else is peripheral'. The content and argument that follows reveal, not unexpectedly, that it is Malinowski ('the outstanding founder of modern anthropology') whom Morgan believes to be sociologically correct (Morgan 1995, pp. 113–14).

The legitimacy principle appears in these texts as a pithy and authoritative statement of fact. Snipped out of its original context and inserted into contemporary political debates about single parenthood, the theory works as if it were a rather speckled but still serviceable mirror of social reality. Anthropological knowledge focuses and reflects back to the contemporary reader an ideal representation of a pure society uncontaminated by modern culture. Conservative discourse represents Malinowski as an unusually wise, perceptive and intelligent man who was able to divine the workings of the social structure as it was in his own time, and as it really is still. The anthropologist is deified as a genius and a prophet, his thoughts enshrined as universal truths.

Although I intend to argue that Malinowski's legitimacy principle may not be the fundamental truth so revered by pro-family advocates, there is no denying that, compared with its predecessors, it did represent a new way of thinking about illegitimacy. Until Malinowski invented the idea of the social father, unmarried fatherhood was seen partly as a moral problem but mainly one that had serious economic consequences. Since Malthus, social scientists have consistently condemned fathers who fail to provide financially for their illegitimate children by making regular maintenance payments to the mother. A child without a father is likely to be a poor child and therefore a drain on state resources. The father's initial and primary relationship to the illegitimate child is perceived to be biological, and his primary contribution to the child's welfare, and thereby to social wellbeing, is economic.

Socialist theory was in part responsible for this economic theory of paternity. Engels' *The Origin of the Family, Private Property and the State* ([1884] 1942) suggested that historically the concept of illegitimacy evolved simultaneously with the move towards the acquisition and transmission of private wealth from one generation to the next. In the patriarchal family form private property passed from father to son. Fathers were determined to confer their personal wealth only on offspring who were their legitimate heirs and hence insisted on monogamous marriage and the sexual fidelity of wives ([1884] 1942, p. 42). Engels predicted that the coming social revolution would transfer the means of production to common ownership and dismantle the patriarchal family unit. Public opinion would be more tolerant of lapses in maidenly honour, and society would take responsibility for the care and education of all children whether they were legitimate or not ([1884] 1942, p. 51). The problem of the destitute fatherless child, Engels suggested, would disappear along with the abolition of private property. Materialist explanations for the persistence of the legitimacy/illegitimacy distinction continue to be popular on the Left and among feminists.

Malinowski's principle of legitimacy, with its stress on the mother–father–child relationship, departs significantly from this tradition. Malinowski proposed that every child needed a father for social reasons; that is, his presence was necessary if the child was to be properly inducted into society. Fathers were necessary for communities to maintain a strong and secure internal structure. The absence of fathers, in Malinowski's theory, was likely to produce not poverty but cultural dissolution. Its appeal to those who argue that illegitimacy threatens social order becomes obvious. If we look at the specific contexts – historical, intellectual, political and personal – out of which the principle emerged, however, the universality of the 'principle of legitimacy', and the argument that in all cultures fathers are sociologically essential, appears more doubtful.

Malinowski was born in Poland in 1884 and in 1908 received a doctorate in philosophy from the Jagiellonian University in Krakow (for biographical details see Firth 1957; Young 1991; Wayne 1984; Wayne 1995). His interest in primitive beliefs about reproduction was evident in his first major anthropological publication, a literature survey, *The Family Among the Australian Aborigines. A Sociological Study* ([1913] 1969). Malinowski was intrigued that some Australian tribes had been found to be 'wholly ignorant of the physiological process of procreation'. A strong individual kinship tie nevertheless existed between father and child, leading Malinowski, in the absence of direct ethnographic data, to risk a 'working hypothesis' that the father–child relationship was sociologically significant in some, as yet unspecifiable, way (Malinowski [1913] 1969, pp. 232–3).

Malinowski continued to ponder over the sociological function of fatherhood during his field-trips to the Trobriand Islands, in the Australian colony of Papua, between 1915 and 1918. A decade elapsed before Malinowski published the results of his research on sexuality, kinship and parenting practices in Trobriand society, but it was this fieldwork that formed the empirical basis of the theories for which he later became famous, including the principle of legitimacy. Malinowski's thoughts on the role of the father appeared in several articles and books that were published and reprinted throughout the 1920s.

Although we can never be sure in what ways or to what extent Malinowski's personal life might have affected his anthropological thinking, the parallels and divergences between his private and public selves are revealing. While in Australia Malinowski met Elsie Masson, and the two married in 1919. Over the next six years Elsie Malinowski gave birth to three daughters. Elsie and Bronislaw led a nomadic life, moving house all over Europe and were often apart because of Bronislaw's work commitments, until in 1923 they established a family home in the South Tirol (which had been ceded to Italy in 1919). Shortly afterwards Bronislaw took up a teaching position at the London

School of Economics. He lived in London during term time, returning to northern Italy to spend vacations with his family. In 1926 he spent several months in the United States. Elsie felt these prolonged separations keenly, especially after 1925 as her health deteriorated (she died of multiple sclerosis in 1935), and his daughters learned to accept that their father would not be a constant physical presence in their lives.

From the recently published letters that passed between Elsie and her husband in the 1920s Malinowski appears to have taken his role as father and head of the family seriously, and was as affectionate and involved as his long absences, scholarly preoccupations and temperament allowed. He wrote fondly of 'the babies', and sent Elsie 'a big hug for each leprechaun' (Wayne 1995, p. 38). Although they both had to struggle to overcome their disappointment that Elsie never gave birth to a son, Bronislaw undertook his paternal duties conscientiously and impartially. Helena, his third child, later credited him for giving his daughters 'the gift of never feeling that women are inferior to men' (Wayne 1984, p. 193). But fatherhood did not come naturally to the anthropologist. His daughter Helena recalled in 1984 that though he wrote so much about the family unit, he was never quite comfortable with fatherhood and wasn't really a family man (Wayne 1984, pp. 198–9). Malinowski candidly admitted that he found the paternal role difficult at times and was aware of his shortcomings: 'At times I catch myself in moments of paternal gaucherie which remind me of my father's rather unfortunate treatment of myself and then I try to unstiffen and above all to drop that surface touchiness' (Wayne 1995, p. 129). He seems to have thought it important to be a good, modern father, but because of physical separation and perhaps some emotional distance was not always able to live up to his ideals.

It was in this period of troubled fatherhood that Malinowski formulated his ideas about legitimacy and fatherhood. Progress towards their transformation into a coherent universal principle was slow and hesitant. In *The Sexual Life of Savages* ([1929] 1968) (some chapters had appeared earlier as journal articles), Malinowski noted that although unmarried Trobriand Island girls were granted considerable sexual freedom illegitimacy was frowned on, and illegitimate children were rare. In the Trobriands, as among Australian Aboriginal tribes, the 'natives' appeared ignorant of the physiological facts of paternity. According to tribal law, however, every child had to have a father who would protect and provide for the mother in pregnancy and childbirth and 'receive the child into his arms', that is, help the mother in nursing and bringing it up (Malinowski [1929] 1968, p. 165–6). This contradiction led Malinowski to conclude that in Trobriand society the meaning of fatherhood was primarily sociological, established and defined independently of any biological meaning. A social dogma declared that 'Every family must have a father; a woman must marry before she may have children; there must be a male to every household' ([1929] 1968, pp. 171–2). Although Malinowski stressed the anthropological significance of what he saw as the basic family structure, he made no specific reference to the 'principle of legitimacy' in *The Sexual Life of Savages*; that is, he did not generalise beyond the Trobriand Islands or refer to it as a law.

In *Sex and Repression* ([1927] 1953), a reply to Freudian psychoanalytic theory, Malinowski elevated his culturally specific observations of fatherhood in Aboriginal and Trobriand societies into a 'principle' or 'rule':

> In all human societies – however they might differ in the patterns of sexual morality, in the knowledge of embryology, and in their types of courtship – there is universally found what might be called the rule of legitimacy. By this I mean that in all human societies a girl is bidden to be married before she becomes pregnant. ([1927] 1953, p. 212.)

It is unclear on what empirical or epistemological grounds Malinowski decided some time between the essays collected in *The Sexual Life of Savages* and *Sex and Repression* to turn a particular observation of specific cultures into a universal principle applicable to all humanity. The only justification he offers is that he knows of no single instance in the anthropological literature of a community in which illegitimate children had the same social status as legitimate ones ([1927] 1953, p. 213).

Once he had formulated his hypothesis Malinowski found evidence from 'savage tribes' in Africa, Australia, Melanesia and Polynesia to strengthen it. He inserted this empirical support into his description of the 'principle of legitimacy' included in the article on 'kinship' for the fourteenth edition of the *Encyclopaedia Britannica* (1929). As the statement of the 'principle' was positioned in the structure of the argument, its meaning remains somewhat ambiguous. It could designate the rule that illegitimate children universally have a lower status than legitimate offspring; or the rule that physiological paternity is irrelevant in determining social fatherhood; or both. Nowhere in the *Encyclopaedia Britannica* entry does Malinowski suggest that the rule is that every child must have a father.

Malinowski's definitive statement of his legitimacy principle appeared in an article on 'Parenthood – the basis of social structure' (1930). It was reproduced and probably received its widest circulation as part of a collection of Malinowski's essays, *Sex, Culture and Myth* (1962). I want to look closely at this fifty-five-page essay, one which

Malinowski claimed represented the culmination of over twenty years' work on parenthood and kinship, because it is here that the universal law receives its most complete exposition. The 1930 essay responds directly to the perceived social problems and debates of Malinowski's own time and culture, and provides some insight into how universal rules might be forged out of historically specific discursive contexts.

The parenthood essay was included in an edited collection of articles on the question of generational change and the problems facing modern parents and their children. The collection as a whole assumed that relations between the family and the state and between parents and children were changing rapidly in the rush towards modernity. *The New Generation. The Intimate Problems of Modern Parents and Children* (Calverton and Schmalhausen 1930) was in part designed to address specific issues such as divorce, unmarried motherhood and the state's responsibility for illegitimate children. One of the book's editors, V. F. Calverton, was a child welfare expert who contributed an essay on 'the illegitimate child' to his own volume.

Malinowski clearly shared this perception that the meaning of parenthood was undergoing radical generational change. He opened his essay with a quote from his 5-year-old daughter Helena, who pronounced in the course of an argument: 'Daddy, what an ass you are!'. Malinowski commented that he could never have said such a disrespectful thing to his own father forty years ago. Malinowski is reported to have referred disparagingly to his own father (also an ethnographer) as a stern patriarch who made little effort to understand his son. By contrast, Malinowski had a deep attachment to his mother which, as a follower of many of Freud's ideas, he readily admitted represented a classic oedipal situation (Wayne 1984, pp. 190–3). The ghost of Malinowski's Victorian father returned in the essay on parenthood to show how much relations between parents and children had changed.

Malinowski claimed he was not too disturbed by his daughter's outburst because as an anthropologist he had encountered the same youthful irreverence in his 'present-day Stone Age savages of the South Seas'. The anthropologist had knowledge of other cultures, and hence:

> remains unmoved even when faced with the most shocking, dangerous and ominous signs of youthful moral decay, with revolts of children against parents, with such symptoms as 'petting parties' and increasing divorce. He teaches us that such things have been before and that they have passed without having killed or poisoned the soul of mankind. And in this lies the comfort of anthropology to the wise conservative. The die-hard who despairs or loses his head and temper in planning all sorts of repressive and reactionary measures of retrogression is beyond consolation, or the reach of any serious argument. (Malinowski 1930 pp. 114.)

From the outset Malinowski signalled his awareness that social theory was not divorced from political questions. His scientific analysis of parenthood was a direct response to 'the most actual and burning question of to-day' – the revolt of modern youth against the social conventions of their parents' generation. By 'the revolt of modern youth' Malinowski and his editors meant primarily the rejection by the 'younger generation' of what they considered to be repressive, moralistic nineteenth-century values in favour of greater freedom in matters to do with sex, marriage, divorce and childbearing. Malinowski's anthropological writings suggest that he held a relatively progressive position on sexual matters and was sympathetic to efforts to talk more openly and less sanctimoniously about sex. His personal experience of the old patriarchal model of fatherhood, not a very happy one, encouraged him to look favourably on the new inter-generational intimacy.

The essay bore the stamp of the political climate of the late 1920s. In his opening Malinowski criticised the repressive measures being taken by various European states to stamp out juvenile delinquency and smother dissent (Malinowski 1930, p. 114). These actions disturbed Malinowski, a political liberal with firm anti-totalitarian sentiments. Bronislaw and Elsie were strongly opposed to the Italian fascist government which in 1926 had prohibited the German language from being used in the kindergarten in the South Tirol attended by their second daughter Wanda (Wayne 1995, p. 86).

The appropriate response to the generational and political crises of the 1920s, according to Malinowski, was to adopt a 'sober, scientific outlook' on the relationship between parents and children, and to establish the fundamental bases of marriage, parenthood and the family (1930, p. 115). In order to determine these fundamentals Malinowski proposed reconciling two sides of a debate about the nature of kinship in past societies that had long preoccupied the anthropological establishment. Engels' *The Origin of the Family*, a tribute to the work of Lewis H. Morgan, an anthropologist who had traced the evolution of different family types in primitive society, was part of this conversation. As Malinowski summarised the argument, there were two opposing schools of anthropological thought on the basic forms of social organisation prevailing in ancient times. One school, closely associated with the nineteenth-century 'armchair' studies of Johann Jakob Bachofen and Lewis Henry Morgan, argued that originally people lived in promiscuous tribes within communitarian forms of marriage and a matriarchal clan system. The other, represented by Malinowski's old mentor Edvard Alexander Westermarck, believed that monogamous marriages and patriarchal kinship systems prevailed, with the family as the basic cell of society.

Malinowski attempted to bridge these two camps, one built around the family, the other around the clan, by suggesting that they were not mutually exclusive. A functionalist approach would suggest that both family and clan systems were parts of an organic whole (1930, p. 130). Malinowski is widely recognised within the discipline as the first major proponent of the functional method in social anthropology. The primary intention of the 1930 essay was to explain and promote the new 'functional' school of anthropology, a label which, Malinowski pointed out in a footnote, he himself had coined (1930, p. 116). To the functionalist, all aspects of a culture were related to one big integral institution – 'the Procreative Institution of Mankind'. The function of this internally self-regulating institution was to propagate the human species and ensure the continuity of human culture (1930, pp. 131, 162). The functionalist anthropologist's task was to set out the laws that defined how the various component parts of the one big system related to each other (1930, p. 162).

The parent–child relationship was at the core of the big procreative institution because it provided the pattern on which broader community ties were based. Malinowski turned to psychoanalysis and behaviourist psychology as relatively new disciplines that placed particular significance on the period of early childhood. Behaviourism suggested that 'all human values, attitudes and personal bonds' could be traced to the earliest period of human development (1930, p. 133). Building on Freud's theory that infantile experiences form the foundation for the later relationship between child and mother, Malinowski argued that in infancy the biological ties between mother and child were 'reinforced, redetermined and remolded' by those of culture (1930, p. 137).

It was only at this point in his argument, about half-way through the article, that Malinowski raised the question of 'The principle of legitimacy and the right to sexual freedom' (1930, pp. 137–9). A father's sole biological function was to impregnate. And yet:

> in all human societies the father is regarded by tradition as indispensable. The woman has to be married before she is allowed legitimately to conceive. Roughly speaking, an unmarried mother is under a ban, a fatherless child is a bastard. This is by no means only a European or Christian prejudice; it is the attitude found amongst most barbarous and savage peoples as well. (1930, p. 137.)

Malinowski rephrased this observation as a general statement of scientific principle:

> The most important moral and legal rule concerning the physiological side of kinship is that no child should be brought into the world without a man – and one man at that – assuming the role of sociological father, that is,

guardian and protector, the male link between the child and the rest of the community. I think that this generalization amounts to a universal sociological law and as such I have called it in some of my previous writings *The Principle of Legitimacy*. (1930, pp. 137–8, emphasis in original.)

The meaning of the 'principle of legitimacy' here is subtly different when compared with its previous manifestations (cited by Malinowski as the entry on 'kinship' in the *Encyclopaedia Britannica* (1929), *Sex and Repression* (1927) and *The Family Among the Australian Aborigines* (1913), in which 'the relevant facts are presented though the term is not used', 1930, p. 138 footnote 7). The parenthood essay redefined the rule more firmly to mean 'every child must have a father', a rule that could be read as a prescription as well as an anthropological observation. Malinowski admitted that the form which the principle of legitimacy takes in any given society may vary, a qualification that contemporary followers tend to ignore. Nevertheless, the general rule persisted that the father was indispensable for the attainment of full legal and sociological status of the child and its family, and that any group consisting of a woman and her offspring was sociologically incomplete and illegitimate (1930, p. 138).

If private correspondence is any guide Malinowski does not seem to have been personally troubled by illegitimacy, at least among his own servants (Wayne 1995, p. 19). There is a suggestion that Elsie had more conventional views, at least where her daughters' education was concerned. She was determined that Jozefa should not be sent to a progressive school run by Bertrand and Dora Russell that she dubbed 'the school for illegitimate parenthood': 'Whatever Dora says about the right to be pregnant, I demand the right to send my child where perfectly sterile spinsters do the teaching' (Wayne 1995, p. 126). Elsie's wry aside notwithstanding, the Malinowskis held more liberal views on sexual matters than many of their peers. In the context of a bourgeois society which still outlawed unmarried motherhood, Bronislaw's attempt to translate what he saw as universal moral disapproval into morally-neutral structural terminology represented a relatively progressive move.

With the sexually-free Trobrianders in mind, Malinowski concluded that the function of marriage was not to legitimate sexual intercourse but to license parenthood (1930, p. 140). Parenthood served a central purpose as 'the only stable force working right throughout life, as the pattern of most relationships' (1930, p. 146). The function of the parent–child relationship was cultural education. It was within the family that tradition, religion, ethical beliefs and social rules were passed on from one generation to another (1930, p. 146). As Elsie put it, she and her husband turned their three children into 'real human beings with the beginnings of knowledge and experience and fitting into the general pattern' (Wayne 1995, p. 112).

It is in Malinowski's discussion of the different functions of mothers and fathers that we begin to detect the limits of his universal theory of legitimacy. In Malinowski's account, each had equally important roles to play in the process of cultural education. Mothers were invariably the main agents in the training of the young, with the father acting as help-mate. Although Malinowski was certain that a sociological father was universally regarded as essential 'to equip the child with a full tribal position' (1930, p. 139) he was vague on how, precisely, fathers did this. Parental training was intimately bound up with a tenderness and affection that was instinctive in mothers, but 'somewhat mysteriously' associated with fathers. Malinowski speculated in a footnote that the 'innate tenderness of the father' possibly derived from his role as a guardian of the woman during her pregnancy (1930, p. 147), but otherwise appears unsure about its functional origins.

'The child' who received this cultural education and the mature 'native' or the 'individual' at the centre of Malinowski's kinship structure was, on the surface, gender-neutral. However, Malinowski's model assumed that culture was transmitted from father to son:

> The training of body and mind, the transmission of standardized behavior and moral ideals in skill, knowledge and values, must go hand in hand with the transmission of material goods. To teach craft you have to provide the tools, to instruct in magic you have to part with your secret formulae and procedures. To impart your family tradition you have to transmit rank, position, even social identity. In this last case, unless you transmit social status, the passing on of its traditional definition is worthless. Thus education, sooner or later, leads to the handing over of material possessions, of social privileges, of a great part of one's moral identity. (1930, p. 147.)

Social rank, possessions, skills, tools, magic – the 'culture' that parents passed on to their children – was, in Malinowski's own culture if not in those he studied, typically associated with men.

Like all his contemporaries Malinowski used the male pronoun to signify both male and female children, but there are passages in which he transparently had boys in mind. For example, he noted that 'the child' would be removed from the protection of its home and made to enter group life by being placed in bachelor houses or men's club houses (a few pages later Malinowski added 'or girls' community' to this list: 1930, p. 152). Or he might undergo initiation ceremonies designed to wean him from the influence of his mother and instruct him in clan mythology and morality. In the process of this separation: 'he forms new bonds, finds himself a member of an Age Grade or other male organization, but above all, when there is a clan, he is taught the solidarity and unity of this group, of which he is now a full member' (1930, p. 148).

Although a son might be prevented from contact with his mother during initiation, he maintains 'close, strongly emotional, though perhaps surreptitious, relations with his mother' (1930, p. 148). Malinowski added briefly that marriage constituted a wrench for both sexes. But his main interest was in what happened to boys:

> With the gradual severance from the household, with his entry into economic cooperation, with his initiation into the mythological and esoteric lore of his people, with his assumption of the legal bonds of citizenship, with his growth, that is, into full participation in the ordinary and ceremonial life of the tribe, the native becomes more and more clearly aware of the validity of the clan and his place in it. (1930, p. 152.)

The 'individual' is a man. Malinowski concluded his descriptive account with the observation that 'The individual whose life history we have followed is now married, at the head of his new household' (1930, p. 156.)

Malinowski's theory implicitly positioned what fathers and sons did in matters of kinship as more significant sociologically than what mothers and daughters did. His account does not ignore women, especially mothers, but it does align the female with Nature and with the private world of the home that has ultimately to be left behind. Mothers and daughters invariably appear in Malinowski's text in the context of what he calls the 'Profane' (1930, p. 156). The Profane realm is associated with the early years of infancy, with family and home, and with the bodily care, affection and nurturing that take place there. Fathers and sons, by contrast, are associated with separation, discipline, maturity and the 'ordeals' and 'privations' of initiation – to the harsher but more culturally advanced public world of the clan, to the Sacred. Men are pivotal to the making and maintaining of (external) culture.

When contemporary anti-illegitimacy writers use Malinowski to bolster their argument that fatherless families are unnatural, they (probably) unwittingly import the idea, unremarkable in the 1920s but anachronistic in the 1990s, that men do the real work of culture. With the androcentrism of Malinowski's universal principle safely shrouded, contemporary readers assume that sex is irrelevant to the sociological work performed by fathers. As Zinsmeister summarises it, Malinowski's principal argument is that 'the main thing a father does is to place his *children* in the broader social context, to help them understand the requirements for living in the world outside the family' (1993, p. 43, my emphasis). This version of Malinowski renders him more palatable for a gender-sensitive contemporary reading public.

It is ironic that Malinowski, who unambiguously stated his opposition to extremist forms of conservative reaction, is now a major prophet of the militantly pro-moral, anti-welfare movement. Malinowski did claim that marriage as a legal contract, and the family as a culturally defined group of parents and children, had existed 'through all the changes and vicissitudes of history'. Any attempt to effect radical change in these institutions, or to abolish them completely, was unlikely to succeed (1930, p. 167). However, for Malinowski this stability was itself a sound reason why conservative forces should resist the temptation to panic at the revolution in social manners or take extreme measures to turn back the clock. The experienced anthropologist knew that 'there is nothing new under the sun' (1930, p. 113) and that even in the face of the rapidly changing values of the early twentieth century, marriage was going to survive. The moral reactionary needed to recognise that 'blind adherence to outworn forms and obsolete habits which survive by mere inertia' did more harm than good to marriage and the family (1930, p. 168). These institutions ought to be supported, but just as importantly, sociological laws indicated that intelligent reform could be undertaken when necessary (1930, p. 168). The family was strong enough to adapt to meet new social conditions.

Replaced within its context, the 'principle of legitimacy' is not a pre-existing independent universal truth that Malinowski somehow had the brilliance and persistence to 'discover'. It was a product of a particular conjunction of random discursive, disciplinary, political and personal events that happened to collide in Malinowski's writing in the 1920s. Malinowski could only think up the principle because he was thinking through other, largely unrelated, issues: the internal split within anthropology; the possibilities of a dialogue between psychology, sociology and anthropology; modern fatherhood; the advent of repressive political regimes in Europe; and the importance of a functionalist analysis. The principle of legitimacy was shaped around the particular sexual division of labour in parenting and the different expectations placed on daughters and sons that were taken for granted in Malinowski's European world of the 1920s. The so-called universal principle is simply a child of its times.

Malinowski has made an enduring contribution to the illegitimacy problem. Scholars have taken up Malinowski's theory of the relationship between legitimacy and paternity, not that of Engels, whose contribution to the illegitimacy question remains ignored (Hendrix 1996, pp. 18—22). Malinowski's principle of legitimacy has been disputed and substantially revised over the past sixty years. But it provided, and continues to provide, the central theoretical starting point for many important social–scientific studies of illegitimacy, including those of Kingsley Davis (1939a, 1939b) and William Goode (1960, 1961). Davis' work, in turn, was seen by the new generation of illegitimacy scholars that began to tackle the question from Left and feminist perspectives in the 1970s and 1980s as marking a major turning point away from older moralistic accounts towards the scientific (that is, functionalist) interpretation of illegitimacy's relationship to social structure (Hartley 1975, pp. 5-6; Laslett et al. 1980, p. 7; Teichman 1982, pp. 8, 16; Kiely 1982, p. 155; Zingo and Early 1994, pp. 16–18). Malinowski makes direct and central appearances in texts like Laslett, Oosterveen and Smith's massive comparative study of illegitimacy rates, a model for all subsequent demographic histories of the subject (1980, pp. 5–7).

In the 1990s Malinowski still sits at the heart of the social study of illegitimacy as a cross-cultural phenomenon. While not uncritical of Malinowski and the way others have interpreted his ideas, a study by Lewellyn Hendrix argues that his concepts of illegitimacy and the social father are implicit, if not explicit, in anthropological and sociological accounts of the universality of the incest taboo, marriage, the nuclear family, male dominance and the division of labour by sex, in fact of all purported family universals (Hendrix 1996, p. 4). Even though many anthropologists as early as the 1940s were unconvinced by Malinowski's functionalist method and sweeping theory of social structure, his account of social fatherhood continues to attract intellectual respect.

In its most recent political reincarnation Malinowski's principle has been strategically redeployed in the service of social conservatism. The pro-fatherhood movement has pulled him out of the archive to back its claim that the postmodern fragmentation of the family is ruining society, precisely the die-hard 'moral reactionary' position to which Malinowski was so vehemently opposed. In the face of postmodern confusion it is perhaps not surprising that conservatives gratefully gravitate towards Malinowski's conclusion that the father-headed family unit is central to all social structures and virtually impregnable. In Torgovnick's terms, Malinowski's work conforms to the primitivist tradition. His 'essential' individual family triad (mother–father–child) was a utopian construction offering comforting proof of the enduring nature of family bonds in the midst of the disruptions and uncertainties of modernity. In the context of the apparent sexual and reproductive anarchy of the 1990s Malinowski's timeless nuclear family is equally reassuring.

CHAPTER 9

Murphy Brown, Feminism and Female Selfishness

Conservative social critics, disturbed by the rise of the concept of the 'unnecessary father', reserve their strongest criticism for those women who deliberately create fatherless families. Most anti-illegitimacy campaigners acknowledge that sometimes a mother has no option but to bring up her child or children alone; her husband may die or desert his family, or she may be forced to leave a partner who is violent or abusive. There is agreement at all points of the political spectrum that in many cases women become single parents 'through no fault of their own' and that they and their children deserve state assistance. Involuntary single motherhood is explicable and forgivable.

The actions of the woman who consciously chooses to bear a child out of wedlock and to bring that child up without a father are far more problematic. If she is poor, not well educated or a member of a racially or ethnically disadvantaged group, the woman who opts for single parenthood may be excused as ignorant or misinformed, but there are no excuses for the relatively well-off single woman who decides to have a child without marrying first. She is patently putting her own desires and personal gratifications ahead of the welfare of her child and of society. She is, according to many social commentators, simply being selfish.

This chapter examines the conservative characterisation of single mothers as selfish and excessively independent women. The 'selfish single mother' constitutes a distinctively post-1980s sub-type of single motherhood. Unlike other varieties – the welfare mother, the teenage mother, the poor mother, the mentally incompetent mother – the selfish mother is perceived to be white, middle-class and mature (typically in her twenties or thirties). It is assumed that she is well educated, heterosexual and a professional, managerial or 'career woman' with a financially secure future who, with some degree of forward planning, has factored in motherhood as one of her personal goals in life. The selfish mother decides to get pregnant in the same materialistic and calculating way she decides to buy a new car. Her primary and purely self-serving consideration is to possess a child. In the pursuit of that objective she cares little for the consequences of depriving a child of a father's involvement and the advantages of a 'normal' family life.

This widespread view that some single mothers are irresponsibly self-centred challenges the widespread belief that these days illegitimacy is fundamentally an economic problem. The selfish mother does not necessarily drain the nation's welfare resources, inflate crime, populate the underclass, lack cognitive ability or contribute to high rates of infant mortality. Her main fault is not even her sexually free lifestyle (many choose to get pregnant by donor insemination). The selfish mother is a moral problem. She is greedy, thoughtless, acquisitive, stubbornly independent, and has actively rejected marriage and a husband. She is more committed to her own pleasures and personal satisfactions than to the welfare of her child. Large numbers of single-mothers-by-choice is a bad thing for society, in this view, because children are being brought into the world at the whim of a new breed of financially and emotionally independent women who believe men are irrelevant to the parenting process.

The trend towards 'single motherhood by choice' is a hot and divisive topic all over the western world. Ric Esther Bienstock's Canadian-produced television documentary 'Ms Conceptions', shown on Australian television in 1997, explored the issue through a series of interviews with women in New York, San Francisco, Toronto and London. Jane Mattes of the Single Mothers by Choice organisation told Bienstock that between 1980 and 1990 the birth-rate among women in their thirties who were single and working in managerial or professional occupations had nearly tripled. These statistics worried critics like psychoanalyst John Munder Ross, who suggested that the woman who uses reproductive technology was acting out a 'queen bee fantasy'. To the queen bee, the males of the species are 'superfluous or unnecessary as active fathers'. David Blankenhorn, President of the Institute for American Values and author of *Fatherless America* (1995), likened single mothers not to bees but to one-armed baseball players. The children of single mothers are disadvantaged in the game of growing-up, and 'There's something frightening and sad about watching parents – mothers – place what is good for "me" ahead of what is good for a child'. A single mother from New York partly agreed: 'Yes, there is a piece [of this whole process] that's selfish. But, so?' (Bienstock 1997).

Opposition to the selfish mother first came to public notice in 1992 in a political controversy surrounding the television series character

Murphy Brown, a single, successful career woman who decided in the show to have a child out of wedlock. The character's actions outraged pro-family political campaigners. In a speech arguing that America's racial conflict and associated social problems would be solved by strengthening marriage and the black family, United States Vice-President Dan Quayle asserted:

> Bearing babies irresponsibly is, simply, wrong. Failing to support children one has fathered is wrong. We must be unequivocal about this. It doesn't help matters when prime time TV has Murphy Brown – a character who supposedly epitomized today's intelligent, highly-paid, professional woman – mocking the importance of fathers by bearing a child alone, and calling it just another 'lifestyle choice'. (Quayle 1992, p. 9.)

What became known as the 'Murphy Brown incident' made the front cover of *Time* magazine on 21 September 1992. Quayle's views were endorsed by conservatives (notably Barbara Dafoe Whitehead's 1993 article entitled 'Dan Quayle was right'), and either ridiculed or seriously critiqued by liberals and feminists.

The debate surrounding Murphy Brown's decision to keep her ex-nuptial child crystallised in spectacular fashion the relatively new notion that there was some causal relationship between the modern woman's right to self-determination and the social problem of illegitimacy. From the late nineteenth century when feminists began to fight to improve the legal, economic and social status of the unmarried mother and her child, until the dawning of the moral backlash in the late 1980s, the goals of feminism have generally been in step with those of the humanitarian, social welfare and social–scientific communities. Professionals concerned with single parenthood did not, at least in print, posit any connection between rising illegitimacy rates and the increasing purchase of feminist ideology.

The recent targeting of feminist ideas by pro-family social scientists and social commentators in Australia, Britain and the United States is unprecedented. In contrast to most of the other illegitimacy problems discussed in this book, the problem of women's selfishness appears to have provoked the most outspoken criticism outside the United States. Noting that some women 'want a child but not a husband or a male partner', a writer for the *Scotsman* newspaper asserts that children in our society have become 'consumer comestibles, status symbols that can be acquired to make adults feel better about themselves or their situations' (*Scotsman* 1997). Feminists are the principal perpetrators of this socially-destructive development: 'I don't care what the sisterhood says, but children SHOULD be paramount' (emphasis in original).

British sociologist Patricia Morgan's *Farewell to the Family?* (1995) directly attacks 'feminist ideologues' and their influence on government social policy. Feminists believe that women's individual autonomy comes before traditional family values. In their determination to overturn the patriarchal family, feminists have spearheaded a vast social experiment designed to replace the father–mother–child family with the mother–child dyad. The feminist anti-family elite tries to impose on society a model 'designed to promote minority political agendas' (Morgan 1995, p. 154). 'Society' here means 'us', the reasonable and normal mainstream forced to defend itself against the political assaults of a marginalised and extremist 'them'. Morgan does not discuss the possibility that mainstream attitudes and social policies have, over the past three decades, assimilated much of the feminist analysis of family and gender relationships that she describes as extremist.

According to Australian philosopher Alan Tapper, academic feminists are responsible for the failure of Australian governments to support two-parent families. In his *The Family in the Welfare State* (1990), written when the Australian Labor Party was in government, Tapper argues that the demands of special interest groups have had an undue influence on Australian family policy. Of these, 'it has been feminism which has prosecuted the case against the family most zealously', attributing to it every kind of social ill from psychosis to bad eating habits (Tapper 1990, p. 79). Arguing that there is no reasonable basis for feminist 'anti-family propaganda' he advocates a conservative version of feminism built around an 'ethics of caring' for dependants. Tapper is not opposed to feminism *per se*, and he does not overtly deny women's right to independence from men. He is critical of 'militant' feminists whom he presents as less rational than more reasonable, sensible and caring feminists.

Social commentator Bettina Arndt (1996) is less subtle in her criticism of Australia's 'laissez-faire attitudes' towards single motherhood. Arndt claims that newspapers, women's magazines, movies, television soap operas and advice books provide abundant evidence that a woman's decision to deliberately have an ex-nuptial child is now socially acceptable. Celebrities 'blithely dismiss the need for fathers in their children's lives' and paternity is treated with contempt. These women, Arndt argues, are 'sentencing their offspring to a lesser life'. Arndt's comments provoked a rash of letters to the editor (*Sydney Morning Herald* 1996b), some readers angered by her attack on single-parent families (one called her the Newt Gingrich of Australian family values), others grateful that she had voiced their own concerns.

American conservatives, especially social scientists, are rarely as overtly critical of women. Charles Murray, for example, blames misguided government policy initiatives and the politics of liberalism, not women or the women's rights movement, for the rise in illegitimate births. This reluctance to publicly attack or disparage feminist viewpoints – and particularly 'women' as a social group – is in part testimony to the movement's success in influencing at least the public rhetoric of the middle ground of politics. Some basic elements of feminist philosophy are accepted even among women and men who believe that single motherhood should not be encouraged.

Nevertheless, the suggestion that feminism is at least partly or tangentially responsible for the rise in illegitimate births, family breakdown and the decline of community can be detected in current American pro-family scholarship. Negative assessments of feminism are presented, indirectly, tentatively and cautiously. Amitai Etzioni's *The Spirit of Community* (1993) gently suggests that America's social problems are in part attributable to women's reluctance to be full-time, home-based mothers. Etzioni sets out the principles of a communitarian movement designed to rectify the assumed loss in America of firmly established moral positions. Etzioni claims that marriage has become a 'disposable relationship' and that millions of teenagers give birth without making a serious commitment to their infants (Etzioni 1993, p. 27). Women as well as men seek satisfaction through their careers and in the acquisition of material goods, with the consequence that there has been 'a mass exodus' of both parents from the home to the workplace (1993, p. 29). Because not enough parents spend time at home fully committed to the care and moral education of their children contemporary society is suffering from a 'parenting deficit'. Instead of wasting time criticising Murphy Brown, Etzioni suggests, Americans would do better to emulate the television sit-com family the Huxtables, parents who are 'actively and deeply involved in their children's upbringing' (1993, pp. 25, 67).

Etzioni is not 'dumping on women'. He is not saying that the parenting deficit is the fault of the women's movement, feminism or mothers (p. 56). Women's search for the same work opportunities as men is only to be expected. The cause, he says, is less important than the result: millions of latchkey children, parents who 'fly the coop', and others whose main commitments lie outside the home. Etzioni denies being opposed in principle to women's pursuit of a career, or of single parenthood – single parents, he says, may actually be more committed to parenting than two-career absentee parents. However, he is critical of institutionalised child care (1993, p. 60), sexual promiscuity (the 'succession of boy- or girlfriends' and 'turnover in partners' that follow divorce) (1993, p. 61), and people (implicitly, feminists) who put down women who choose to be homemakers (1993, p. 64). In expressing the opinion that 'women are obviously entitled to all the same rights men are, including the pursuit of greed' (1993, p. 63), Etzioni implies that women have unthinkingly adopted a morally flawed model of success. His argument strongly suggests that modern mothers, distracted by the desire for a successful career and superficial material comforts, are not as committed to child-rearing as they were before the advent of feminism. Etzioni may not be anti-feminist but he does lament the loss, to both mothers and fathers, of the pre-1960s maternal ideal: the self-sacrificing, domesticated, completely involved parent, wholly devoted to spouse and children.

Pro-family advocates locate the origins of the idea that women have a right to pursue motherhood independently of marriage and conventional family commitments in the wider libertarian and amoral climate that overtook western societies in the 1960s. Historian Christopher Lasch's *The Culture of Narcissism* (1978) was one of the first intellectual attempts to articulate what was going wrong with the direction of American life in the 1970s. Lasch argued that an older authoritarian model of 'economic man' had been replaced by 'psychological man'. The new narcissist was the ultimate product of bourgeois individualism. He is 'haunted not by guilt but by anxiety. He seeks not to inflict his own certainties on others but to find a meaning in life ... [He] demands immediate gratification and lives in a state of restless, perpetually unsatisfied desire' (Lasch 1978, p. xvi). Among other worrying social consequences, the narcissist's determination to live for the moment had led to the deterioration of stable family life. The family of the late 1970s was marked symbolically by the loss of traditional paternal authority (1978, pp. 188–9).

What Lasch called the culture of narcissism became more popularly known as the sexual revolution, the era of liberation ideologies, the rise of social movements (left-wing student protest, women's rights, anti-racist and postcolonialist struggles) or the counter-culture movement. The 1960s, 1970s and 1980s have acquired a bad reputation among conservatives as the time when western culture lost its sense of moral purpose. Charles Krauthammer refers to the 1960s as a period of 'moral deregulation' (1993, p. 20). In conservative discourse this repudiation of strict moral codes led to an explosion of deviancy in family life, criminal behaviour, the erosion of traditional values governing sexual continence and the loss of a collective sense of commonly-agreed social values.

The moral reaction against counter-culture values and 'liberation ideology' is most clearly articulated in the United States, but is also evident in the words of British and Australian social conservatives including Patricia Morgan (1995, p. 115) and Barry Maley (Maley et al.

1996, p. 21). In an interview conducted just before he became Prime Minister of Australia, John Howard stated his belief, one he knew would 'probably sound like the ravings of a social conservative', that the Me Generation of the 1970s and its assault on traditional norms of behaviour carried much of the responsibility for social disintegration, family breakdown, economic dependency and poverty in Australia (Duffy 1996, p. 36).

Etzioni (1993, p. 25) argues that the loss of the moral absolutes that were taken for granted until the 1950s created a moral vacuum filled by the 1980s by a 'radical individualism' in which the celebration of the self became a virtue. The post-1960s ethos sanctions selfish individual behaviour. According to Stanley Rothman, the (implicitly good) ethics of nineteenth-century liberal capitalism, characterised by restraint and commitment to community, have been replaced by (an implicitly bad) culture of 'expressive individualism'. Post-1960s culture centres on 'the exploration of experience and sensation – unfettered, impulsive and nonrational' (Rothman 1996, p. 12). The result has been: 'an erosion of the capacity to sublimate both aggressive and erotic drives in the service of civilization, and the replacement of bourgeois commitments to achievement and constancy by an increase in defensive projection, "acting out", and drives for power and control' (Rothman 1996, p. 15). Myron Magnet argues that the sexual liberation and counter-culture movements of the 1960s encouraged members of the middle and wealthy classes to reject traditional bourgeois culture, including marriage and family life, as 'sick, repressive and destructive'. Instead the 'Haves' of society were urged to act upon their true feelings, to express themselves and 'let it all hang out' (Magnet 1993, p. 17).

The resurgence of a militant women's movement and the feminist critique of marriage and the patriarchal family is seen as partly, if not substantially, responsible for the general disintegration of moral and family values that began in the 1960s and 1970s. Feminism was clearly implicated in the devaluing of restraint, duty, deferral of gratification and the 'disciplines of work and family and citizenship' (Magnet 1993, p. 18). While Etzioni acknowledges that pre-revolutionary social institutions and authoritarian values needed to be challenged, he argues that 'the waning of traditional values was not followed by a solid affirmation of new values' (Etzioni 1993, p. 24), such as the restoration of the father–mother–child family unit welded by an ideal of parental unselfishness. What has been lost is a liberal individualism, derived from religion, that emphasised the restraint of impulse, the acceptance of discipline and hierarchy, and the accumulation of wealth (Rothman 1996, p. 11).

The underlying 'problem' of modern society, from this conservative perspective, is the ascendancy of a philosophy built on the unfettered expression of personal feelings and the pursuit of individual satisfactions – most notoriously, the blind following of sexual and maternal desires heedless of the consequences. The current rise in illegitimate births and increasing social acceptance of single motherhood by choice is seen as the direct legacy of a post-1960s libertarianism that actively encouraged women to be selfish.

Unlike the other problems examined in this book, some of which date back to the early nineteenth century, the problem of illegitimacy as a product of women's excessive independence has a very brief discursive history. It is a specific product of the reaction (some would say backlash) that began in the mid-1980s against feminism's influence on popular culture, social inquiry and much social policy. What does exist in the illegitimacy archive are statements that question the conservative assumption that the counter-culture endorsed permissive attitudes towards unmarried parenthood. An alternative reading of this period based on social–scientific studies of illegitimacy produced between 1960 and the early 1980s suggests that the liberation decades were not as universally morally bankrupt as conservative critics suggest.

There is some evidence of a discursive shift towards libertarian philosophies centred on the pursuit of personal and political liberation from oppressive ideologies and social institutions. Social welfare professionals and academics noted the spread of a less punitive, more tolerant attitude towards pre-marital sexuality, contraception (the pill became available in the early 1960s) and abortion. From the 1970s there was a growing perception that being pregnant and single was a situation in which a woman could legitimately exercise some degree of personal choice (termination, adoption or keeping the child) without fear of moral condemnation. It was in the 1970s that the terms 'illegitimate child' and 'unmarried mother' began to be replaced by 'single mother', 'single parent', and 'out-of-wedlock birth'. The legal distinction between legitimate and illegitimate children was removed in many jurisdictions. By the early 1970s a significant group of social scientists had adopted a relatively liberal position on illegitimacy. Their liberalism was indicated more by what they did not say, and by what they were opposed to, than by what they actually said or did. Progressive social scientists did not suggest, for example, that rising levels of ex-nuptial births had to be stopped or prevented, and they did not assume it was a priority to 'solve' the problem of unmarried motherhood.

Largely as a reaction against the psychological constructions of unmarried motherhood that were prominent in the 1950s and 1960s, progressive social scientists refused to treat the unwed mother as someone with a pathology. Rachel Zinober Forman argued that social workers' overwhelming reliance on Freudian frameworks had distorted the reality of the lives of unmarried mothers. She found it impossible to believe that 'there is not one whose pregnancy was the result of strength and will, and whose mothering was an example of resilience and competence' (Forman 1982, p. 29). Sociologist Shirley Foster Hartley consciously departed from the welfare and psychologically oriented focus on individual deviancy. Her cross-national study presented illegitimacy in Durkheimian fashion as a 'social fact'. Hartley and many sociologists who came after her placed illegitimacy firmly within a morally-neutral structural context, viewing it 'as a reflection of the patterns of human group life – the social structure – and the related beliefs, values, and expectations – the culture – of a whole society or of a subcultural group within it' (Hartley, S. 1975, p. 17).

Others adopting a progressive position represented the individual unmarried mother as a 'normal' woman. Prudence Mors Rains, in her *Becoming an Unwed Mother. A Sociological Account* (1971), examined the unwed mother's experiences and her 'moral career' in the context of the usual concerns of unmarried girls, particularly their attempts to come to terms with the competing forces of sexuality and respectability (Rains 1971, p. 4). A group of Australian experts simply refused to recognise marital status as a relevant factor in sexuality and fertility issues. They drew no distinction between married and unmarried mothers but instead referred to the problem of pregnancies that were 'unplanned and unwanted' (Royal Commission on Human Relationships 1977, ch. 3).

Influenced to a greater or lesser extent by feminism and the lifting of the taboo against premarital sexuality, many social scientists criticised traditional attitudes towards illegitimacy as being politically unacceptable, morally inappropriate, outdated or inaccurate. Benjamin Schlesinger's 1973 review of the situation of unmarried mothers, one of the first Australian sociological studies, found statistical evidence that the number of single women retaining their ex-nuptial children was increasing throughout the industrialised English-speaking world. He outlined the legal, social and economic problems faced by unmarried mothers and their children, argued the need for more child-care facilities, and supported the work of organisations like the Council for the Single Mother and her Child (Schlesinger 1973). The problem for Schlesinger and many of his colleagues was insufficient knowledge about this 'new pattern of family life' and the lack of social support for the single mother. According to American sociologist Phillips Cutright, a better understanding of the factors causing variations in illegitimacy rates would allow the design of 'a preventive program which would benefit the individual as well as society' (Cutright 1971, p. 26). In these accounts the social problem of illegitimacy was replaced by a focus on the personal problems experienced by the unmarried mother.

Another strand of liberal social inquiry found that, despite the major change that had taken place in sexual mores, illegitimacy was still perceived as a problem for society. Those social scientists who in the 1960s took up the new field of research into premarital sexuality argued that, analytically speaking, premarital sexual behaviour had to be distinguished from premarital pregnancy. Malinowski's 'principle of legitimacy' appeared implicitly or explicitly in several of these sex studies. According to American sex researcher Ira Reiss, 'the key societal function of marriage is to legitimise parenthood, not to legitimise sexuality'. Premarital relations that resulted in a conception without the probability of marriage were almost universally condemned (Reiss 1967, p. 173). Sex researchers explained this persistent social disapproval of illegitimacy primarily as a structural problem in which births out of wedlock represented an intolerable deviation from accepted patterns of family formation and reproduction. Social investigators noted that although by 1980 sexual attitudes had changed markedly, illegitimacy was still seen in the United States as 'a threat to the integrity and continuity of society' (Zelnick et al. 1981, p. 169).

It was in the 1960s and 1970s that social scientists began to focus their attention on the creation and impact of various myths, stereotypes and negative images of single mothers and their children. Those who worked directly with these women, in social administration or social welfare, argued that in their experience American society had not progressed beyond the punitive 'scarlet letter' era: the labels 'unmarried mother' and 'unwed mother' continued to brand the pregnant girl with her assumed sin (Jeffers 1971, p. 11). Australian social workers reported frequent encounters with clients who, because of society's attitudes, were too afraid to tell their parents, employers or friends of their pregnancy (Roberts, P. 1969). Rose Bernstein (1960), a Boston director of social services, suggested that social workers themselves, in their ready acceptance of the psychological interpretation of illegitimacy to the exclusion of other hypotheses, were in danger of stereotyping the unmarried mother as emotionally disturbed. Although comparable studies of unmarried fathers were much rarer, men too, were portrayed as victims of social stereotyping, having no perceived function for welfare workers 'except as an object of blame' (Barber 1975, ch. 1).

Social scientists began in this period to apply the theory of 'stigma' outlined by the American sociologist Erving Goffman (1964) to unmarried motherhood. Phyllis Day of Western Michigan University argued that women on public welfare suffered from a dual stigmatisation: 'the very fact of a woman seeking public support brands her not only with the taint of laziness but with the taint of sexual immorality' (1977, p. 872). British social policy expert Robert Page (1984) argued that although the harshest forms of disapproval and punishment of unmarried motherhood had withered away since 1900, implicit forms of secular stigmatisation continued to operate in the form of inappropriate or inadequate welfare services (Page 1984, p. 79). The growth of psychological, sociological and social administration studies of the problem since the 1940s had inadvertently reinforced this process of stigmatisation by representing unmarried mothers as either psychologically disturbed, locked into a working-class culture, belonging to an inferior racial group, or unsatisfactory parents (1984, p. 123). Page's study provides abundant evidence that, two decades after the dawning of the sexual revolution, illegitimacy continued to be represented as highly undesirable by both expert and non-expert publics.

Studies of sexual behaviour suggested that no matter how permissive society appeared to be on the surface, traditional ideas about marriage and proper family formation constrained the activities of many members of the younger generation. Most parents were morally opposed to illegitimacy and passed their antipathy on to their children. Of the 985 men and women aged between 18 and 23 interviewed by American researchers John DeLamater and Patricia MacCorquodale, 90 per cent of the women and 86 per cent of the men said that their fathers would react negatively to the news that their child was either pregnant, or was responsible for an out-of-wedlock pregnancy. The interviewees perceived their mothers to be only marginally less opposed (DeLamater and MacCorquodale 1979, pp. 196–7).

The influence of middle-class expectations of respectable behaviour was, according to sex researchers, particularly noticeable among white Americans. Robert Bell found that whereas there was a relative absence of social stigma attached to illegitimacy among lower-class Negroes, 'in the middle class, and for many in the white lower class the values toward premarital coitus are strongly influenced by the fear of pregnancy' (Bell 1966, p. 123). Young women's sexual attitudes and ideas about illegitimacy were determined by their religious beliefs. A Kinsey Institute for Sex Research study of pregnancy, birth and abortion found that the more devout a woman was, the less likely she was to become pregnant before marriage (Gebhard et al. 1958, p. 66). A later study of 109 single white women from the southeastern States confirmed that religious faith continued to be a relevant factor, with evidence that women who went to church regularly were more likely to continue with their pregnancies than have an abortion (Butts and Sporakowski 1974, p. 113).

Far from promoting the joys of unfettered maternity, social science presented a sober and discouraging portrait of the unmarried mother.

The southern white women who proceeded with their pregnancy, the majority of whom gave up their babies for adoption, were reported to have subsequently experienced more dissatisfaction and unhappiness with their decision than those who terminated their pregnancy. Compared with the thirty-five women who opted for abortion, researchers found in the seventy-four maternity-home women a significant degree of 'conflict, discomfort and anxiety' (Butts and Sporakowski 1974, p. 114). Unmarried mothers in Melbourne, Australia, exhibited similar signs of shame and guilt. They were 'aware that premarital pregnancy is not socially acceptable and expressed remorse concerning their situation' (Shanmugam and Wood 1970, p. 53). Another Australian study found that the single largest cause of maternal deaths in New South Wales between 1964 and 1969 was suicide. The risk of suicide was especially high among single teenage girls (McMurdo 1975, p. 49).

American welfare work organisations, advice-givers and journalists clearly promoted the message that illegitimacy was wrong, or at least should be strenuously avoided. According to Glenn Matthew White, writing in the *Ladies Home Journal,* 'there is no poetry and little romance or love in the true stories of illegitimately pregnant schoolgirls; neither did they pause to debate the consequences of their behavior'. It was the innocent child who suffered (White 1960, p. 102). The Child Welfare League of America's Standards for Services to Unmarried Parents stated its belief that unmarried parenthood was 'a specific form of social dysfunctioning which is a problem in itself and which in turn creates social and emotional problems for parent and child' (Gallagher 1963, p. 402).

Advice books drawing on the latest research, like Chicago sociologist Evelyn Millis Duvall's *Why Wait Till Marriage?*, warned that young people might be enjoying considerable freedom, but: 'there are still harsh penalties for the couple who step out of line. The pregnant unmarried girl is still disapproved of by adults, pitied by her classmates, asked to leave school, and/or drop out of normal social activities, and is often sent packing to have her baby among strangers' (Duvall 1966, p. 67). Termination, a shot-gun marriage, or having the baby all 'have their problems and their pain' (1966, p. 60). Even enthusiastic supporters of the new sexual openness had serious reservations about the reproductive consequences. According to prolific sex writer Dr Eustace Chesser, in his book on *Unmarried Love*: 'How two consenting individuals, without pressure on either side, behave in private is not the concern of society unless their actions lead to social consequences – such as the bringing of an unwanted child into the world. With this exception I fail to see that any moral issue is raised' (Chesser 1965, p. 32). This significant group of relatively enlightened professionals acknowledged, even welcomed, the new sexual freedom while simultaneously voicing moral objections to unmarried parenthood.

Some welfare professionals unequivocally disapproved of illegitimacy on moral grounds. A British study of the unmarried mother and her child, published by the Catholic Truth Society, condemned the open celebration of lust in plays and films, the spread of contraceptive knowledge, and social acceptance of immorality and other 'selfish acts' (Walsh 1954, pp. 2–3). Moral unease was not confined to the religious community. There was a perception within some sectors of the social welfare profession that the consequences of the sexual revolution – 'increased illegitimacy, prolific illicit sex, and pregnant brides' (Delamarter 1962) – had ominous consequences for American youth. An appropriate response, according to Walter Delamarter, speaking at the National Conference on Social Welfare in New York in 1962, was to ensure that traditional family life was strengthened, and to remember that 'goodness, love, charity, mercy, truth, humility, brotherliness, and human dignity need never be obsolete' (1962, p. 4). The Louisiana Youth Commission attributed the increase in illegitimacy in large part to the change in attitude towards illicit relations and 'the greater freedom from parental supervision, the general availability of liquor and automobiles, the use of narcotics, gang influences, and stimulation from certain types of literature, movies and television' (Webb 1961, p. 11). The report concluded with the words of an anonymous State Governor describing illegitimacy as one of the nation's 'great moral and spiritual problems' (Webb 1961, p. 15). Particularly in the United States, politicians and welfare workers' ideas about illegitimacy continued to be influenced directly or indirectly by religious beliefs.

The work of sociologist Clark Vincent (1959–60; 1961; 1963) is a good example of the subtlety with which moral schema continued to influence even secular, objective and sympathetic accounts of illegitimacy. Vincent's *Unmarried Mothers* (1961) has had a major impact on understandings of illegitimacy in the second half of the twentieth century. Vincent's research methodology was based on Kingsley Davis' (1939a) statement that a truly scientific study would analyse, rather than take for granted, the moral norms by which illegitimacy was judged wrong. The study is viewed today as a 'classic' representing the first full exposition of a modern scientific method that explicitly distances itself from moral judgements (for example, Bennett 1992, p. 1181; Teichman 1982, pp. 17–18). Vincent's work is cited in some current American encyclopaedia entries on illegitimacy (Furstenberg 1992).

Previous research had, according to Vincent, reflected middle-class values in artificially compartmentalising illicit coition and illicit pregnancy. Premarital pregnancies were viewed as a more overt and serious threat to traditional family life than covert premarital sexual relationships (Vincent 1961, p. 18). Because early researchers had not linked sex and unwed pregnancy, they had studied only those women who had been 'caught', a small and unrepresentative group. Vincent's study sought to position middle- and working-class unmarried mothers' attitudes and behaviours in the context of those of the 'normal' female population. He argued that favourable definitions of illicit sex were promoted by the commercialisation of sex, the publication of sex research and the philosophy of 'fun morality' – the idea that a child learns more effectively if he or she is happy and having fun – that dominated child-rearing practices from 1940 until the mid-1950s. That generation of children, adolescents at the time Vincent was writing, were predisposed to believe that 'anything which is fun and wanted is good and needed. And they read, hear, and see progressively fewer denials that *sex is fun*' (1961, p. 8). Young people were encouraged to believe, moreover, that they had a '*right*' to fun and enjoyment (1963, p. 803, emphases in original).

The implicit rules of the fun morality stated, however, that one should not enjoy more than one can afford and that one should not allow one's own fun to detract from the fun of others. Consequently, poor, unwed mothers came in for particular censure (Vincent 1961, p. 15). Unwed mothers of all social backgrounds were expected to do what society was not able to do itself: reconcile the contradictory attitudes toward illicit coition and illicit pregnancy (1961, p. 51). The cause of unmarried motherhood (illicit coition) was encouraged, while its result (illicit pregnancy) was condemned (1961, p. 244).

Unmarried Mothers appears at one level to adopt a liberal position on illegitimacy. Vincent attempts to normalise unmarried motherhood. He acknowledges and seeks to analyse the contradictory nature of society's attitudes to premarital sex and pregnancy, and he takes illegitimacy to be a socially complex, constructed social problem, one that is not solved because society does not want to solve it (Vincent 1961, p. 25). Contemporaries praised the book's 'thoroughness, its freedom from evaluative judgments and its objectivity'. Extracts were selected for inclusion in a volume on *Problems of Sex Behavior* on the grounds that the study was 'a model for a social–scientific approach to any aspect of human sexuality' (Sagarin and MacNamara 1968, p. 32).

Vincent's work nevertheless conveys a clear message that illegitimacy and premarital sexual activity is morally undesirable. Vincent describes both illegitimate pregnancies and sex outside marriage as 'illicit', a nineteenth-century, morally loaded term, and favours twentieth-century equivalents such as 'permissive sexual behaviour'. He is clearly opposed to a modern society that 'inundates young people with sexual stimuli' and condones social practices that 'instill [sic] permissive attitudes toward illicit sexual behaviour' (Vincent 1963, p. 804).

The book's underlying assumptions are just as revealing as its language. Vincent assumes that society will want to continue to try to prevent illegitimacy and suggests a number of measures that might contribute to such a project. He argues, firstly, that the 'learning sources' that define illicit coition favourably and which weaken traditional sex mores have to be critically examined (Vincent 1961, p. 249). He believes it is better for society to withdraw the sexual stimuli than make contraceptive advice more widely available (Vincent 1963, p. 804). Secondly, he claims that: 'The concerted efforts to understand, aid, support, and rehabilitate those whose illicit sexual behavior undermines the normative supports for legitimate family life must be balanced by equal, if not greater, efforts to emphasize and provide positive sanctions for those whose licit sexual behavior supports legitimate marriage and family life' (1961, p. 249).

Prefiguring the arguments of contemporary conservative critics like Patricia Morgan and Alan Tapper, Vincent claims that governments provide 'greater rewards for those who undermine than for those who support legitimate or normative family life'. Vincent does not want to reduce assistance to needy 'deviant individuals' but does point out that insufficient attention is paid to strengthening legitimate families at a time when the breakdown of family life was causing mental illness, illegitimacy, delinquency and crime (1961, p. 250). The most vexing problem facing society was how to deter behaviour that undermined the family while rehabilitating the unwed mother and facilitating the development of her child into a good and useful citizen (1961, p. 251).

In pitting bourgeois society's need to preserve accepted moral standards against its philanthropic impulse to rescue the illegitimate child, Vincent identified precisely the same problem that had troubled his more moralistic forebears. This was the value dilemma faced by mid-nineteenth-century scholars trying to weigh up the social advantages and moral disadvantages of establishing foundling hospitals or employing fallen women as wet-nurses, for example. The reappearance of this old moral conundrum in a study that otherwise appeared well-suited to its revolutionary times indicates how little the climate of 'moral deregulation' had affected the social prohibition on illegitimacy.

Despite the apparent revolution in sexual mores, contemporary feminist scholars make it abundantly clear that they are still engaged in a battle against prejudice, discrimination and misinformation. In 1986 the (British) National Council for One Parent Families published extracts from 230 letters expressing the 'sense of shame, of feeling different and inferior, which has been the experience of so many non-marital children in the past' (National Council for One Parent Families 1986, p. 16). One correspondent wrote:

> The word illegitimate should be taken out of the English Dictionary, should not be allowed to be used on radio or television. Yes, I know what I am talking about – I was one of those children. I beg of you please get a law passed to wipe that word out once and for all. It is heartbreaking. I shall die brokenhearted. (1986, p. 57.)

Rosemary Kiely (1982), an Australian political scientist and founding member of the Council for the Single Mother and her Child in Victoria, noted the emergence of a new 1980s stereotype that she called the 'superdoll syndrome', the idea that teenagers deliberately got pregnant so that they would have something to love. In a book published in 1997, Nancy E. Dowd devotes a chapter to 'The stories of stigma: what we say about single-parent families'. Dowd argues that the law supports nuclear marital families materially and ideologically. The stigma currently attached to single-parent families functions as 'a necessary badge of social scorn and economic penalty' (Dowd 1997, p. 15).

Hence I would argue that the libertarian shift has been nowhere near as definitive, pervasive or uncontested as conservatives imply. Some social groups and individuals embraced the new culture, some staunchly opposed it. Probably the majority were unsure or accepted some ideas but not others. I suspect that liberation ideologies infiltrated popular culture, political rhetoric and the arts more easily than they did the sciences, social sciences and the professions. Even if magazines, films, plays, novels and television shows disseminated a new set of libertarian values, and even if the various social movements, including feminism, promoted liberation from repressive sexual, social and political ideologies, social scientists and welfare professionals generally did not. Theirs was a far more hesitant and cautious response, one that indicated how complex and contradictory and resistant to change western cultures are.

The response to illegitimacy in the 1960s and 1970s does need to be analysed as a western-culture-wide phenomenon. Jane Lewis and Kathleen Kiernan, focusing exclusively on Britain, argue that while commentators adopted a generally positive attitude towards the separation of sex and marriage in this period, they paid 'surprisingly little explicit attention' to the increase in the extra-marital birth-rate (Lewis and Kiernan 1996, p. 384). The separation of marriage and parenthood attracted notice only in the 1980s when it sparked the unprecedented moral panic that surrounds lone motherhood today. British and Australian social scientists and commentators did seem to be less preoccupied in the 1960s and 1970s with illegitimacy than their American colleagues. Although their interest in illegitimacy was less intense, I would argue that non-American social scientists did contribute to a general pool of negative images of unmarried mother-hood. To treat the sex and illegitimacy literatures of Britain, the United States and other English-speaking countries in isolation from one another is to draw an arbitrary distinction based on geographical borders. Ideas about social problems simply refuse to stay on their own side of the border. By the 1960s social inquiry practitioners rarely restricted their reading or thinking about a particular problem to their own country, with the result that the social inquiry discourses of one western nation were almost indistinguishable from those of another. The American literature on illegitimacy was certainly read and had some influence in Britain and Australia.

Where Lewis and Kiernan detect a radical shift between the values of one period and the next, my survey of British, American and Australian literatures indicates a continuing ambivalence concerning the immorality or otherwise of illegitimacy. Social scientists writing between 1960 and the mid-1980s were, as they are now, divided on the question of unmarried motherhood's moral status. Experts' views on the increase in illegitimate births ranged along a continuum from a neutral, deliberately non-moralistic stance at one end to outright disap-proval of both premarital sexuality and illegitimacy at the other.

One group of social scientists did adopt feminism's egalitarianism, refusing to draw a qualitative distinction between married and single mothers and proposing that single-parent families be seen as an alter-native family structure just as socially valid as their two-parent equiva-lents. Lorraine Fox Harding (1993, pp. 176–7) argues that some feminists writing in the 1980s and 1990s characterise lone parenthood as 'liberating' in that single parenthood frees women from marriage and marriage-like relationships with men which are patriarchal and oppressive. I would suggest that if there is a 'single parenthood as "liberation"' view, it is not a naive celebration of women's freedom but a critique of gender imbalance within the two-parent family. Feminists who claim that a woman is often better off on her own than tied to a bad husband and father are not necessarily advocating single parent-hood as a preferred lifestyle. Their main purpose is to explain why, given the unsatisfactory relationship existing between the sexes in contemporary society, women would choose to end a marriage, or not marry, or not live with the father of their child in the first place. Single parenthood, in some circumstances, is better than the alternative but not necessarily liberating *per se*. Not one of the feminist-influenced and otherwise progressive social scientists in my survey of the literature produced in the 1960–85 period argued that single parenthood was a good thing, either for women or for society.

On the contrary, the majority of experts were convinced that the new sexual permissiveness and the growing recognition of women's right to lead an independent life free of patriarchal constraints had done little to soften traditional condemnation of pregnancy and birth outside marriage. The retreat from traditional sexual moral values and family discipline in the 1960s and 1970s was nowhere as universal or as even as conservatives imply. To claim that post-1960s feminism and a counter-culture philosophy that celebrates selfishness are responsible for the normalisation of single-parent families is, to say the least, to construct a very specific and highly contestable version of historical truth.

CHAPTER 10

The Possibilities of a Postmodern Illegitimacy

Why is illegitimacy considered to be a social problem? Not, as the fore-going chapters have shown, for any single reason. On close examination the problem of high rates of illegitimate birth appears to be a constellation of other social problems. Illegitimacy represents an unbearable expense for the state, it leads to welfare dependency, it deprives children of fathers and devalues fatherhood, it raises levels of crime and poverty thereby producing social unrest, it is associated with racial inferiority, it contributes to high rates of infant death and phys-ical incapacity, it is a sign of female selfishness and irresponsibility and it makes parents out of people with poor emotional-management skills and low cognitive ability. And these are only the most frequently cited reasons. The list could be expanded to include illegitimacy's association with low educational achievement and other social consequences that I have been unable to cover here.

There is no pure essence of illegitimacy at the centre of the debate, only a series of reflections. It is precisely this multiplicity that creates illegitimacy's considerable rhetorical force. Because each sub-problem exists in a harmonious partnership with its neighbours, the overall effect is powerfully cumulative. If illegitimacy has so many negative consequences in different areas of social life, according to all kinds of experts, then it must be very bad indeed.

The spread of the problem across such a wide and varied discursive terrain discourages dissent. It is hard to imagine a space outside this discursive universe in which an alternative, non-problematic conceptu-alisation might be constructed. If feminists and liberals find a way to dispute the idea that single-parent families contribute to high crime levels, for example, the idea that single mothers have low IQs persists. Historians might counter anthropological accounts of the universality

of the nuclear family structure with evidence that there have always
been single-parent families; meanwhile medical accounts of high
mortality rates among ex-nuptial infants remain virtually unchallenged.
Reinforcing this discursive back-up system, each sub-problem is
strengthened by its own dense history. Any attempt to think more positively, or just differently, about illegitimacy inevitably comes up against
the sheer weight of culture that precedes it. This and other comparable
social phenomena – poverty, suicide, interpersonal violence, for
example – has been made into a problem to be solved or prevented, for
many different reasons, for nearly two centuries by scholars working in
every discipline from statistics to psychiatry. That degree of cultural
infiltration makes illegitimacy's bad reputation difficult to argue against
and almost impossible to eradicate.

Illegitimacy's stigma is not, as feminists have tended to assume,
equivalent to Hester Prynne's scarlet letter, a 'thing' that can be
unpicked and discarded to allow the female body to return to a natural
state unsullied by social attitudes. Immoral meanings are not external
to and separate from, the concept of illegitimacy, but are intrinsic to it.
This is not to say that illegitimacy's meaning is fixed. Illegitimacy has
meant different things to different social groups at different moments
in history. No matter how much the precise meanings have varied, they
have never exceeded the limit defining illegitimacy as 'not good',
whether for the individual mother, the individual child, 'the family', the
community, the nation or western society. Thus it seems to me that
while the pursuit of a de-stigmatised, de-mythologised and de-stereo-
typed representation of single parenthood may have strategic value, the
ideal of a pure scientific representation stripped of all moral meaning
may be unachievable.

By concentrating on ironing out specific distortions in the representation of single parenthood, liberal and feminist analysts may miss the
wider cultural significance of anti-illegitimacy discourses. Illegitimacy
functions as a metaphor for socially undesirable reproduction.
Although, technically speaking, only births that occur outside of
marriage can be described as illegitimate, other forms of parenting,
family structure and population growth are constructed as socially illegitimate. Women who are considered for various reasons to pose a
medical or social risk to the health and wellbeing of their foetus or
child, and who are thereby deemed improper, unwise or unfit mothers,
comprise one group of metaphorically illegitimate parents. These
include alcoholic and drug-dependent mothers, mothers who are HIV-
positive, mothers with a physical or intellectual disability and mothers
who have female partners. A second group of socially illegitimate
parents has been created by the introduction of fertility treatments

such as in-vitro fertilisation and artificial donor insemination. These include single women, unmarried heterosexual couples, lesbian couples, gay men and married heterosexual women past normal child-bearing age. On a larger scale, poverty stricken or racially disadvantaged populations, or communities with scarce natural resources, can be illegitimate populations. Women living in countries whose governments are anxious to control population growth, for example, are perceived as having produced an offspring who is both legally and socially illegitimate. Biological illegitimacy provides a cultural model upon which these and other variants of illicit reproduction are based.

There is a particularly close rhetorical relationship between illegitimacy and homosexuality. The Christian church has traditionally been reluctant to endorse both homosexuality and single motherhood as behaviours that undermine marriage and the nuclear family. The same linkage occurs in secular conservative rhetoric in which single-parent families and gay relationships are seen to pose a similar threat to social wellbeing. In an article published in the *Washington Post* in 1993, William Raspberry drew a somewhat improbable analogy between the problem of out-of-wedlock births and the issue of whether gays should be permitted to serve in the defence forces. He argued that it was reasonable to support the rights of individuals who depart from normal practice while opposing social policies and attitudes that weaken the two-parent heterosexual norm, thereby damaging society:

> I know hundreds of single mothers – some divorced or widowed, some never married. Many have earned my admiration for the way they have managed to raise strong, decent children with solid values. I would be appalled if anyone suggested withholding from these admirable women any opportunity or privilege based solely on their status as single mothers. And yet I'd worry about any policy that seemed likely to produce very many more single mothers – not because I don't like single mothers but because I have serious concerns for a society that does not see the importance of encouraging two-parent families. (Raspberry, 1993 p. A21.)

As the title of Raspberry's piece ('Courage to say the obvious') suggests, conservatives associate support for single parenthood and homosexuality with the so-called 'political correctness' movement. According to one British critic, the average Labour councillor is likely to endorse all of the following principles: 'the acceptance of homosexuality as a legitimate "option"; the marginalisation of marriage as a status-conferring choice, the acceptance and rewarding of illegitimacy, the advocacy of easy divorce, the feminist conception of women and their role' (Scruton 1997).

Gay parents, like single mothers, are represented as irresponsibly selfish individuals. In Britain, in the mid-1990s two gay men advertised for a surrogate mother so that they could have a child. One Conservative member of parliament opposed the move on the grounds that babies ought not to be used as 'pawns' that allowed individuals to 'gratify their emotions' (Vallely 1997). Australian social studies lecturer Brian Trainor is wary of an 'emerging adultist variety of gay ideology' that endorses 'the "right" of homosexual couples to have a family by means of reproductive technology as a legitimate lifestyle choice' (Trainor 1995, p. 42). Gay men and lesbians who want to be parents are just as 'selfish' as the heterosexual women who have followed in the footsteps of Murphy Brown.

Conservatives argue that it is bad for a child to be brought up by a parent or parents of only one sex. An important part of seeking the best for our children is to ensure that they are provided with appropriate role models: children need 'actually to experience a mother and father interacting with each other as husband and wife' (Trainor 1995, p. 42). Or, as one clergyman commented in relation to the two gay men seeking a child: 'It must be very confusing to have two mums and two dads' (*Guardian* 1997). The fear that haunts both homophobic and anti-illegitimacy campaigners is that children will be brought up in a non-heterosexual environment.

Widespread concern with the social impact of endemic fatherlessness betrays a fear that heterosexual culture is failing to reproduce itself. Conservatives argue that without a father a girl is likely to find it difficult to form 'comfortable and durable relations with men', while boys are at risk of engaging in activities traditionally considered feminine and 'playing like girls' (Zinsmeister 1993, p. 44). Sociologist David Popenoe expresses concern about the trend towards 'parental androgyny' and the suggestion that it is possible for 'daddies to become mommies'. Recognition of the 'very real biological differences between men and women' in aggression and activity levels, cognitive skills, sensory sensitivity and sexual and reproductive behaviour will result in better parenting and greater marital stability (Popenoe 1994). Complementary heterosexual partnerships based on these differences are, according to conservative logic, natural and genetically designed to perpetuate the species. To grow up into whole, properly functioning adults, children must have access to both male and female parenting styles. If children do not mature into respectable adults, society will suffer.

Illegitimacy debates suggest how deeply the homosexual/heterosexual divide permeates western culture. Eve Kosofsky Sedgwick's *Epistemology of the Closet* (1990) shows how the homosexual/

heterosexual binary opposition maps on to other dualisms basic to modern cultural organisation. These pairings, condensed in the figures of 'the closet' and 'coming out', include masculine/feminine, majority/minority, innocence/initiation, health/illness and same/ different (Sedgwick 1990, p. 72). I would add legitimacy/illegitimacy to these closeted pairings. The illegitimate/legitimate opposition in turn informs those of dangerous/safe, single/married, patholog- ical/normal, accidental/planned, maternal/paternal, profligate/ restrained, delinquent/disciplined, seduced/consented, casual/com- mitted, promiscuous/monogamous, unknowable/intelligible, igno- rant/informed, young/mature, reckless/responsible, transient/ permanent and corporeal/intellectual. Because the homosexual/ heterosexual binary is firmly affixed to that of the illegitimate/ legitimate, being gay or lesbian in our culture means being illegitimate. Acknowledging illegitimacy (either as a mother, father or offspring) does not imply a homosexual lifestyle but it often involves similar experiences of shame, secrecy, disclosure, pride and 'coming out'. A legitimate culture is, literally, a straight one.

Homosexuality and illegitimacy have different genealogies. Sedgwick traces the homosexual/heterosexual divide to the invention in western cultures of a medical model of homosexual social identity in the late nineteenth century. Illegitimacy, in the specific sense of a problem for society and for population management, emerged in the late eigh- teenth and early nineteenth century coincident with the emergence of statistical discourse. The prototypical illegitimate social identity, the 'mother of the illegitimate child', was female (compared with the homosexual figure, who was male) and had her origins in mid-nine- teenth-century medicine, philanthropy and social science. The illegiti- mate individual predated and may have provided one of the discursive templates for the making of the homosexual.

Philosopher Jenny Teichman argued in 1982 that what needed to be investigated were not the causes of illegitimacy but 'the institutions which give rise to the legitimate/illegitimate distinction' (Teichman 1982, p. 10). Opposition to illegitimacy functions covertly as support for its binary opposite – legitimacy. Martine Spensky's (1992) account of homes for unmarried mothers in 1950s England suggested that their adoption programs were designed to produce socially legitimate chil- dren, marriages and families. The legitimation project extends far beyond the individual family. What is legitimated by the concept of ille- gitimacy is western, white bourgeois culture itself.

Legitimacy nominally refers to being born in wedlock. However, legit- imate birth status can stand in for cultural legitimacy. As a consequence of their various discursive heritages, contemporary debates about natal illegitimacy are deeply coloured by, and to a certain extent just as much 'about', sexual, social and racial illegitimacy as they are about the failure to marry. From this perspective, natal illegitimacy becomes a social metaphor for all kinds of cultural deviance. Its opposite, natal legitimacy, stands for all that is socially normal, stable and natural.

The concept of illegitimacy makes possible the definition, not just of legitimate parenthood and legitimate family structure, but of culture itself. Far from being a meaningless remnant from the dead past or the signifier of a marginal form of human reproduction, the notion of illegitimacy continues to be crucial to how modern western cultures define their own legitimacy. The ideal legitimate culture can only be white, of Anglo origin, racially pure, rational, intelligent, middle-class, Christian, sexually continent, financially prudent, law-abiding, monogamous, married and heterosexual. Irrespective of whether any given individual is born in or out of wedlock, if they fail to adhere to any of these tenets their legitimacy as a citizen and their right to call themselves a member of 'normal society' is placed in question. The greater the number of transgressions, the more illegitimate a person becomes.

This discursive theory of cultural legitimacy differs from Malinowski's principle of legitimacy. Malinowski's theory proposed that it is a universal requirement in all societies that each child be legitimated by providing *him* with a father, whether natural or social. As Vicki Bell suggests in her analysis of a comparable anthropological concept, the incest prohibition, the legitimacy principle's 'existence and status are frequently taken for granted and assumed to be a fact of societies' (Bell 1993, p. 117). But there is no legitimacy principle intrinsic to society: legitimacy exists 'only to the extent that we talk about it' (1993, p. 123). Like the concept of 'incestuous desires' (1993, p. 119), the concept of the 'social father' as the key to cultural cohesion obscures the different political positioning of mothers and fathers, sons and daughters, within discourses of marriage, sexuality and the family. The legitimacy principle normalises heterosexual marriage and the idea that there are natural sex differences in parenting behaviour.

Discourse analysis proposes that the concept of legitimacy is not a universal principle but a specific historical product of western intellectual culture. Rather than serving to reinforce a social structure that is by nature legitimate, social condemnation of illegitimacy exposes a myriad of internal disturbances and quietly unresolved political tensions around race, class, gender, sexuality and colonialism. Making visible these internal fractures reveals the extent to which they actually constitute the cultural fabric itself. The discursive activity that threatens to rent that fabric apart is precisely what propels its constant remaking as an image of the legitimate.

Although my argument here is heavily dependent on discourse analysis, it differs in some respects from a conventional Foucauldian interpretation of the function of sexual discourses. The persistent western determination to name, know and control illegitimacy through a proliferation of intellectual and practical strategies could be seen as one of Foucault's biopolitical techniques of population management (Foucault [1976] 1981). Within such an explanatory schema, anti-illegitimacy statements become a means of channelling, regulating and managing individual sexual and reproductive behaviour to produce 'legitimate' populations. The self-government thesis stresses the negative constraints exerted by discursive forces on human practices and tends to represent discourse as a particularly covert and refined technique of social control. Foucault does consider the productive potential of discourse: for example, in his argument that there emerged in the nineteenth century, not repression of sexuality but a positive explosion of speech about sex. But for Foucault those multiple discursive constructions ultimately set limits on thinking about sex and sexual identities. According to the regulatory framework set up in *The History of Sexuality vol. 1* ([1976] 1981), the main function of the ongoing conversation about the illegitimacy problem is to persuade citizens through non-coercive means to conform to the two-parent norm.

Biopolitical interpretations run the risk of reducing illegitimacy's richly variegated discursive history to a single explanatory apex that stresses discourse's repressive effects. Rather than viewing the discursive process as one that primarily inhibits the full range of possible human actions, the construction of social problems can be conceptualised as a mechanism by which certain socially validated actions, values and beliefs are given shape and meaning. From this productive perspective, social inquiry's engagement with the illegitimacy problem may have reinforced the nuclear family ideal but, just as significantly, it actively and energetically made the various illegitimacy problems and thereby defined what constitutes a legitimate culture.

Social–scientific inquiries, in particular, lent authority to the legitimising process. Social science is, by definition, concerned with ordering the world according to social categories such as socioeconomic status, racial origin, intellectual ability, religion, marital status and sexual identity. In so doing it inevitably draws distinctions between centre and margin, normal and abnormal. Social scientists' habitual presentation of their work as rational and objective, at least until very recently, has given its constructions of society and its problems considerable weight. Political debate depends heavily upon social–scientific accreditation. Those in power and those who seek power – politicians, bureaucrats, political activists, dinner-party ideologues – selectively appropriate the language of social–scientific truth (by drawing on statistics, referring to relevant research studies or quoting the ideas of reputable scholars) to further their own particular political goals.

Canadian philosopher and political theorist John Ralston Saul argues that the social sciences are fully implicated in the corporatism that, he argues, dominates modern western societies. In *The Unconscious Civilization* (1997) Saul proposes that a corporatist society such as ours adheres firmly to the ideals of reason, certainty, absolute values and efficiency. It has implicit faith in, and is dictated to by, the discipline of economics: hence, in corporatist rhetoric, the market is destiny. The ultimate source of political legitimacy in a corporatist regime is the group – not God, not kings, as in the past, not the individual citizenry acting as a whole as it might be – but individual corporations.

The corporatist elite, Saul argues, sends up what amounts to an ideological smokescreen of jargon. Each group has its own specialised language, or dialect. There is, for example, a medical dialect, a linguist dialect, an artist dialect. 'Thousands and thousands of them', says Saul, 'purposely impenetrable to the non-expert, with thick defensive walls that protect each corporation's sense of importance' (Saul 1997, p. 49). Obscurity suggests complexity, which suggests authority. The core of this disease is to be found in what Saul calls the well-intentioned, potentially useful false sciences, the social sciences. In place of scientific evidence the social sciences are 'obliged to pile up overwhelming weights of documentation relating to human action – none of which is proof, little of it even illustration'. Social scientists have to work with circumstantial evidence that they subsequently establish as a social truth (1997, pp. 71–2). Social–scientific dialect encourages the passivity and social conformity that characterise the 'unconscious' state of contemporary civilisation.

Where Saul presents the social–scientific dialect as monolithic, I want to stress the internal heterogeneity of social–scientific language on any given social problem. Eugenics, psychology, psychoanalytic theory, quantitative sociology and brain science all, in certain circumstances, come under the social science umbrella, but each has a distinct way of talking about illegitimate births – each is a sub-dialect, perhaps. And, as I have shown, the credibility that social scientists accord particular varieties of 'circumstantial evidence' changes over time. So if social science is a corporation in Saul's sense, it is a corporation in a constant state of flux and an active site of border disputes, changes in position, adaptation and self-criticism.

Saul's analysis of the corporatist character of social science is only the latest move in a long tradition of criticism directed at social–scientific positivism. Much of Foucault's work (for example 1973, [1975] 1991) shows how various forms of scientific knowledge and their associated practices have functioned in a disciplinary and therefore political fashion. Particularly as a consequence of poststructuralist criticism, social inquiry is under siege. The sciences and human sciences as we know them have until now been conducted in the Enlightenment faith that a complete and properly conducted pursuit of social knowledge will inevitably lead to social justice. As Jane Flax (1992) argues, western culture is now sceptical of the rationalist project. We have reached 'the end of innocence' in social inquiry.

What then is illegitimacy's future? Can we take heart from Foucault's observation that we are witnessing the end of the modern episteme based on the assumption that Man can be known empirically (Foucault 1973, p. 385)? Conceivably the modernist distinction between legitimate and illegitimate birth will become redundant with the growth of postmodern scepticism or simply with increasing numbers of ex-nuptial births. On the other hand, illegitimacy's long history as an inherently problematic social phenomenon, and its important function in defining cultural legitimacy, make its complete erasure from public discourse unlikely, at least in the short term.

In that case, feminism will need to develop strategies that will be effective in a post-innocence discursive climate. Feminism might reconsider the extent of its commitment to positivist social science and structuralism. Countering one set of statistics with another, pointing out empirical inaccuracies and distortions, revealing flawed methodologies or providing alternative sets of facts, is not, in certain circumstances, without political value. It is just that this process of contestation over the nature of 'reality' is inevitable, interminable and ultimately unresolvable. Dispute and methodological refinement is part-and-parcel of what the social sciences are all about and highly predictable. Any opposition to the dominant paradigm is in danger of being trumped at the last moment by those whose power is legislative, as was recently demonstrated in the United States welfare debate. Shifts in perspective do happen, and contestation may result in an internal rearrangement of the discursive territory, but only rarely is external ground gained. Empirical engagements between conservatives and feminists can too easily be dismissed by opponents as scholarly squabbles, minor territorial disputes and professional point-scoring.

Feminism has been one of the driving forces behind the twentieth-century move towards a value-free social science, but even the most 'scientifically neutral' accounts of single parenthood cannot help but hint at the problem's nineteenth-century moral heritage. A moral schema lies behind statistics that differentiate marital from non-marital births. A certain normative view of the family informs the common assumption of feminists and the liberal welfare sector that the problems of female-headed households are structural – that is, their disadvantages are the result of economic and social inequalities.

As Joy Puls suggests, conservatives and their opponents share a remarkably similar vision of the 'broken family' as a structural problem. Even feminist-oriented research implies, if grudgingly, that 'single parent families would be better off if they weren't single parent families' (Puls 1996a, p. 19). Intentionally or not, the considerable research output of the feminist–liberal social science establishment, much of which points to the negative effects on children, has contributed to the widespread concern over family breakdown. In this sense, Puls argues, feminist as well as non-feminist empirical studies implicitly support the nuclear family form. The nuclear family constitutes the 'unmoving reference point', the centre of meaning, in relation to which any difference is automatically problematised (Puls 1996b, p. 6). Feminist thought inadvertently constructs single parenthood primarily in terms of disadvantage, deprivation or as the consequence of male irresponsibility, thereby helping to entrench the normalcy and desirability of the nuclear family form. Puls suggests that feminism could more usefully critique the manner in which the traditional family – and, I would add, heterosexuality – centres meaning and marginalises others (1996b, p. 10).

Social inquiry's persistent attempts over the past two centuries to 'measure immorality' have played a large part in the implicit privileging of the heterosexual nuclear family. Feminist social inquiry wants to distance itself from its conservative 'other', but can do so only partially because it relies on the same techniques, methodologies, disciplinary rules, and – perhaps most importantly – the same vocabulary. In Jean-Francois Lyotard's terms ([1979] 1984), no matter what their political allegiances, social scientists play the same language game. The extent to which feminism can deviate from the social–scientific norm is constrained by its adherence to an intellectual–moral heritage which it shares with conservatives and liberals. The contest over women's reproductive rights is consequently enacted as a series of empirical skirmishes. If positivist approaches cannot be abandoned entirely, they might be limited to specific local engagements where a resort to 'facts and figures' is unavoidable. As a universal strategy or epistemological position, however, the inherent value of feminist social science can no longer be assumed.

Since the early 1980s poststructuralist feminists have shown that it is possible for feminists to intervene in public debates affecting women without having to depend on moral categories and hidden heterosexual centres of meaning. Poststructuralist methods are generally occupying more space in the academy, a development that conservative social scientists find worrying. It is not coincidental that social scientists concerned with the loss of moral standards are also opposed to what they see as the loss of value judgements and structuralist certainties and the rise of relativism in their own disciplines (for example, Himmelfarb 1997). Positivism and a moralistic world view go together. Himmelfarb directly equates postmodernism with the demoralisation of society evident in high rates of illegitimacy (Himmelfarb 1994–5, p. 43), suggesting the extent to which the study of illegitimacy is a modernist enterprise.

Critical interventions into the illegitimacy debate would ideally uncouple the relationship between morals and facts. Like Puls, I would urge feminists to consider strategies that avoid problematising single parenthood, even in sympathetic and politically supportive ways, and instead to try to positively disassemble the category itself. The starting point of this de-problematising project would be to affirm the right of a single woman to bear a child and to make public discourse and government policy recognise that 'female-headed families are a viable, normal, and permanent family form, rather than something broken and deviant that policy should eradicate', as Iris Marion Young (1994, p. 90) puts it. Young's proposals for changes that would 'make single motherhood normal' are conventionally economic and policy related in character: the state provision of job training, employment opportunities, child care, education, accommodation and physical support schemes; programs which make fathers pay child support and encourage them to be actively involved in their child's upbringing; and acceptance of the principle that the whole community has a responsibility for the welfare of children.

The normalisation of single-parent families should, just as importantly, proceed at a discursive level by questioning, for example, the need for statistical demographic categories that separate nuptial from ex-nuptial children, and single-parent from two-parent families. A balance needs to be kept between de-problematising single motherhood, on the one hand and, on the other, ensuring that individual single mothers receive the full measure of state and public support they deserve. Nevertheless, there seems no reason why single-parent families could not be included in groups deemed disadvantaged by virtue of their income level, housing or transport usage, access to social services or other categories that do not refer to marital status. What single-parent families have in common, economically and socially, with other disadvantaged groups might be stressed more than what is perceived to be especially problematic about their situation. Instead of getting caught up in the problematisation of single parenthood, feminists and the social welfare sector might think about what needs to be done to make single parenthood not a problem.

Those who are more creatively inclined might turn their attention to the language of illegitimacy and how it might be deliberately and perversely refigured. Can illegitimacy mean power (for women) instead of a problem (for society)? In her famous 'Manifesto for cyborgs' ([1985] 1990), Donna Haraway uses what de Certeau might call 'tactics' and what Foucault might call 'reverse discourse' to refigure illegitimacy as a positive symbol of disruption. Haraway's cyborg is an insubordinate, destabilising, subversive figure. It is a hybrid creature, part ourselves, part machine. Cyborgs are 'the illegitimate offspring of militarism and patriarchal capitalism, not to mention state socialism'. But, Haraway points out, 'illegitimate offspring are often exceedingly unfaithful to their origins. Their fathers are, after all, inessential' ([1985] 1990, p. 193). Not only does the postmodern illegitimate attach little consequence to the absence of a father, as Haraway indicates, it flouts the law of permanent heterosexual coupling. The hybrid illegitimate cyborg is more than likely queer.

Such playful reversals of meaning are more likely to happen in the non-scientific realm of fiction, art and performance than within the constraints of critical discourse. In a postmodern world there may be more to be gained by re-imagining immorality than by continuing to measure it.

References

Acton, William 1859, 'Observations on illegitimacy in the London parishes of St. Marylebone, St. Pancras, and St. George's, Southwark, during the year 1857: deduced from the returns of the Registrar-General', *Journal of the Statistical Society of London* 22: 491–505.

Adelson, Pamela L., Frommer, Michael S., Pym, Margaret A. and Rubin, George L. 1992, 'Teenage pregnancy and fertility in New South Wales: an examination of fertility trends, abortion and birth outcomes', *Australian Journal of Public Health* 16 (3): 238–44.

Adair, Richard 1996, *Illegitimacy and Marriage in Early Modern England, Manchester and New York*, Manchester, Manchester University Press.

Adler, Jerry 1996, 'Building a better dad', *Newsweek* 17 June: 58–64.

Allan, Robert Marshall 1928, 'Report on maternal mortality and morbidity in the State of Victoria', *Medical Journal of Australia* 2 June: 668–84.

Anderson, Digby (ed.) 1992, *The Loss of Virtue: Moral Confusion and Social Disorder in Britain and America*, [printed in the United States of America, no place of publication], Social Affairs Unit.

Anderson, Margo 1992, 'The history of women and the history of statistics', *Journal of Women's History* 4 (1): 14–36.

Appignanesi, Lisa and Forrester, John 1992, *Freud's Women*, New York, Basic Books.

Arndt, Bettina 1993, 'When baby comes first', *Weekend Australian* 13–14 November: 23.

— 1996, 'Time to make fathers matter', *Sydney Morning Herald* 30 July: 17.

Arney, William Ray and Bergen, Bernard J. 1984, 'Power and visibility: the invention of teenage pregnancy', *Social Science and Medicine* 18 (1): 11–19.

Ashby, Hugh T. 1922, *Infant Mortality*, 2nd edn, Cambridge, Cambridge University Press.

Atrash, Hani K., Koonin, Lisa M., Lawson, Herschel W., Franks, Adele L. and Smith, Jack C. 1990, 'Maternal mortality in the United States, 1979–1986', *Obstetrics and Gynecology* 76 (6): 1055–60.

Australasian Medical Gazette 1886, 'Private lying-in establishments', October: 23.

Australian Bureau of Statistics 1991, *Australia's One Parent Families*, Canberra, catalogue no. 2511.0.

— 1996, *Year Book Australia*, Canberra, catalogue no. 1301.0.

— 1997, *Births Australia 1995*, Canberra, catalogue no. 3301.0.

Australian Labor Party 1997, 'The story on families', at http://www.alp.org.au/news/97budfam.htm.

Australian Medical Journal 1879, [untitled news items], March: 145.

Baber, Ray E. 1955, Review of Leontine Young's *Out of Wedlock*, in *Marriage and Family Living* 17 (4): 377–9.

Bagnall, Diana 1994, 'Children of a lesser mode', *Bulletin* 8 March: 29–32.

— 1996, 'Higher anxieties. Crisis of confidence', *Bulletin* 1 October: 16–18.

Balls-Headley, Walter 1894, *The Evolution of the Diseases of Women*, London, Smith, Elder & Co.

Barber, Dulan 1975, *Unmarried Fathers*, London, Hutchison.

Barlow, T. W. Naylor 1916, 'Illegitimacy in relation to infant mortality', *Medical Officer* 17 June: 235–6.

Barnes, Annie E. 1917, 'The unmarried mother and her child', *Contemporary Review* 112: 556–9.

Basavarajappa, K. G. 1968, 'Premarital pregnancies and ex-nuptial births in Australia, 1911–66', *Australian and New Zealand Journal of Sociology* 4: 126–45.

Beale, Octavius Charles 1910, *Racial Decay. A Compilation of Evidence from World Sources*, Sydney, Angus & Robertson.

Beaver, William 1996, 'Illegitimacy and television', *Journal of Social, Political and Economic Studies* 21 (1): 101–11.

Bell, Robert R. 1966, *Premarital Sex in a Changing Society*, Englewood Cliffs NJ Prentice-Hall.

Bell, Shannon 1994, *Reading, Writing and Rewriting the Prostitute Body*, Bloomington, Indiana University Press.

Bell, Vicki 1993, *Interrogating Incest. Feminism, Foucault and the Law*, London and New York, Routledge.

Bennett, Trude 1992, 'Marital status and infant health outcomes', *Social Science and Medicine* 35 (9): 1179–87.

Bernstam, Mikhail S. and Swan, Peter L. 1989, *Malthus and the Evolution of the Welfare State: An Essay on the Second Invisible Hand*, Kensington, Australian Graduate School of Management, University of New South Wales, Working Paper 89–012.

Bernstein, Rose 1960, 'Are we still stereotyping the unmarried mother?', *Social Work* 5 (3): 22–8.

Besharov, Douglas J. 1994, 'Working to make welfare a chore', *Wall Street Journal* 9 February: A14.

Besharov, Douglas J. with Gardiner, Karen N. 1993, 'Teen sex: truth and consequences. Part 1', *American Enterprise* January/February: 52–9.

Besharov, Douglas J. and Sullivan, Timothy S. 1996, 'Welfare reform and marriage', *Public Interest* 125: 81–94.

Bethell, Tom 1996, 'We're not alright, Jack', *American Spectator* 29 (January): 20–1.

Bienstock, Ric Esther 1997, 'Ms Conceptions', television documentary program broadcast by the Australian Broadcasting Corporation, 6 May.

Bingham, Annie T. 1922–3, 'Determinants of sex delinquency in adolescent girls based on intensive studies of 500 cases', *Journal of the American Institute of Criminal Law and Criminology* 13: 494–586.

Bisset-Smith, George T. 1918, 'Illegitimacy: is it increasing? I. Views of yesterday and to-day', *Poor Law Magazine* 163–8. 'II. Illegitimacy and its causes. Some general observations', *Poor Law Magazine* 355–63.

Blaikie, Andrew 1993, *Illegitimacy, Sex, and Society. Northeast Scotland, 1750–1900*, Oxford, Clarendon Press.

— 1996, 'From "immorality" to "underclass": the current and historical context of illegitimacy', in Jeffrey Weeks and Janet Holland (eds), *Sexual Cultures. Communities, Values and Intimacy*, New York, St Martin's Press, pp. 115–36.

Blankenhorn, David 1995, *Fatherless America. Confronting Our Most Urgent Social Problem*, New York, Basic Books.

Blum, Linda M. and Deussen, Theresa 1996, 'Negotiating independent motherhood: working-class African–American women talk about marriage and motherhood', *Gender and Society* 10 (2): 199–211.

Bogert, Carroll 1997, 'Life with mother', *Newsweek* [European edn.] 20 January: 41–6.

Bork, Robert H. 1996, *Slouching Towards Gomorrah. Modern Liberalism and American Decline*, New York, Regan Books.

Bowen, Louise de Koven 1914, *A Study of Bastardy Cases. Taken from the Court of Domestic Relations in Chicago*, Chicago, Juvenile Protective Association of Chicago.

Bowlby, John 1952, *Maternal Care and Mental Health. A Report Prepared on Behalf of the World Health Organization as a Contribution to the United Nations Programme for the Welfare of Homeless Children*, Geneva, World Health Organization.

Brignell, Lyn 1990, 'Illegitimacy in New South Wales, 1875–1972', PhD thesis, University of Sydney.

Brindle, David 1993, 'Lone mothers face benefits onslaught', *Guardian Weekly* 14 November: 11.

— 1996, 'Defiance may cost lone mothers dear', *Guardian* 3 April: 6.

Brinton, Crane 1936, *French Revolutionary Legislation on Illegitimacy 1789–1804*, Cambridge, Harvard University Press, Harvard Historical Monographs no. 9.

British Medical Journal 1880a, [untitled news item], 23 October: 668.

— 1880b, 'Infant mortality at Worcester', 24 April: 635.

— 1881, 'Protection of infant life', 12 March: 400.

— 1882, 'Illegitimacy in Salford', 25 February: 282.

Broder, David S. 1994, 'Illegitimacy: an unprecedented catastrophe', *Washington Post* 22 June: A21.

Browning, Don 1996, 'Diagnosis, maybe; solution, no', Symposium on Illegitimacy and Welfare, *Society* 33 (5): 28–9.

Brownlee, John 1926, 'On the probability that the distribution of illegitimacy in the British Isles depends upon survival from definite racial invasions', *Man* 26 (119): 181–4.

Brumberg, Joan Jacobs 1984, ' "Ruined girls": changing community responses to illegitimacy in upstate New York 1890–1920', *Journal of Social History* 18: 247–72.

Burbank, Victoria K. 1989, 'Premarital sex norms: cultural interpretations in an Australian Aboriginal Community', *Ethos* 15 (2): 226–34.

Burman, Sandra and Preston-Whyte, Eleanor 1992 (eds), *Questionable Issue: Illegitimacy in South Africa*, Cape Town, Oxford University Press.

Burman, Sandra and van der Spuy, Patricia 1996, 'The illegitimate and the illegal in a South African city: the effects of apartheid on births out of wedlock', *Journal of Social History* 29 (3): 613–35.

Burns, Ailsa and Scott, Cath 1994, *Mother-Headed Families and Why They Have Increased*, Hillsdale NJ, Lawrence Erlbaum Associates.

Butler, Judith 1993, *Bodies That Matter. On the Discursive Limits of 'Sex'*, New York and London, Routledge.

Butts, Robert Y. and Sporakowski, Michael J. 1974, 'Unwed pregnancy decisions: some background factors', *Journal of Sex Research* 10 (2): 110–17.

Calverton, V. F. and Schmalhausen, Samuel D. (eds) 1930, *The New Generation. The Intimate Problems of Modern Parents and Children*, London, George Allen & Unwin.

Campbell, Beatrix 1993, *Goliath. Britain's Dangerous Places*, London, Methuen.

Canberra Times 1995, 'New baby thrown out of window', 7 January: 7.

Capp, W. M. 1890, 'Statistics of illegitimate births', *Medical and Surgical Reporter* LXIII: 424–6.

Carmichael, Gordon A. 1995, 'From floating brothels to suburban semi-respectability: two centuries of nonmarital pregnancy in Australia', *Working Papers in Demography* no. 60, Research School of Social Sciences, Australian National University, Canberra.

Carr Brown, David 1997, *Dispatches – The Blair Project*, Four Corners, Australian Broadcasting Corporation television program, 19 May.

Cass, Bettina 1993, 'Sole parent family policy in Australia: income support and labour market issues', *Social Policy Journal of New Zealand* 1 (November): 3–16.

Cass, Bettina, Wilkinson, Marie and Webb, Anne, with the assistance of Caggegi, Carmel and Whitfield, Emma 1992, *The Economic, Labour Market and Social Circumstances of Sole Parents of Non-English Speaking Backgrounds: Implications for the Development of Social Policies to Enhance Education, Training and Employment Opportunities. Final Report to the Office of Multicultural Affairs*, Canberra, Australian Government Publishing Service.

Chaille, Stanford E. 1879, 'State medicine and state medical societies', *Transactions of the American Medical Association* 30: 305–6.

Chapman, Stephen 1991, 'Mere money won't solve our infant mortality problem', *Chicago Tribune* 31 March: 3.

Chesser, Eustace 1947, *Unwanted Child*, London and New York, Rich & Cowan.

—— 1965, *Unmarried Love*, London, Jarrolds.

Chicago Tribune 1994, 'The coming apart of America' (editorial), 23 July: 18.

Chidester, David 1992, 'The politics of exclusion: Christian images of illegitimacy', in Sandra Burman and Eleanor Preston-Whyte (eds), *Questionable Issue. Illegitimacy in South Africa*, Cape Town, Oxford University Press, pp. 145–70.

Chira, Susan 1994, 'In the name of the father', *New York Times*, reproduced in *Sydney Morning Herald* 20 June: 9.

Church of England, Board for Social Responsibility of the National Assembly 1966, *Fatherless by Law? The Law and the Welfare of Children Designated Illegitimate*, London.

Clothier, Florence 1943, 'Psychological implications of unmarried parenthood', *American Journal of Orthopsychiatry* 13: 531–49.

Coglan, T. A. 1889–90, *The Wealth and Progress of New South Wales*, Sydney, Government Printer.

—— 1903, *The Decline of the Birth-Rate of New South Wales and Other Phenomena of Child-Birth. An Essay in Statistics*, Sydney, Government Printer.

Condit, Celeste Michelle 1990, *Decoding Abortion Rhetoric. Communicating Social Change*, Urbana and Chicago, University of Illinois Press.

Consumer Contact 1992, *The Women's View. Market Research Study on Women's Perceptions of Themselves and Government Programs and Policies*. Conducted for the Office of the Status of Women, Department of the Prime Minister and Cabinet, Sydney.

Cook, Lady C. (Tennessee Celeste, 'née Tennessee Claflin') *c* 1890, 'Illegitimacy', *Essays on Social Topics*, Gerritsen Collection of Women's History microfiche B584, pp. 70–85. Reprinted in ?1898, *Lady Cook's Talks and Essays*, vol. 3, London, National Union Publishing Co.

— 1900, *Children of Scorn and Medical Papers*, London, National Union Publishing Co.

Cook, Margaret 1994, 'Beer pressure – getting a handle on teenage drinking', *Age* 5 September (Reuters News Service).

Cowlishaw, Gillian 1978, 'Infanticide in Aboriginal Australia', *Oceania* XLVIII (4): 262–83.

Cramond, William 1888, *Illegitimacy in Banffshire: Facts, Figures and Opinions*, Banff, Banffshire Journal Office (reprinted from the *Banffshire Journal* 10, 17, 24 and 31 January, 7 and 14 February 1888).

Crisp, Lyndall 1990, 'The underclass: Australia's social time bomb', *Bulletin* 3 April: 48–56.

Cullen, M. J. 1975, *The Statistical Movement in Early Victorian Britain. The Foundations of Empirical Research*, New York, Harvester Press.

Cummings, Peter, Theis, Mary Kay, Mueller, Beth A. and Rivara, Frederick P. 1994, 'Infant injury death in Washington State, 1981 through 1990', *Archives of Pediatrics and Adolescent Medicine* 148 (October): 1021–6.

Curgenven, John Brendon 1871, *On the Laws of France Relating to Illegitimate Children, Foundlings and Orphans*, London, Head, Hole & Co.

Curthoys, Ann 1989, 'Eugenics, feminism, and birth control: the case of Marion Piddington', *Hecate* 15 (1): 73–89.

Cutright, Phillips 1971, 'Illegitimacy: myths, causes and cures', *Family Planning Perspectives* 3 (1): 26–48.

Dahlgren, Elza Virginia 1940, 'Attitudes of a group of unmarried mothers toward the Minnesota Three Months' Nursing Regulation and its application', MA thesis, University of Minnesota.

Daily Telegraph 1997a, 'Absent fathers to blame for rise in crime, says report', 2 January: 12.

— 1997b, 'Editorial – Thank Evans', 6 March: 25.

Daley, Janet 1997, 'New Labour – the party of the single-parent family', *Daily Telegraph* 8 July: 20.

Daley, Paul 1997, 'MP slams women's "children for profit"', *Sunday Age* 2 February: 3.

Daly, Anne 1992, 'Replacement ratios for female single sole parents: the position of Aboriginal women', *Australian Bulletin of Labour* 18 (4): 297–311.

Danforth, W. C. 1940, 'The doctor and the unmarried mother', *Illinois Medical Journal* 77: 588–92.

Darwin, Major Leonard 1918, *Divorce and Illegitimacy*, London, Eugenics Education Society.

Davidson, Kenneth 1997, 'Which families? Exposing the Lyons Forum', *Australian Rationalist* 43: 2–7.

Davies, Christie 1992, 'Moralization and demoralization: a moral explanation for changes in crime, disorder and social problems', in Digby Anderson (ed.), *The Loss of Virtue: Moral Confusion and Social Disorder in Britain and America*, UK, Social Affairs Unit, pp. 1–13.

Davis, James E. 1904, 'Illegitimacy an economic problem', *Journal of the America Medical Association* 42 (30 April): 1135–8.

Davis, Kingsley 1939a, 'Illegitimacy and social structure', *American Journal of Sociology* 45 (2): 215–33.

— 1939b, 'The forms of illegitimacy', *Social Forces* 18 (1): 77–89.

Day, Phyllis J. 1977, 'The scarlet "W": public welfare as sexual stigma for women', *Journal of Sociology and Social Welfare* 4 (6): 872–81.

Deacon, Desley 1985, 'Political arithmetic: the nineteenth-century Australian census and the construction of the dependent woman', *Signs* 11 (1): 27–47.

— 1989, *Managing Gender. The State, the New Middle Class and Women Workers 1830–1930*, Melbourne, Oxford University Press.

Dean, Mitchell 1991, *The Constitution of Poverty. Toward a Genealogy of Liberal Governance*, London and New York, Routledge.

de Certeau, Michel 1986, *Heterologies. Discourse on the Other*, Manchester, Manchester University Press.

— 1988, *The Writing of History*, New York, Columbia University Press.

Delamarter, Walter 1962, 'Values and goals of youth in our culture: their impact on the problem of illegitimacy among adolescents', paper presented at the National Conference on Social Welfare, 31 May, New York City.

DeLamater, John and MacCorquodale, Patricia 1979, *Premarital Sexuality. Attitudes, Relationships, Behavior*, Madison, University of Wisconsin Press.

Dennis, Norman and Erdos, George 1993, *Families Without Fatherhood*, 2nd edn, London, Institute of Economic Affairs.

Detroit News and Free Press 1995, 'The crisis of public order', 15 July: 5.

Deutsch, Helene 1945, *The Psychology of Women. A Psychoanalytic Interpretation*, vol. 2, New York, Grune & Stratton.

Dickerson, Bette J. (ed.) 1995, *African American Single Mothers. Understanding Their Lives and Families*, Thousand Oaks, Sage Publications.

Dixon, Sue-Graham 1981, *Never Darken My Door. Working for Single Parents and their Children*, London, National Council for One Parent Families.

Doherty, Sheelagh 1995, 'Single mothers: a critical issue', *Feminism and Psychology* 5 (1): 105–11.

Douglas, David C. (ed.) 1959, *English Historical Documents vol 11. 1783–1832*, London, Eyre & Spottiswoode.

Dowd, Nancy E. 1997, *In Defense of Single-Parent Families*, New York and London, New York University Press.

Dublin Review 1858, 'Child murder – obstetric morality', 45 (September): 4–106.

Ducrocq, Francoise 1986, 'From Poor Law to jungle law: sexual relations and marital strategies (London, 1850–1870)', in Judith Friedlander, Blanche Wiesen Cook, Alice Kessler-Harris and Carroll Smith-Rosenberg (eds), *Women in Culture and Politics: A Century of Change*, Bloomington, Indiana University Press, pp. 32–51.

Duffy, Michael 1996, 'Who is John Howard and why are they saying these things about him?', *Independent Monthly* (February): 28–37.

Duvall, Evelyn Millis 1966, *Why Wait Till Marriage?*, London, Sydney, Auckland and Toronto, Hodder & Stoughton.

Eberstadt, Nicholas 1988, 'Is illegitimacy a public health hazard?', *National Review* 40 (25) 30 December: 36–9.

— 1989, 'Out of wedlock and into danger?', *Los Angeles Times* 3 November: 7.

— 1991a, 'America's infant-mortality puzzle', *Public Interest* 105: 30–47.

— 1991b, 'Why are so many American babies dying?', *American Enterprise* 2 (5): 37–45.

— 1994, 'Why babies die in D.C.', *Public Interest* 115: 3–16.

— 1996, 'Prosperous paupers and affluent savages', *Society* 33 (2): 17–25.

Edelman, Murray 1988, *Constructing the Political Spectacle*, University of Chicago Press.

Eden, Sir Frederick Morton [1797] 1966, *The State of the Poor; Or An History of the Labouring Classes in England. A Facsimile of the 1797 Edition*, London, Frank Cass.

Edgar, Patricia 1996, 'Thinking with the heart' (review of *Emotional Intelligence*), *Weekend Australian*, review section, 30–31 March: 7.

Ellis, Havelock 1912, *The Task of Social Hygiene*, London, Constable.

Ellwood, David T. 1996, 'The end of work', *New Republic* 12 August: 19.

Emerick, Sarah J., Foster, Laurence R. and Campbell, Douglas T. 1986, 'Risk factors for traumatic infant death in Oregon, 1973 to 1982', *Pediatrics* 77 (4): 518–22.

Encyclopaedia Britannica 1771, 1791, 1854, 1875, 1910, 1929, 1958, 1964.

Encyclopaedia of Religion and Ethics 1914 [latest imp. 1971], Edinburgh, T. & T. Clark.

Encyclopaedia of the Social Sciences 1932, New York, Macmillan.

Engels, Frederick [1884] 1942, *The Origin of the Family, Private Property and the State, in the Light of the Researches of Lewis H. Morgan*, Sydney, Current Book Distributors.

Ensor, George 1818, *An Inquiry Concerning the Population of Nations; Containing a Refutation of Mr. Malthus's Essay on Population*, London, Effingham Wilson.

Etzioni, Amitai 1993, *The Spirit of Community. Rights, Responsibilities, and the Communitarian Agenda*, New York, Crown Publishers.

Everett, Alexander [1826] 1994, *New Ideas on Population: With Remarks on the Theories of Malthus and Godwin*, 2nd edn, London, Routledge/Thoemmes Press.

Fagan, Patrick F. 1996, 'Disintegration of the family is the real root cause of violent crime', *USA Today* (May): 36–8.

Farr, William 1877, 'On some doctrines of population', *Journal of the Statistical Society of London*, December: 568–81.

Field, Frank 1995, *Making Welfare Work: Reconstructing Welfare for the Millenium*, London, Institute of Community Studies.

Finch, Lynette 1993, *The Classing Gaze. Sexuality, Class and Surveillance*, St Leonards, Allen & Unwin.

Firth, Raymond 1957, 'Introduction: Malinowski as scientist and as man', in Raymond Firth (ed.), *Man and Culture. An Evaluation of the Work of Bronislaw Malinowski*, London, Routledge & Kegan Paul, pp. 1–14.

Fisher, Arthur 1992, 'Sociobiology: science or ideology?', *Society* 29 (5): 67–79.

Fison, Lorimer and Howitt, A. W. [1880] 1967, *Kamilaroi and Kurnai: Group-Marriage and Relationship, and Marriage by Elopement. Drawn Chiefly from the Usage of the Australian Aborigines. Also the Kurnai Tribe. Their Customs in Peace and War*, Oosterhout, Anthropological Publications.

Flax, Jane 1992, 'The end of innocence', in Judith A. Butler and Joan W. Scott (eds), *Feminists Theorise the Political*, New York and London, Routledge, pp. 445–63.

Fletcher, David 1997, 'Sex education "is best way" to cut teen pregnancies', *Daily Telegraph* 15 February: 5.

Flowers, Rev. Field 1875, 'Infanticide', *National Association for the Promotion of Social Science. Transactions*: 366.

Forman, Rachel Zinober 1982, *Let Us Now Praise Obscure Women. A Comparative Study of Publicly Supported Unmarried Mothers in Government Housing in the*

United States and Britain, Washington DC, University Press of America.

Forrest, Alan 1981, *The French Revolution and the Poor*, Oxford, Basil Blackwell.

Forsyth, Craig J. and Palmer, C. Eddie 1990, 'Teenage pregnancy: health, moral and economic issues', *International Journal of Sociology of the Family* 20 (1): 79–95.

Forster, Colin and Hazlehurst, Cameron, n.d., *Australian Statisticians and the Development of Official Statistics*, Canberra, Australian Bureau of Statistics.

Foucault, Michel 1972, *The Archaeology of Knowledge and the Discourse on Language*, New York, Pantheon.

— 1973, *The Order of Things. An Archaeology of the Human Sciences* (A translation of *Les Mots et les Choses*), New York, Vintage Books.

— [1975] 1991, *Discipline and Punish. The Birth of the Prison*, London, Penguin.

— [1976] 1981, *The History of Sexuality vol. 1. An Introduction*, London, Penguin.

— 1977, *Language, Counter-Memory, Practice. Selected Essays and Interviews*, Oxford, Basil Blackwell.

— 1981, 'Questions of method: an interview with Michel Foucault, *I & C* 8: 3–14.

— 1988, *Politics, Philosophy, Culture. Interviews and Other Writings 1977–1984*, Lawrence D. Kritzman (ed.), New York and London, Routledge.

Fraser, James 1860, 'On the excessive infant mortality occurring in cities and large towns', *National Assocation for the Promotion of Social Science. Transactions*: 648–54.

Fraser, Nancy 1989, *Unruly Practices. Power, Discourse and Gender in Contemporary Social Theory*, Cambridge, Polity Press.

— and Gordon, Linda 1994, 'A genealogy of dependency: tracing a keyword of the U.S. welfare state', *Signs* 19 (2): 309–336.

Freeman, Rev. E. G. D. 1919, 'Illegitimacy, immorality and poverty', *Public Health Journal* 10 (July): 334–8.

Fuchs, Rachel G. 1992, *Poor and Pregnant in Paris. Strategies for Survival in the Nineteenth-Century*, New Brunswick, NJ, Rutgers University Press.

Furstenberg, Frank F. Jr. 1992, 'Illegitimacy', *Encyclopedia of Sociology*, New York and Toronto, Macmillan.

Fyffe, C. A. 1877, 'The punishment of infanticide', *Nineteenth Century* 1 (June): 583–95.

Gairdner, W. T. 1860, 'On infantile death rates, in their bearing on sanitary and social science', *National Association for the Promotion of Social Science. Transactions*: 632–48.

Gallagher, Ursula M. 1963, 'What of the unmarried parent?', *Journal of Home Economics* 55 (6): 401–5.

Gallichan, Mrs W. M. 1918, 'Notes on illegitimacy', *American Journal of Sexology* 14: 417–21 (see also Hartley, C. Gasquoine).

Gans, Herbert J. 1995, *The War Against the Poor. The Underclass and Antipoverty Policy*, New York, Basic Books.

Gartner, Rosemary 1991, 'Family structure, welfare spending and child homicide in developed democracies', *Journal of Marriage and the Family* 53 (February): 231–40.

Gebhard, Paul H., Pomeroy, Wardell B., Martin, Clyde E. and Christenson, Cornelia V. 1958, *Pregnancy, Birth and Abortion*, New York, Harper & Bros. and Paul B. Hoeber Inc.

Geronimus, Arline T. 1991, 'Teenage childbearing and social and reproductive disadvantage: the evolution of complex questions and the demise of simple answers', *Family Relations* 40: 463–71.

— Korenman, Sanders and Hillemeier, Marianne M. 1994, 'Does young maternal age adversely affect child development? Evidence from cousin comparisons in the United States', *Population and Development Review* 20 (3): 585–609.

Gibbs, Nancy 1994, 'The vicious cycle', *Time* 20 June: 25–33 (cover story).

Gigerenzer, Gerd, Swijtink, Zeno, Porter, Theodore, Daston, Lorraine, Beatty, John and Kurger, Lorenz 1989, *The Empire of Chance. How Probability Changed Science and Everyday Life*, Cambridge, Cambridge University Press.

Gill, Derek 1977, *Illegitimacy, Sexuality and the Status of Women*, Oxford, Blackwell.

Gillis, John R. 1979, 'Sevants, sexual relations and the risks of illegitimacy in London, 1801–1900', *Feminist Studies* 5 (1): 142–73.

Godwin, William 1820, *Of Population. An Enquiry Concerning the Power of Increase in the Numbers of Mankind. Being an Answer to Mr. Malthus's Essay on That Subject*, London, Longman, Hurst, Rees, Orme & Brown.

Goffman, Erving 1964, *Stigma. Notes on the Management of Spoiled Identity*, Englewood Cliffs NJ, Prentice Hall.

Goldstein, Jan 1984, 'Fouault among the sociologists: the "disciplines" and the history of the professions', *History and Theory* 23 (1): 170–92.

Goleman, Daniel 1996, *Emotional Intelligence. Why It Can Matter More Than IQ*, London, Bloomsbury.

Goode, William J. 1960, 'Illegitimacy in the Caribbean social structure', *American Sociological Review* 25 (1): 21–30.

— 1961, 'Illegitimacy, anomie, and cultural penetration', *American Sociological Review* 26 (6): 911–25.

— 1967, 'A policy paper for illegitimacy', in Mayer N. Zald (ed.), *Organizing for Community Welfare*, Chicago, Quadrangle Books, pp. 262–312.

Gordon, Linda 1994, *Pitied But Not Entitled. Single Mothers and the History of Welfare*, New York, Free Press.

Gordon, Ronald R. 1990, 'Postneonatal mortality among illegitimate children registered by one or both parents', *British Medical Journal* 300 (27 January): 236–7.

Gould, Stephen Jay 1995, 'Curveball', in Steven Fraser (ed.), *The Bell Curve Wars. Race, Intelligence, and the Future of America*, New York, Basic Books, pp. 11–22.

Grahame, James [1816] 1994, *An Inquiry into the Principle of Population*, London, Routledge and Thoemmes Press.

Grant, Linda 1993, 'Too little, too late', *Guardian* 5 July: 10–11.

Great Britain. National Birth Rate Commission 1920, *Problems of Population and Parenthood, Being the Second Report and the Chief Evidence Taken by the National Birth-Rate Commission, 1918–1920*, London, Chapman & Hall.

Grimes, David A. 1994, 'The morbidity and mortality of pregnancy: still risky business', *American Journal of Obstetrics and Gynecology* 170 (5, part 2): 1489–94.

Gross, Leonard 1960, 'Are we paying an illegitimacy bonus?', *Saturday Evening Post* 30 January: 30, 69–70.

Guardian 1997, 'Gay pair insist on right to "family child" ', 28 May: 3.

Guibord, Alberta S. B. and Parker, Ida R. 1922, *What Becomes of the Unmarried Mother? A Study of 82 Cases*, Boston, Research Bureau on Case Work.

Hacking, Ian 1990, *The Taming of Chance*, Cambridge, Cambridge University Press.

Haldane, Charlotte 1927, *Motherhood and its Enemies*, London, Chatto & Windus.

Hannan, Daniel 1997, 'I believe in masculinity', *Daily Telegraph* 22 February: 17.

Hannan, Martin 1997, 'Concern at teenage pregnancy', *Scotsman* 29 May: 4.

Haralambos, Michael, van Krieken, Robert, Smith, Philip and Holborn, Martin 1996, *Sociology. Themes and Perspectives. Australian Edition*, South Melbourne, Longman.

Haraway, Donna [1985] 1990, 'A manifesto for cyborgs: science, technology, and socialist feminism in the 1980s', in Linda J. Nicholson (ed.), *Feminism/Postmodernism*, New York and London, Routledge, pp. 190–233.

— 1989, *Primate Visions. Gender, Race and Nature in the World of Modern Science*, New York and London, Routledge.

— 1991, *Simians, Cyborgs, and Women. The Reinvention of Nature*, New York, Routledge.

Harding, Lorraine Fox 1993, ' "Alarm" versus "liberation"? Responses to the increase in lone parents', parts 1 and 2, *Journal of Social Welfare and Family Law* 2: 101–12; 3: 174–84.

Hartley, C. Gasquoine (Mrs W. M. Gallichan) 1914, 'The unmarried mother', *English Review* 18: 78–90.

— 1921, 'The child of the unmarried mother', *Nineteenth Century* September: 511–20.

Hartley, Shirley Foster1967, 'The amazing rise of illegitimacy in Great Britain', *Social Forces* (44): 533–45.

— 1975, *Illegitimacy*, Berkeley, University of California Press.

Hayami, Akira 1980, 'Illegitimacy in Japan', in Laslett et al. (eds), pp. 397–402.

Hazlitt, William 1807, *A Reply to the Essay on Population, by the Rev. T. R. Malthus. In a Series of Letters. To Which Are Added, Extracts from the Essay, with Notes*, London, Longman, Hurst, Rees & Orme.

Healey, Kaye (ed.) 1995, *Parenting. Issues for the Nineties vol. 39*, Sydney, Spinney Press.

Hein, H. A., Burmeister, L. F. and Papke, K. R. 1990, 'The relationship of unwed status to infant mortality', *Obstetrics and Gynecology* 76 (5, part 1): 763–8.

Heise, L. L. 1994, 'Gender-based violence and women's reproductive health', *International Journal of Gynecology and Obstetrics* 46: 221–9.

Hendrix, Lewellyn 1996, *Illegitimacy and Social Structure: Cross-Cultural Perspectives on Nonmarital Birth*, Westport Conn., Bergin & Garvey.

Herrnstein, Richard and Murray, Charles 1994, *The Bell Curve. Intelligence and Class Structure in American Life*, New York, Free Press.

Hewett, Jennifer 1996, 'Farewell to welfare: U.S. busts its bonds', *Sydney Morning Herald* 2 August: 13.

— 1997, 'Howard faces jobs crusade', *Sydney Morning Herald* 15 September: 17.

Higginbotham, Ann R. 1989, ' "Sin of the age": infanticide and illegitimacy in Victorian London', *Victorian Studies* 32 (3): 319–38.

Himmelfarb, Gertrude 1994–5, 'A de-moralized society: the British/American experience', *American Educator* 18 (4): 14–21, 40–3.

— 1995, *The De-Moralization of Society. From Victorian Virtues to Modern Values*, New York, Alfred A. Knopf.

— 1997, 'Beyond method', in Alvin Kernan (ed.), *What's Happening to the Humanities?*, Princeton, Princeton University Press, pp. 143–61.

Holden, Constance 1997, 'The power of IQ', *Science* 276 (13 June): 1651.

Holland, Steve 1997, 'Clinton launches strategy to stop teen pregnancies', 4 January (Reuter News Service).

Horn, Wade F. 1995, 'Why fathers count', interview in *Men's Health* September: 48, reproduced at http://www.execpc.com/wismen/wadehorn.html.

Hufton, Olwen H. 1974, *The Poor of Eighteenth Century France 1750–1789*, Oxford, Clarendon Press.

— 1992, *Women and the Limits of Citizenship in the French Revolution*, Toronto, University of Toronto Press.

Human Rights and Equal Opportunities Commission, Australia, 1997. *Bringing Them Home. Report of the National Inquiry into the Separation of Aboriginal and Torres Strait Islander Children from their Families*, Sydney, Human Rights and Equal Opportunities Commission.

Husband, W. D. 1864, 'Infant mortality', *National Association for the Promotion of Social Science. Transactions*: 498–508.

Hutchins, John H. 1940, *Jonas Hanway 1712–1786*, London, Society for Promoting Christian Knowledge.

Hyde, John 1994, 'Child casualties of the extended family', *Australian* 7 January: 9.

Ibister, Clair 1990, 'The family and children in the year 2000 or the basic unit of society', *Australian Family* 11 (1): 6–16.

Jacoby, Jeff 1994, 'Illegitimacy – a deadly risk for infants', *Boston Globe* 19 May: 19.

James, Patricia 1979, *Population Malthus. His Life and Times*, London, Boston and Henley, Routledge & Kegan Paul.

Jeffers, Camille 1971, 'The single-parent family: "blackenizing" the Scarlet Letter', in National Conference on Social Welfare, *Illegitimacy. Today's Realities*, New York, National Council on Illegitimacy, pp. 9–17.

Johnson, Boris 1995, 'The male sex is to blame for the appalling proliferation of single mothers', *Spectator* 19 August: 6.

Johnson, Lesley 1993, *The Modern Girl. Girlhood and Growing Up*, St Leonards, Allen & Unwin.

Johnson, Paul 1996, 'America stops throwing money at problems – a lesson for us too', *Spectator* 24 August: 8.

Johnston, Philip 1997, 'Blair tests the waters to cut £100bn bill – the welfare debate', *Daily Telegraph* 3 June: 4.

Jonas, Oswald, Roder, David and Chan, Annabelle 1992, 'The association of maternal and socioeconomic characteristics in metropolitan Adelaide with medical, obstetric and labour complications and pregnancy outcomes', *Australian and New Zealand Journal of Obstetrics and Gynaecology* 32 (1): 1–5.

Jones, Gareth Stedman 1996, 'The determinist fix: some obstacles to the further development of the linguistic approach to history in the 1990s', *History Workshop Journal* 42: 19–35.

Jones, Hugh R. 1894, 'The perils and protection of infant life', *Journal of the Royal Statistical Society* LVII (March, part 1): 1–103.

Jones, Michael 1993, 'Wedded to welfare – unmarried mothers', *Sunday Times* 11 July (Reuter Australasian Briefing).

Jopson, Debra 1995, 'Divorce rights push for Jewish women', *Sydney Morning Herald* 27 November (Reuters Business Briefing).

Jordens, Ann-Mari 1993, 'Migrant supporting mothers and the state 1938–54', *Women and the State*, special issue of *Journal of Australian Studies*, pp. 47–57.

Journal of the Statistical Society of London 1865, 'Infanticide and illegitimacy', September: 420–3.

Judge, Ken and Benzeval, Michaela 1993, 'Health inequalities: new concerns about the children of single mothers', *British Medical Journal* 306 (13 March): 677–80.

Jury, Louise 1994, 'EU survey has Britain third in list for illegitimacy', *Guardian* 25 May: 3.

Kammerer, Percy Gamble [1918] 1969, *The Unmarried Mother. A Study of Five Hundred Cases*, Montclair NJ, Patterson Smith.

— 1920, 'The social consequences of illegitimacy', *Social Hygiene* 6 (2): 161–80.

Kasanin, J. and Handschin, Sieglinde 1941, 'Psychodynamic factors in illegitimacy', *American Journal of Orthopsychiatry* 11: 66–84.

Kenworthy, Marion E. 1921, 'The mental hygiene aspects of illegitimacy', *Mental Hygiene* 5: 499–508.

Key, Ellen 1911, *Love and Marriage*, New York and London, G. P. Putnam & Sons.

— 1914, *The Renaissance of Motherhood*, New York and London, G. P. Putnam & Sons.

Kiely, Rosemary 1982, 'Single mothers and supermyths', *Australian Journal of Social Issues* 17 (2): 155–61.

Kingston, Margo 1996, 'Family policy anything but child's play', *Sydney Morning Herald* 1 February: 10.

Kirsta, Alix 1994, *Deadlier Than the Male. Violence and Aggression in Women*, London, HarperCollins.

Knapp, Patricia and Sophie T. Cambria 1947, 'The attitudes of Negro unmarried mothers towards illegitimacy', *Smith College Studies in Social Work* 17 (3): 185–203.

Krauthammer, Charles 1993, 'Defining deviancy up. The new assault on bourgeois life', *New Republic* 22 November: 20–5.

— 1994, 'The scourge of illegitimacy. 1. Stop the subsidy', condensed from *Washington Post*, *Reader's Digest* March: 49–50.

— 1995, 'A social conservative credo', *Public Interest* 121: 15–22.

Kunzel, Regina 1993, *Fallen Women, Problem Girls. Unmarried Mothers and the Professionalization of Social Work*, New Haven, Yale University Press.

— 1995, 'Pulp fictions and problem girls: reading and rewriting single pregnancy in the postwar United States', *American Historical Review* 100 (December): 1465–87.

LaCapra, Dominick 1989, *Soundings in Critical Theory*, Ithaca NY, Cornell University Press.

Lamb, Kevin 1995, 'The causal factors of crime: understanding the sub-culture of violence', *Mankind Quarterly* XXXVI (1): 105–16.

Lamm, Richard D. 1997, 'Why we must restigmatize the institution of illegitimacy', *Humanist* 57 (2) March/April: 35–6.

Lamont, Leonie 1997, 'Gay, lesbian families stand to be counted', *Sydney Morning Herald* 15 September: 3.

Lancet 1860, 'A way of help for the fallen', 4 February: 125.

— 1866, 'Infanticide: the Committee of the Harveian Society', 29 September: 367.

— 1867, 'Committee of the Harveian Society on Infanticide', 12 January: 61–3.

— 1881, 'Remarkable case of early maternity', 9 April: 601–2.

Lankester, Edwin 1867, 'Infanticide, with reference to the best means of its prevention', *National Association for the Promotion of Social Science. Transactions*: 216–24.

Lapham, Lewis H. 1997, 'In the garden of tabloid delight. Notes on sex, Americans, scandal, and morality', *Harper's Magazine* August: 35–43.

Laqueur, Thomas 1989, 'Bodies, details, and the humanitarian narrative', in Lynn Hunt (ed.), *The New Cultural History*, Berkeley, University of California Press, pp. 176–204.

Lasch, Christopher 1978, *The Culture of Narcissism. American Life in an Age of*

Diminishing Expectations, New York, W. W. Norton.

Laslett, Peter, Oosterveen, Karla, and Smith, Richard M. (eds) 1980, *Bastardy and its Comparative History. Studies in the History of Illegitimacy and Marital Nonconformism in Britain, France, Germany, Sweden, North America, Jamaica and Japan*, London, Cambridge Group for the History of Population and Social Structure.

Laster, Kathy 1989, 'Infanticide: a litmus test for feminist criminological theory', *Australian and New Zealand Journal of Criminology* 22 (3): 151–66.

— 1990, 'Infanticide and feminist criminology: "strong" or "weak" women', *Criminology Australia* 2 (1): 14–15, 18.

Laws, John 1997, 'Keep the bastards down', *Sunday Telegraph* 29 June: 49.

Laws, Sophie 1996, 'The "single mothers" debate: a children's rights perspective', in Janet Holland and Lisa Adkins (eds), *Sex, Sensibility and the Gendered Body*, Basingstoke and London, Macmillan Press, pp. 60–77.

Lecky, William Edward Hartpole [1877] 1892, *History of European Morals from Augustus to Charlemagne*, 10th edn, London, Longmans, Green & Co.

Leffingwell, Albert 1892, *Illegitimacy and The Influence of the Seasons Upon Conduct. Two Studies in Demography*, 2nd edn, London, Swan Sonnenschein & Co.

Legitimation League, London 1895, *The Bar Sinister and Licit Love. The First Biennial Proceedings of the Legitimation League*, Oswald Dawson (ed.), London, W. Reeves, microfilm copy in 'The History of Women' collection, no. 4440, Rutgers University Library.

Lenroot, Katharine F. 1921, 'Social responsibility for the protection of children handicapped by illegitimate birth', *Annals of the American Academy of Political and Social Science* 98 (November): 120–8.

— 1924, 'Social responsibility for the care of the delinquent girl and the unmarried mother', *Journal of Social Hygiene* 10 (2): 74–82.

'Lens' 1920, 'The unmarried mother', *New Statesman* 6 March: 639–40.

Lewis, Jane and Kiernan, Kathleen 1996, 'The boundaries between marriage, nonmarriage, and parenthood: changes in behavior and policy in postwar Britain', *Journal of Family History* 21 (3): 372–87.

Lewittes, Mendell 1994, *Jewish Marriage. Rabbinic Law, Legend, and Custom*, Northvale NJ and London, Jason Arsonson.

Link-Up (NSW) and Wilson, Tikka Jan 1997, *In the Best Interest of the Child? Stolen Children: Aboriginal Pain/White Shame*, Canberra, Australian National University, *Aboriginal History* monograph no. 4.

Litchfield, W. F. 1899, 'The infants under "The New South Wales Children's Protection Act", with some remarks on infants' asylums', *Australasian Medical Gazette* 20 January: 23–6.

Lowe, Charlotte 1927, 'The intelligence and social background of the unmarried mother', *Mental Hygiene* 11: 783–94.

Luff, David and Barnsley, Gail 1997, 'A nation of bastards', *Daily Telegraph* 23 September: 1–2.

Luker, Kristin 1996, *Dubious Conceptions. The Politics of Teenage Pregnancy*, Cambridge Mass. and London, Harvard University Press.

Lumley, W. G. 1862, 'Observations upon the statistics of illegitimacy', *Journal of the Statistical Society of London* 25: 219–74.

Lundberg, Emma O. 1918, 'The illegitimate child and war conditions', *American Journal of Physical Anthropology* 1 (3): 339–52.

— 1921, 'The illegitimate mother as a delinquency problem', *American Sociological Society. Papers Presented* 16 (December): 201–8.

— 1926, *Children of Illegitimate Birth and Measures for their Protection*, Washington,

US Department of Labor, Children's Bureau, Bureau Publication no. 166.

Lyotard, Jean-Francois [1979] 1984, *The Postmodern Condition: A Report on Knowledge*, Manchester, Manchester University Press.

McCloy, Shelby T. 1946, *Government Assistance in Eighteenth-Century France*, Durham NC, Duke University Press.

McGuinness, Padraic 1995, 'The true conservatives are those who deny our welfare policies have failed', *Sydney Morning Herald* 26 October (Reuters Australasian Briefing).

— 1996, 'Old-style families at a financial loss', *Sydney Morning Herald* 21 September: 34.

McIniscon, John 1825, *Principles of Political Economy, and of Population; Including an Examination of Mr. Malthus's Essay on Those Subjects*, London, Sherwood, Jones & Co.

Mackellar, Sir Charles 1903, *State Children's Bill and Infants' Protection Bill: Address by the Hon. C. K. Mackellar, MLC (President of the State Children Relief Board) to the Women's Progressive Association on 20th April, 1903, at the Sydney School of Arts*, Sydney, Government Printer.

Mackellar, Sir Charles and Welsh, D. A. 1917, *Mental Deficiency. Medico-Sociological Study of Feeble-Mindedness*, Sydney, Government Printer.

McLanahan, Sara and Sandefur, Gary 1994, *Growing Up With a Single Parent. What Hurts, What Helps*, Cambridge, Mass. and London, Harvard University Press.

McMurdo, Robin 1975, 'Pregnancy and suicide', *Modern Medicine of Australia* 17 February: 49–52.

Magnet, Myron 1992, 'The American family, 1992', *Fortune* 10 August: 56–61.

— 1993, *The Dream and the Nightmare. The Sixties' Legacy to the Underclass*, New York, William Morrow & Co.

Maley, Barry 1992, 'Babies – a national resource', *Australian Family* 13 (1): 20–9.

Maley, Barry, Berger, Brigitte, Morgan, Patricia, Sullivan, Lucy and Tapper, Alan 1996, *Home Repairs. Building Stronger Families to Resist Social Decay*, St Leonards, Centre for Independent Studies, Policy Forum no. 13.

Malinowski, Bronislaw [1913] 1969, *The Family Among the Australian Aborigines. A Sociological Study*, New York, Schocken Books.

— [1927] 1953, *Sex and Repression in Savage Society*, London, Routledge & Kegan Paul.

— 1929 'Kinship', *Encyclopaedia Britannica*, 14th edn.

— [1929] 1968, *The Sexual Life of Savages in North-Western Melanesia. An Ethnographic Account of Courtship, Marriage and Family Life Among the Natives of the Trobriand Islands, British New Guinea*, London, Routledge & Kegan Paul.

— 1930 'Parenthood – the basis of social structure', in Calverton and Schmalhausen (eds), *The New Generation. The Intimate Problems of Modern Parents and Children*, pp. 113–68.

— 1962 *Sex, Culture and Myth*, New York, Harcourt, Brace & World.

Mallet, Sir Bernard 1918, 'Vital statistics as affected by the war', *Journal of the Royal Statistical Society* 81 (1): 1–36.

Malthus, Thomas Robert [1803] 1986, *An Essay on the Principle of Population*, 6th edn (1826) with variant readings from the 2nd edn (1803), E. A. Wrigley and David Soudon (eds), London, William Pickering.

Mangold, George 1921, *Children Born Out of Wedlock. A Sociological Study of Illegitimacy, With Particular Reference to the United States*, Columbia, University of Missouri.

Marcus, Sharon 1992, 'Fighting bodies, fighting words: a theory and politics of rape prevention', in Judith Butler and Joan W. Scott (eds), *Feminists Theorise the Political*, New York and London, Routledge, pp. 385–403.

Mead, Lawrence M. 1992, *The New Politics of Poverty. The Nonworking Poor in America*, New York, HarperCollins.

— 1996, 'Welfare reform at work', *Society* vol. 33 (5): 37–40.

Meiss, Margaret L. 1952, 'The oedipal problem of a fatherless child', *The Psychoanalytic Study of the Child* 7: 216–29.

Meliora. A Quarterly Review of Social Science in its Ethical, Economical, Political and Ameliorative Aspects 1863, 'Infanticide and illegitimacy', 5: 323–42.

Mencken, Alice D. 1922, 'A social aspect of the unmarried mother', *Journal of Delinquency* 7 (2): 99–103.

Meyerson, Adam 1997, 'Family, faith, freedom – how conservatives can set the cultural agenda', *Policy Review* 83 (Reuters Business Briefing, Information Access Company Trade and Industry Database 15 May).

Mitchison, Rosalind and Leneman, Leah 1989, *Sexuality and Social Control, Scotland 1660–1780*, Oxford, Blackwell.

Moran, Alan and Chisholm, Andrew 1994, 'Welfare no substitute for a job', *Australian Financial Review* 12 July (Reuter Australasian Briefing).

Morgan, Patricia 1995, *Farewell to the Family? Public Policy and Family Breakdown in Britain and the USA*, London, Institute of Economic Affairs Health and Welfare Unit.

Morris, E. Sydney 1925, 'An essay on the causes and prevention of maternal morbidity and mortality', *Medical Journal of Australia* 2 (12 September): 301–45.

Morrison, Joseph L. 1965, 'Illegitimacy, sterilization, and racism. A North Carolina case history', *Social Service Review* 39 (1): 1–10.

Morton, Marian J. 1993, *'And Sin No More': Social Policy and Unwed Mothers in Cleveland, 1855–1990*, Columbus, Ohio University Press.

Moynihan, Daniel Patrick 1993, 'Defining deviancy down', *American Scholar* (Winter): 17–30.

Muehlenberg, Bill 1993, 'The case for two-parent families', *Australian Family* 14 (2): 3–17.

Mullins, Claud 1940, 'The illegitimate child', *Quarterly Review* 275 (545, July): 13–27.

Mullins, G. L. 1892, 'The registration of still-births and the protection of infants', *Intercolonial Medical Congress of Australasia*, third session: 605.

Murray, Charles 1984, *Losing Ground: American Social Policy, 1950–1980*, New York, Basic Books.

— 1989, 'The American experience with the welfare state', in Michael James (ed.), *The Welfare State. Foundations and Alternatives*, St Leonards, Centre for Independent Studies.

— 1993, 'Welfare and the family: the U.S. Experience', *Journal of Labor Economics* 11 (1, part 2): S224–62.

— 1994a, 'Does welfare bring more babies?', *American Enterprise* 5 (1): 54–9.

— 1994b, 'Society cannot tolerate illegitimacy', *Wall Street Journal*, reprinted in *St Croix Review* 27 (4): 61–5.

— 1994c, 'Underclass – the crisis deepens', *Sunday Times* 22 May (Reuters Australasian Briefing).

— 1995, 'The partial restoration of traditional society', *Public Interest* no. 121 (Fall): 122–34.

Murray, Charles with Frank Field, Joan C. Brown, Nicholas Deakin and Alan

Walker 1990, *The Emerging British Underclass*, London, Institute of Economic Affairs Health and Welfare Unit, Choice in Welfare Series no. 2.

Murray, David W. 1994, 'Poor suffering bastards', *Policy Review* 68: 9–15.

Nahan, Mike, Rutherford, Tony and Tapper, Alan 1993, *Reform and Recovery. An Agenda for the New Western Australian Government*, West Perth, Institute for Public Affairs.

Nathan, P. R. 1996, 'Is it necessary to be brutal?', *Society* vol. 33 (5): 15–16.

Nation. A Weekly Journal Devoted to Politics, Literature, Science and Art 1865, 'England – infanticide among the poor', 1 (31 August): 270–1.

National Council for One Parent Families 1986, *Illegitimate. The Experience of People Born Outside Marriage*, London.

National Office of Vital Statistics, United States Public Health Service 1947, *Vital Statistics of the United States 1945. Part 1*, Washington DC, US Government Printing Office.

Neubauer, Peter 1960, 'The one-parent child and his oedipal development', *The Psychoanalytic Study of the Child* 15: 286–309.

New Dictionary of Statistics 1911, London, George Routledge & Sons.

Newman, George 1906, *Infant Mortality. A Social Problem*, London, Methuen.

New Republic 1915, 'War babies', 8 May: 6.

New South Wales 1857, 1862, 1869,1895 *Annual Report from the Registrar-General on Vital Statistics*, Colonial microfiche series, Canberra, Australian Bureau of Statistics.

— 1900, *Statistician's Report on the Vital Statistics of New South Wales*, Colonial microfiche series, Canberra, Australian Bureau of Statistics.

New South Wales Legislative Assembly 1904, *Royal Commission on the Decline of the Birth-Rate and on the Mortality of Infants in New South Wales. Report. Vol. 1*, Sydney, Government Printer.

New York Academy of Medicine Committee on Public Health Relations, Ranson S. Hooker, Director of the Study, [1933] 1987, *Maternal Mortality in New York City. A Study of all Puerperal Deaths 1930–1932*, New York and London, Commonwealth Fund and Humphrey Milford, Oxford University Press.

Nixon, J. W. 1913–14, 'Some factors associated with the illegitimate birth-rate' *Journal of the Royal Statistical Society* LXXVII (July): 852–62.

Nottingham, Ruth D. 1937, 'A psychological study of forty unmarried mothers', *Genetic Psychology Monographs* 19: 155–228.

Omolade, Barbara 1994, *The Rising Song of African American Women*, New York and London, Routledge.

Osofsky, Howard J. 1968, *The Pregnant Teen-ager: A Medical, Educational and Social Analysis*, Springfield Ill., C. C. Thomas.

Page, Robert 1984, *Stigma*, London, Routledge & Kegan Paul.

Parr, Robert J. 1909, *Beyond the Law. Some Facts on Illegitimacy in Ireland*, London, National Society for the Prevention of Cruelty to Children.

Perrot, Jean-Claude and Woolf, Stuart J. 1984, *State and Statistics in France, 1789–1815*, New York, Harwood Publishers

Peuchet, Jacques et al. 1799, *Dictionnaire Universel de la Géographie Commercante*, Paris, Blanchon.

— 1815, *Sketch of the Geography, Political Economy and Statistics of France*, translated by James N. Taylor, Washington City, Joseph Milligan.

Phoenix, Ann 1993, 'The social construction of teenage motherhood: a black and white issue?', in Annette Lawson and Deborah L. Rhode (eds), *The Politics of Pregnancy. Adolescent Sexuality and Public Policy*, New Haven and

London, Yale University Press, pp. 74–97.

— 1996, 'Social constructions of lone motherhood. A case of competing discourses', in Silva (ed.), *Good Enough Mothering?* pp. 175–90.

Piddington, Marion 1923, *The Unmarried Mother and Her Child*, Sydney, Moore's Bookshop.

Politician's Dictionary, The; or a summary of political knowledge: containing remarks on the interests, connections, forces, revenues, wealth, credit, debts, taxes, commerce and manufactures of the different states of Europe, 1775, London, Geo. Allen.

Pollitt, Katha 1996, 'What we know', *New Republic* 12 August: 20.

Poovey, Mary 1988a, 'Feminism and deconstruction', *Feminist Studies* 14 (1): 51–65.

— 1988b, *Uneven Developments. The Ideological Work of Gender in Mid-Victorian England*, Chicago, University of Chicago Press.

— 1990, 'Speaking of the body: mid-Victorian constructions of female desire', in Mary Jacobus, Evelyn Fox-Keller and Sally Shuttleworth (eds), *Body/Politics. Women and the Discourses of Science*, New York and London, Routledge, pp. 29–46.

— 1993, 'Figures of arithmetic, figures of speech: the discourse of statistics in the 1830s', *Critical Inquiry* 19 (Winter): 256–76.

Popenoe, David 1994, 'Parental androgyny', *Australian Family* 15 (1): 35–47 (reprinted from *Society* September/October 1993).

— 1996a, 'Family caps', *Society* 33 (5): 25–7.

— 1996b, *Life Without Father*, New York, Martin Kessler Books/Free Press.

Popenoe, David, Norton, Andrew and Maley, Barry 1994, *Shaping the Social Virtues*, St Leonards, Centre for Independent Studies Monographs no. 28.

Porter, Theodore M. 1986, *The Rise of Statistical Thinking 1820–1900*, Princeton, Princeton University Press.

Powell, Miriam 1949, 'Illegitimate pregnancy in emotionally disturbed girls', *Smith College Studies in Social Work* 19 (3): 171–9.

Proctor, Candice E. 1990, *Women, Equality, and the French Revolution*, New York, Westport and London, Greenwood Press.

Puls, Joy 1996a, 'Re-forming the single parent family – the way of the future?', *Just Policy* 7 (August): 15–21.

— 1996b, 'Broken family values', paper presented at the Australian Women's Studies Association Conference, Perth, 27 November.

Purdy, J. S. 1922, 'Infantile mortality in New South Wales', *Medical Journal of Australia* 1 (11), 18 March: 287–96.

Quayle, Dan 1992, 'The value of families', speech delivered in San Francisco 19 May 1992, reproduced in *Australian Family* 13 (2): 3–10.

Queensland 1893, *Registrar-General's Report on Vital Statistics*, Colonial microfiche series, Canberra, Australian Bureau of Statistics.

Quetelet, Adolphe [1842] 1969, *A Treatise On Man and the Development Of His Faculties*, facsimile of the English translation of 1842, Gainesville Fla., Scholars' Facsimiles and Reprints.

Rains, Prudence Mors 1971, *Becoming an Unwed Mother. A Sociological Account*, Chicago and New York, Aldine.

Raspberry, William 1993, 'Courage to say the obvious', *Washington Post* 5 April: A21.

— 1994, 'Marriage as cultural base, neglected at great risk', *Washington Post*, reproduced in *International Herald Tribune* 14 April: 5.

Rawson, Beryl 1989, 'Spurii and the Roman view of illegitimacy', *Antichthon* 23: 10–41.

Read, Peter 1984. *The Stolen Generations. The Removal of Aboriginal Children in New South Wales 1883 to 1969*, Sydney, New South Wales Ministry of Aboriginal Affairs, Occasional Paper no. 1.

Reader's Digest 1994, 'The ominous rise in illegitimacy' (October): 139.

Reese, D. Meredith 1857, 'Infant mortality in large cities: the sources of its increase, and means for its diminution', *Transactions of the American Medical Association* 10: 93–107.

Refractory Girl no 52, 1997.

Registrar-General of Births, Deaths and Marriages 1844, 'Sixth Annual Report', Great Britain, House of Commons, *Parliamentary Papers* vol. 19.

Reiss, Ira L. 1967, *The Social Context of Premarital Sexual Permissiveness*, New York, Holt, Rinehart & Winston.

Reuter, Edward Byron 1923, *Population Problems*, Philadelphia, J. B. Lippincott.

Reuter News Service 1996, 'Third of births in U.S. to unmarried women – study', 11 December.

— 1996, 'Honestly, "bastard" won't do in Queensland', 21 February, Canberra.

Riley, Denise 1988, *'Am I That Name?' Feminism and the Category of 'Women' in History*, Minneapolis, University of Minnesota Press.

Roberts, Ian and Pless, Barry 1995, 'Social policy as a cause of childhood accidents: the children of lone mothers', *British Medical Journal* 7 October: 925–8.

Roberts, P. 1969, ' "One in thirteen": a reconsideration of the problems of the unmarried mother and her child', *Social Service* May/June: 9–14.

Roberts, Robert W. 1966, 'Introduction and theoretical overview of the unwed mother', in Robert W. Roberts (ed.), *The Unwed Mother*, New York and London, Harper & Row, pp. 3–22.

Roberts, Yvonne 1996, 'Holding the baby', cover story, *Sunday Times Magazine* 28 July: 18–25.

Rodis, Themistocles C. 1968, 'Morals: marriage, divorce and illegitimacy during the French Revolution, 1789–1795', PhD thesis, Case Western Reserve University.

Romero, D. James 1997, 'Fear and ignorance seed a bitter harvest', *Los Angeles Times* 9 February: 3.

Rose, Nikolas 1989a, *Governing the Soul. The Shaping of the Private Self*, London and New York, Routledge.

— 1989b, 'Individualizing psychology', in John Shotter and Kenneth J. Gergen (eds), *Texts of Identity*, London, Sage Publications, pp. 119–32.

Rothman, Stanley 1996, 'The decline of bourgeois America', *Society* 33 (2): 9–16.

Routh, C. H. F. 1858, 'On the mortality of infants in foundling institutions, and generally, as influenced by the absence of breast-milk', *British Medical Journal* 16 January: 46–50, 23 January: 65–8, 6 February: 103–5 and following.

Royal Commission on Human Relationships, Australia 1977, *Final Report vol. 3. Sexuality and Fertility*, Canberra, Australian Government Printing Service.

Ryan, John A. 1910, 'Illegitimacy', *Catholic Encyclopedia* vol. VII, New York, Robert Appleton.

Ryan, William Burke 1862, *Infanticide: Its Law, Prevalence, Prevention, and History*, London, J. Churchill.

Sadler, Michael Thomas 1830, *The Law of Population: A Treatise, in Six Books; In Disproof of the Superfecundity of Human Beings, and Developing the Real Principle of Their Increase*, vol. 2, London, John Murray.

Safford, Herbert A. 1870, 'Infanticide', *National Association for the Promotion of Social Science. Transactions*: 208–10.

Sagarin, Edward and MacNamara, Donal E. J. (eds) 1968, *Problems of Sex Behavior*, New York, Thomas Y. Cromwell.

Santamaria, B. A. 1995, 'Family law act lacks moral content', *Weekend Australian* 14–15 January: 26.

Saul, John Ralston 1997, *The Unconscious Civilization*, Ringwood, Penguin.

Saunders, Edward 1989, 'Neonaticides following "secret" pregnancies: seven case reports', *Public Health Reports* 104 (5): 368–72.

Schlesinger, Benjamin 1973, 'Unmarried mothers in Australia: a review', *Australian Journal of Social Issues* 8 (1): 58–69.

Schumacher, Henry C. 1927, 'The unmarried mother: A socio-psychiatric viewpoint', *Mental Hygiene* 11: 775–82.

Scotsman 1997, 'Leave single mothers alone to care for their families', 3 June: 7 (Reuters Business Briefing).

Scott, Joan W. 1988a, *Gender and the Politics of History*, New York, Columbia University Press.

— 1988b, 'Deconstructing equality-versus-difference: or, the uses of poststructuralist theory for feminism', *Feminist Studies* 14 (1): 33–50.

— 1991, 'The evidence of experience', *Critical Inquiry* 17 (Summer): 773–97.

— 1993, 'Women's history', in Linda S. Kaufmann (ed.), *American Feminist Thought at Century's End. A Reader*, Cambridge Mass. and Oxford, Blackwell Publishers, pp. 234–57.

Scruton, Roger 1997, 'Blair's bogus claim to the high moral ground', *Sunday Telegraph* 20 April: 36 (Reuters Business Briefing).

Seccombe, Mike 1997, 'Break-ups "the main cause of poverty" ', *Sydney Morning Herald* 22 September: 6.

Sedgwick, Eve Kosofsky 1990, *Epistemology of the Closet*, Berkeley, University of California Press.

Seelye, Katharine Q. 1995, 'Gingrich looks to Victorian age to cure today's social failings', *New York Times* 14 March: 19.

Seton, George 1860, *The Causes of Illegitimacy, Particularly in Scotland*, Edinburgh, Edmonston & Douglass.

Shanmugam, N. and Wood, C. 1970, 'Unwed mothers: a study of 100 girls in Melbourne, Victoria', *Australian and New Zealand Journal of Sociology* 6 (1): 51–5.

Shirk, Martha 1991, 'Infanticide increasing, experts fear', *St Louis Post-Dispatch* 7 April: 1.

Shorter, Edward, Knodel, John and Van de Wall, Etienne 1971, 'The decline of non-marital fertility in Europe, 1880–1940', *Population Studies* 25: 375–93.

Sidel, Ruth 1996, *Keeping Women and Children Last. America's War on the Poor*, New York, Penguin.

Silva, Elizabeth Bortolaia 1996 (ed.), *Good Enough Mothering? Feminist Perspectives on Lone Motherhood*, London and New York, Routledge.

Sinclair, Sir John 1791, *The Statistical Account of Scotland. Drawn from the Communications of the Ministers of the Different Parishes*, Edinburgh, William Creech.

Singer, Linda 1993, *Erotic Welfare. Sexual Theory and Politics in the Age of Epidemic*, New York, Routledge.

Skrine, Mary J. H. 1917, 'The little black lamb', *Spectator* 11 August: 137.

Smart, Carol 1996, 'Deconstructing motherhood', in Silva (ed.), *Good Enough Mothering?*, pp. 37–57.

Smart, Carol and Sevenhuijsen, Selma 1989 (eds), *Child Custody and the Politics of Gender*, London and New York, Routledge.

Smith, Enid Severy 1935, *A Study of Twenty-five Adolescent Unmarried Mothers in New York City*, New York, Salvation Army Women's Home and Hospital.

Smith, Kenneth 1951, *The Malthusian Controversy*, London, Routledge & Kegan Paul.

Smith, Daniel Scott and Hindus, Michael 1975, 'Premarital pregnancy in America, 1640–1971: an overview and interpretation', in Robert I. Rotberg and Theodore K. Rabb (eds), *Marriage and Fertility. Studies in Interdisciplinary History*, Princeton, Princeton University Press, pp. 339–72.

Smithers, Rebecca 1996, 'Adoption law aims at single mothers', *Guardian* 25 March: 3.

Smyth, R. Brough 1878, *The Aborigines of Victoria. With Notes Relating to the Habits of the Natives of Other Parts of Australia and Tasmania. Compiled from Various Sources for the Government of Victoria*, vol. 1, Melbourne and London, Government Printer and Trubner & Co.

Society July/August 1996.

Solinger, Rickie 1992, *Wake Up Little Susie: Single Pregnancy and Race Before Roe v. Wade*, New York, Routledge.

Spectator 1890, 'The Judges' opinion upon child-murder', 12 July: 44.

— 1993, 'The family way' leading article, 17 July: 5.

Spensky, Martine 1992, 'Producers of legitimacy: homes for unmarried mothers in the 1950s', in Carol Smart (ed.), *Regulating Womanhood. Historical Essays on Marriage, Motherhood and Sexuality*, London, Routledge, pp. 100–18.

Standard Library Cyclopaedia of Political, Constitutional, Statistical and Forensic Knowledge, 1853, London, H. G. Bohn.

Stangeland, Charles Emil 1904, *Pre-Malthusian Doctrines of Population: A Study in the History of Economic Theory*, New York, Columbia University Press.

Stevenson, Alan Carruth 1950, *Recent Advances in Social·Medicine*, London, J. & A. Churchill.

Strachan, John M. n.d. ?1859, *Address Upon Illegitimacy to the Working Men of Scotland*, Edinburgh, Religious Tract and Book Society of Scotland.

Sullivan, Barbara 1997, *The Politics of Sex. Prostitution and Pornography in Australia Since 1945*, Cambridge, Cambridge University Press.

Sullivan, John 1992, 'Foreword', in Anderson (ed.), *The Loss of Moral Virtue*, pp. ix–xiv.

Sundt, Eilert [1856–66] 1993, *Sexual Customs in Rural Norway. A Nineteenth-Century Study*, translated and edited by Odin W. Anderson, Ames, Iowa University Press.

Swain, Shurlee with Howe, Renate 1995, *Single Mothers and Their Children. Disposal, Punishment and Survival in Australia*, Cambridge, Cambridge University Press.

Swan, Peter L. and Bernstam, Mikhail S. 1988, 'The political economy of the symbiosis between labour market regulation and the social welfare system', *Australian Journal of Management* 13 (2): 177–201.

Sweet, Melissa 1996, 'Children of single mothers "more at risk"', *Sydney Morning Herald* 28 June: 4.

Sydney Morning Herald 1996a, 'News and Features/Briefs', 6 April: 2.

— 1996b,'Bringing up a child on your own', letters page, 3 August: 32.

Tapper, Alan 1990, *The Family in the Welfare State*, North Sydney, Allen & Unwin in association with the Australian Institute for Public Policy.

— 1993, 'Juvenile crime and family decline', *IPA Review* 46 (1): 46–8.

— 1993–4, 'Supporting mothers twenty years on', *Policy. A Journal of Public Policy and Ideas*, 9 (4): 24–6.

Teagarden, Florence M 1946, *Child Psychology for Professional Workers*, New York, Prentice-Hall.

Teichman, Jenny 1982, *Illegitimacy. A Philosophical Examination*, Oxford, Basil Blackwell.

Thompson, Barbara 1956, 'A social study of illegitimate maternities', *British Journal of Preventive and Social Medicine* 10: 75–87.

Torgovnick, Marianna 1990, *Gone Primitive. Savage Intellects, Modern Lives*, Chicago and London, University of Chicago Press.

Townsend, Joseph [1786] 1817, *A Dissertation on the Poor Laws, by a Well-Wisher to Mankind*, London, Ridgways.

Trainor, Brian T. 1995, 'The forgotten children', *IPA Review* 47 (3): 40–2.

Turnbull, W. M. 1864, 'A contribution to Victorian statistics', *Medical and Surgical Review* 21 July: 97.

United States Bureau of the Census, US Department of Commerce, *Statistical Abstract of the United States* 1923–95, Washington DC, Bureau of the Census.

United States Department of Health and Human Services 1995, *Executive Summary. Report to Congress on Out-of-Wedlock Childbearing*, Hyattsville, Maryland.

United States Senate, Committee on Finance 1995, *Teen Parents and Welfare Reform. Hearing Before the Committee on Finance, United States Senate, One Hundred Fourth Congress, First Session*, US Government Printing Office, Washington DC

Universal Jewish Encyclopedia 1948, Isaac Landman (ed.), New York.

US News & World Report 1959, 'Illegitimacy – growing problem for the taxpayer', 15 June: 86–9.

Vallely, Paul 1997, 'They all want to be left holding the baby', *Independent* 28 May: 19.

Vincent, Clark E. 1959–60, 'Ego involvement in sexual relations: implications for research on illegitimacy', *American Journal of Sociology* 65: 287–95.

— 1961, *Unmarried Mothers*, New York, Free Press of Glencoe.

— 1963, 'Illegitimacy and value dilemmas', *Christian Century* 80 (19 June): 801–4.

Vinovskis, Maris 1988, *'An Epidemic' of Adolescent Pregnancy? Some Historical and Policy Considerations*, New York, Oxford University Press.

Waite, D. 1936, 'The role of the physician in the care of unmarried mothers and adoptive children', *Wisconsin Medical Journal* 35: 59–64.

Wakefield, Colonel Sir Charles Cheers 1919, *The Care of the Unmarried Mother and Her Child*, London, John Bale, Sons & Danielsson Ltd.

Wallace, Victor H. 1946, *Women and Children First. An Outline of a Population Policy for Australia*, Melbourne, Oxford University Press.

Walsh, Mary 1954, *The Unmarried Mother and Her Child*, London, Catholic Truth Society.

Warden, Ian 1997, 'Social snapshot shows Australia changing', *Canberra Times* 20 June: 1.

Watson, Amey Eaton 1918, 'The illegitimate family', *Annals of the American Academy of Political and Social Science* LXXVII: 103–15.

Wayne (Malinowska), Helena 1984, 'Bronislaw Malinowski: the influence of various women on his life and works', *Journal of the Anthropological Society of Oxford* 15: 189–203.

— (ed.) 1995, *The Letters of Bronislaw Malinowski and Elsie Masson vol. 2 1920–1935*, London and New York, Routledge.

Webb, Clarence 1961, *The Problem of Illegitimacy*, Baton Rouge, Louisiana, Louisiana Youth Commission.

Weeks, Jeffrey 1989, *Sex, Politics and Society. The Regulation of Sexuality since 1800*, London and New York, Longman.

— 1995, *Invented Moralities. Sexual Values in an Age of Uncertainty*, Cambridge, Polity Press.

West, Rosemary 1991, 'How single mothers overcame discrimination', in Eileen Baldry and Tony Vinson (eds), *Actions Speak. Strategies and Lessons from Australian Social and Community Action*, Melbourne, Longman Cheshire, pp. 168–86.

Wheelwright, Julie 1995, 'A moment as mother', *Guardian* 13 May (Reuters Australasian News Service).

Wheen, Francis 1994, 'The typically British way of bastardy', *Guardian* 25 May: sec. 2, p. 7.

White, Glenn Matthew 1960, 'The truth about illegitimacy', *Ladies Home Journal* 77 (December): 76–7, 102.

Whiteford, Peter 1995, 'Does Australia have a ghetto underclass?', *Social Security Journal* (June): 3–19.

Whitehead, Barbara Dafoe 1993, 'Dan Quayle was right', *Atlantic Monthly* April: 47–84 (cover story).

White House, Office of Press Secretary 1995a, 'Remarks by the President in State of the Union Address', 24 January, White House Virtual Library at http:/www.whitehouse.gov/.

— 1995b, 'Remarks by the President at Nga [sic] National Summit on Young Children', 6 June, White House Virtual Library at http:/www.whitehouse.gov/.

— 1996a, 'Remarks by the President in statement on teen pregnancy', 29 January, White House Virtual Library at http://www/whitehouse.gov/.

— 1996b, 'Radio address of the President to the nation', 4 October, White House Virtual Library at http://www.whitehouse.gov/.

Whitman, David and Friedman, Dorian et al. 1994, 'The white underclass', *US News & World Report* 17 October: 40–53.

Wickert, Christl, Hamburger, Brigitte and Lienau, Marie 1982, 'Helen Stocker and the Bund fuer Mutterschutz (Society for the Protection of Motherhood)', *Women's Studies International Forum* 5 (6): 611–18.

Wilczynski, Ania 1994, 'Why do parents kill their children?', *Criminology Australia* 5 (3): 12–13.

Wilks, J. C. 1859, 'On bastardy in the rural districts', *National Association for the Promotion of Social Science. Transactions*: 733–4.

Will, George 1993, 'It's time, again, to judge single parents', *Australian Financial Review* 9 November: 18.

Willoughby, W. G. et al. 1942, 'Preserving the race in post-war reconstruction', *British Medical Journal* February–May: 196, 565, 624, 655.

Wilson, James Q. 1993, *The Moral Sense*, New York and Toronto, Free Press.

Wimperis, Virginia 1960, *The Unmarried Mother and Her Child*, London, George Allen & Unwin.

Winch, Donald 1987, *Malthus*, Oxford and New York, Oxford University Press.

Winspinger, K. A. et al. 1991, 'Risk factors for childhood homicides in Ohio: a birth-certificate-based case-control study', *American Journal of Public Health* 81 (8): 1052–4.

Wollaston, Tullie C. 1917, *Compulsory Marriage*, Adelaide, G. Hassell & Son.

Woolf, Stuart 1989, 'Statistics and the modern state', *Comparative Studies in Society and History* 31: 588–604.

Woolsey, Theodore D. 1881, 'The moral statistics of the United States', *Journal of Social Science* 14 (1): 129–35.

Worrell, Judith 1988, 'Single mothers: from problems to policies', *Women and Therapy* 7 (4): 3–14.

Yeo, Eileen Janes 1996, *The Contest for Social Science. Relations and Representations of Gender and Class*, London, Rivers Oram Press.

Young, Iris Marion 1994, 'Making single motherhood normal', *Dissent* (Winter): 88–93.

Young, Leontine 1954, *Out of Wedlock. A Study of the Problems of the Unmarried Mother and Her Child*, New York, McGraw-Hill.

Young, Michael 1991, 'Malinowski', *International Dictionary of Anthropologists*, New York and London, Garland Publishing.

Zelnick, Melvin, Kantner, John F. and Ford, Kathleen 1981, *Sex and Pregnancy in Adolescence*, Beverley Hills, Sage Publications.

Zhang, Baoping and Chan, Annabelle 1991, 'Teenage pregnancy in South Australia, 1986–1988', *Australian and New Zealand Journal of Obstetrics and Gynaecology* 31 (4): 291–8.

Zingo, Martha T. and Early, Kevin E. 1994, *Nameless Persons. Legal Discrimination Against Non–Marital Children in the United States*, Westport, Conn. and London, Praeger.

Zinsmeister, Karl 1993, 'The need for fathers', *IPA Review* 46 (1): 43–6.

Zucchino, David 1997, *Myth of the Welfare Queen. A Pullitzer Prize-Winning Journalist's Portrait of Women on the Line*, New York, Scribner.

Index